Fix It!™
Grammar

Frog Prince
TEACHER'S MANUAL
LEVEL 5

Pamela White

Fourth Edition, January 2022
Institute for Excellence in Writing, L.L.C.

The purchase of this book allows its owner access to e-audio resource talks by Andrew Pudewa.
See blue page for details and download instructions.

Additional copies of this Teacher's Manual may be purchased from IEW.com/FIX-L5-T

Institute for Excellence in Writing (IEW®)
8799 N. 387 Road
Locust Grove, OK 74352
800.856.5815
info@IEW.com
IEW.com

Printed in the United States of America

IEW® and Structure and Style® are registered trademarks of the Institute for Excellence in Writing, L.L.C.

Fix It!™ is a trademark of the Institute for Excellence in Writing, L.L.C.

Accessing Your Downloads

The purchase of this book entitles its owner to a free download of the following:

- *Mastery Learning, Ability Development, and Individualized Education* e-audio

- *But, but, but ... What about Grammar?* e-audio

- *Fix It! Grammar: Frog Prince* vocabulary list with definitions

To download these e-resources, please follow the directions below:

1. Go to our website: IEW.com

2. Log in to your online customer account. If you do not have an account, you will need to create one.

3. After you are logged in, go to this web page: IEW.com/FIX-E

4. Click the red arrow, and then click the checkboxes next to the names of the files you wish to place in your account.

5. Click the "Add to my files" button.

6. To access your files now and in the future, click on "Your Account" and click on the "Files" tab (one of the gray tabs).

7. Click on each file name to download the files onto your computer.

If you have any difficulty receiving these downloads after going through the steps above, please call 800.856.5815.

Institute for Excellence in Writing
8799 N. 387 Road
Locust Grove, OK 74352

Instructions

The list below shows the components to each *Fix It! Grammar* weekly exercise.

Although in Levels 1–4 students could choose to either Mark It or Fix It first, in Levels 5 and 6, students must complete the passages in this order: **Read It, Mark It, Fix It.** After Week 4 students should number the sentence openers after the passage has been marked and fixed.

Students should discuss their work with the teacher after working through each daily passage. However, older students may work with their teacher on a weekly basis. Students should actively be involved in comparing their work with the Teacher's Manual. The repetition of finding and fixing their own mistakes allows them to recognize and avoid those mistakes in the future.

Fix It! Grammar should be treated as a game. Keep it fun!

Learn It! On the first day of the new Week, read through the Learn It section. Each Learn It covers a concept that the student will practice in future passages. Instructions for marking and fixing passages are included in each Learn It.

Read It! Read the day's passage.

Look up the bolded vocabulary word in a dictionary and pick the definition that fits the context of the story. Maintain a list of vocabulary words and their definitions.

The vocabulary definitions are printed in the Teacher's Manual.

Mark It! Mark the passage using the guide at the top of the daily practice page.

Fix It! Correct the passage using the guide at the top of the daily practice page.

The Teacher's Manual includes detailed explanations for grammar concepts and punctuation in each daily passage.

Rewrite It! After marking, correcting, and discussing the passage with the teacher, copy the corrected passage on the lines provided or into a separate notebook.

- Copy the corrected story, not the editing marks.
- Indent and use capital letters properly.
- Copy the corrected punctuation.

Editing Marks

¶ indent

∧ insert

ꝺ delete

t̲ capitalize

ꬵ lowercase

⌒ reverse order

add a space

⌣ close the space

Helpful Hints

Use different colors for **Mark It** and **Fix It**.

When you complete the book, remove the daily passages.

Use the remaining **Learn It** pages as a quick grammar reference.

Appendix I Complete Story Familiarize yourself with the story that you will be editing by reading the complete story found in Appendix I.

Appendix II Collection Pages Look for strong verbs, quality adjectives, and -ly adverbs in this book and write them on the collection pages in Appendix II.

Appendix III Lists Refer to the lists found in Appendix III to quickly identify pronouns, prepositions, verbs, conjunctions, clauses, phrases, and sentence openers.

Appendix IV Grammar Glossary Reference the Grammar Glossary found in Appendix IV of the Teacher's Manual for more information about the concepts taught in the *Fix It! Grammar* series.

Fix It! Grammar Cards are an optional product that will enhance the *Fix It! Grammar* learning experience.

Fix It! Grammar Cards

Thirty full color grammar cards highlight key *Fix It! Grammar* concepts for quick and easy reference.

For a more relaxed and entertaining way to drill and review grammar concepts learned, instructions for a download of multiple game ideas are included in the card pack.

Fix It! Grammar Cards are beautifully designed and come in a sturdy card box for easy storage.

IEW.com/FIX-GC

On the chart below *Fix It! Grammar Cards* are listed in the order that the information is taught in this book.

WEEK	**Fix It! Grammar Cards for *Frog Prince* Level 5**
1	Editing Marks, Capitalization, Indentation, Subject-Verb Pair, Preposition, Prepositional Phrase
2	Conjunction, Coordinating Conjunction
3	Clause, Dependent Clause, www Word
4	Sentence Openers, #3 -ly Adverb Opener
5	#4 -ing Opener, Quotation, Apostrophes, Verb, Linking Verb, Helping Verb
6	Adjective, Commas with Adjectives before a Noun
7	Interjection
10	Run-On
11	Noun
12	Pronoun
13	Indefinite Pronoun
14	Number Words and Numerals
15	Adverb
18	Title
25	Comparative and Superlative Adjectives and Adverbs

Scope and Sequence

Week numbers indicate when a concept is introduced or specifically reinforced in a lesson. Once introduced the concept is practiced throughout the book.

Parts of Speech

	1	2	3	4	5	6	7	8	9	10	11	12	13	14	15	16	17	18	19	20	21	22	23	24	25	26	27	28	29	30
Noun											11														25					
Pronoun												12	13					18							25					
Preposition	1													14																
Verb					5																			24						
Conjunction																														
coordinating conjunction		2																		20							27			
subordinating conjunction			3																											
Adjective						6									15										25	26				
Adverb															15															
Interjection							7																							

Capitalization

	1	2	3	4	5	6	7	8	9	10	11	12	13	14	15	16	17	18	19	20	21	22	23	24	25	26	27	28	29	30
First Word of Sentence	1																													
Proper Noun	1																													
Proper Adjective	1																													
Personal Pronoun I	1																													
Title	1																													
Quotation Marks					5					10																	27			
Noun of Direct Address					5																									
Interjection							7																							
Literary Titles																		18												

Punctuation

	1	2	3	4	5	6	7	8	9	10	11	12	13	14	15	16	17	18	19	20	21	22	23	24	25	26	27	28	29	30
End Marks	1				5					10																				
quote					5					10																	27			
interjection							7																							
attribution										10																	27			
Commas																														
prepositional phrase	1																													
coordinating conjunction		2								10																				
dependent clause			3				7									16														
sentence adverb				4																										
sentence openers				4	5																									
quotation marks					5					10																				
noun of direct address					5																									
phrases	1						7	8																						

Commas, cont.

	Week 1	2	3	4	5	6	7	8	9	10	11	12	13	14	15	16	17	18	19	20	21	22	23	24	25	26	27	28	29	30
adjectives						6																								
interjection							7																							
unnecessary commas									9																			28		
comma splice										10																				
contrasting items																					21									
Apostrophe					5																									
Quotation Marks					5					10							17					22					27			
Semicolon										10														24						

Clauses

	Week 1	2	3	4	5	6	7	8	9	10	11	12	13	14	15	16	17	18	19	20	21	22	23	24	25	26	27	28	29	30
Main Clause	1		3																											
Dependent Clause			3																											
Who/Which Clause			3				7	8			11				15				19											
That Clause			3											14		16		18												
Adverb Clause			3	4											15	16	17				21									
Adjective Clause															15	16	17					22								

Phrases

	Week 1	2	3	4	5	6	7	8	9	10	11	12	13	14	15	16	17	18	19	20	21	22	23	24	25	26	27	28	29	30
Prepositional Phrase	1			4			7							14	15															
Verb Phrase					5																									
Participial (-ing) Phrase					5			8						14	15			18					23							
Appositive											11											22								

Other Concepts

	Week 1	2	3	4	5	6	7	8	9	10	11	12	13	14	15	16	17	18	19	20	21	22	23	24	25	26	27	28	29	30
Indentation	1																													
Subject-Verb Pairs	1																													
Numbers														14																
Usage																														
who/whom/whose																			19											
affect/effect																								24						
among/between																									25					
than/then																										26				
accept/except																													29	
Words as Words																						22								

Week 1–30

	1	2	3	4	5	6	7	8	9	10	11	12	13	14	15	16	17	18	19	20	21	22	23	24	25	26	27	28	29	30

Run-On

	1	2	3	4	5	6	7	8	9	10	11	12	13	14	15	16	17	18	19	20	21	22	23	24	25	26	27	28	29	30
Fused Sentence										10																				
Comma Splice										10																				
Fix																														
period										10	11																			
semicolon										10	11													24						
comma + cc										10	11									20										
adverb clause																					21									

Stylistic Techniques

	1	2	3	4	5	6	7	8	9	10	11	12	13	14	15	16	17	18	19	20	21	22	23	24	25	26	27	28	29	30
Strong Verb	1															16														
Quality Adjective							7								15	16														
Who/Which Clause			3				7				11								19											
-ly Adverb							7								15	16														
Adverb Clause			3												15	16	17				21									
#1 Subject Opener				4																									29	
#2 Prepositional Opener				4			7							14								22							29	
#3 -ly Adverb Opener				4																									29	
#4 -ing Opener					5			8										18					23						29	
#5 Clausal Opener				4																		22							29	
#6 Vss Opener				4																									29	

Vocabulary

1 decorous compassion esteemed devotion	**2** obstinate courtiers roe repulsed	**3** chic fastidiousness court dwindling	**4** charge tractable gratify resemble	**5** minuscule conservatory eyeing roamed	**6** stately regrettable inconsolable benefactor
7 honored proposed inquisitiveness stipulation	**8** retrieve salvage hastily wheezed	**9** sumptuously hastened hospitably audacious	**10** deficiencies despicable theatrics audibly	**11** sire whined integrity complied	**12** unceremoniously relish deduced pretentious
13 daunting oblivious decency plummeting	**14** humility fated sequestered conjectured	**15** substantial inadvertently feigned mortified	**16** dangled convalescence sullen resolved	**17** imperial marveled proffered hesitantly	**18** responded stump reputation suspicious
19 ignobly futilely hampering brimming	**20** evaded brandished prominent gallant	**21** mourned bona fide snickered testily	**22** toady repulsive pattered luster	**23** commiserate humane regaled demeanor	**24** odious chastise empathy discontent
25 rummaged precise mute emphatically	**26** credible undaunted mere noxious	**27** agitated parched detect jiggled	**28** callously insubordination grievingly laborious	**29** arrogant contritely coveted entrusting	**30** poignantly abhorrent remorse reversed

Contents

Weekly Lessons

Appendices

Appendix I: Complete Story

Appendix II: Collection Pages

Appendix III: Lists

Appendix IV: Grammar Glossary

Learn It!

Capitalization

Capitalize the first word of a sentence.

Capitalize proper nouns and proper adjectives.

Capitalize the personal pronoun *I*.

Capitalize a title when it is used with a person's name.

End Mark

Use a period at the end of a statement.

Use a question mark at the end of a question.

Use an exclamation mark at the end of a sentence that expresses strong emotion.

Indentation

An **indentation** shows the start of a new paragraph. In fiction (stories) there are four reasons to start a new paragraph: new speaker, new topic, new place, new time.

Fix It!   Place three short lines below letters that should be capitalized.

Draw a slanted line through letters that should be lowercase.

Place the correct end mark at the end of each sentence.

Add the ¶ symbol (known as a pilcrow) in front of each sentence that should start a new paragraph. When you rewrite the passage, indent. Start the sentence on the next line and write ½ inch from the left margin.

¶ Dorinda's new dress cost king morton an outrageous amount of money. The ᶄing was not pleased!

Subject and Verb

A **verb** shows action, links the subject to another word, or helps another verb. Every verb has a subject. The subject and verb (*s v*) belong together.

A **subject** is a noun or pronoun that performs a verb action. It tells who or what the clause is about.

Main Clause

A **main clause** contains a subject and a verb and expresses a complete thought, so it can stand alone as a sentence. Every sentence must have a main clause.

Find It!   Read the sentence and look for the verb.
Ask, "Who or what _____ (verb)?"

Mark It!   Write *v* above each verb and *s* above each subject.
Place square brackets around the main clause *[MC]*.

      s   *v*
[King Morton ruled wisely].

Strong Verb

A **strong verb** dresses up writing because it creates a strong image or feeling. A strong verb is an action verb, never a linking or a helping verb. Look for strong verbs in this book and write them on the Strong Verb collection page, Appendix II.

Titles capitalized before a person's name include mister and missus as well as job titles like doctor, king, and president.

The **k**ing was **K**ing Morton.

For more information about indentation, see page G-31.

Clause Overview: Appendix III

For more information about clauses, see pages G-20 to G-22.

Ask students to identify the subject and verb.

What is the verb? ***ruled***

Who ruled? ***King Morton***

Phrase Overview:
Appendix III

For more information about prepositional phrases, see pages G-8 and G-18.

A prepositional phrase always follows the **PATTERN preposition + noun (no verb)**.
after dinner

If a word on the preposition list is followed by a subject and a verb, the word functions as a subordinating conjunction (www word) and begins an adverb clause.
after we ate

If a word on the preposition list is at the end of a phrase or clause, it is probably functioning as an adverb.
We sat down.

Ask students to identify each prepositional phrase and explain how it follows the pattern.

In what? **castle**
In a charming ancient castle begins with a preposition (in) and ends with a noun (castle). It has an article and adjectives in between but no verb.

With whom? **daughters**
with his daughters begins with a preposition (with) and ends with a noun (daughters). It has a possessive adjective in between but no verb.

With whom? **him**
with him begins with a preposition (with) and ends with an objective case pronoun (him).

Prepositional Phrase

A **prepositional phrase** begins with a preposition and ends with a noun or pronoun, which is called the object of the preposition.

A **preposition** is the first word in a prepositional phrase. It shows the relationship between its object (a noun or pronoun) and another word in the sentence. Review the prepositions in Appendix III.

An **object of the preposition** is the last word in a prepositional phrase. It is always a noun or pronoun.

A prepositional phrase adds imagery or information to a sentence because the entire phrase functions as an adjective describing a noun or as an adverb modifying a verb or an adjective.

Formal gardens <u>near a large conservatory</u> featured exotic plants.

Near is the first word in the prepositional phrase. *Near* is a preposition. *Conservatory* is the noun at the end of the prepositional phrase. It is the object of the preposition.

Near shows the relationship between conservatory (its object) and gardens (another word in the sentence). *Near* tells which gardens featured exotic plants. They are not the gardens behind, inside, or past a large conservatory. They are the gardens near a large conservatory.

The king's daughters often explored the gardens <u>with him</u>.

With is the first word in the prepositional phrase. *With* is a preposition. *Him* is the pronoun at the end of the prepositional phrase. It is the object of the preposition.

When a personal pronoun follows a preposition and functions as the object of the preposition, use an objective case pronoun. It is incorrect to write *with I* or *with he* because *I* and *he* are not objective case pronouns.

			Objective Case
			object of preposition
singular		1st	me
		2nd	you
		3rd	him, her, it
plural		1st	us
		2nd	you
		3rd	them

If a prepositional opener has five words or more, follow it with a comma.

If two or more prepositional phrases open a sentence, follow the last phrase with a comma.

Do not put a comma in front of a prepositional phrase.

Mark It!   Underline each prepositional phrase.
Write *prep* above the preposition.
Write *op* above the object of the preposition.

Fix It!   Insert or remove commas. Follow the comma rules.

    prep   op   prep   op
<u>In a charming ancient castle</u>, [King Morton lived <u>with his daughters</u>].

                 prep op
[They dined, <u>with him</u>].

Do not include the opener in the main clause square brackets.

Students complete the passage in this order: Read It! Mark It! Fix It!

In the recent past, in an obscure Kingdom, among the alps a **decorous** King reigned faithfully. His family line of monarchs stretched back to the middle ages

5 <u>prepositional phrases</u>	1 indent
2 [main clauses]	5 capitals
2 subject-verb pairs (s v)	3 commas
	1 end mark

decorous
dignified in conduct and manners

¶ In the recent past, in an obscure Kingdom, among the alps, [a **decorous** King reigned faithfully]. [His family line of monarchs stretched back to the middle ages].

This is the only week that an explanation about capitalization is provided.

Indentation	new topic
Capitalization	*kingdom*; *king* lowercase, common noun *Alps*; *Middle Ages* uppercase, proper noun *Middle Ages* is a compound noun. Because the compound noun forms a proper noun, both words are capitalized.
Prep Phrase	Each prepositional phrase begins with a preposition and ends with a noun, the object of the preposition. The words between the preposition and its object are article adjectives (a, an, the) or adjectives that describe the noun. What kind of past? *recent* What kind of kingdom? *obscure*
Note	After marking a prepositional phrase, mentally remove it. Neither subjects nor verbs are found inside a prepositional phrase. Week 15 students will learn that a prepositional phrase functions as either an adjective or an adverb.
S V Pairs MC	*king reigned* When a prepositional phrase opens (begins) a sentence, do not include the phrase in the main clause square brackets. Week 4 students will begin marking this as a #2 prepositional opener.
MC	*line stretched*
Commas	Do not use a comma in front of a prepositional phrase. If two or more prepositional phrases open a sentence, follow the last phrase with a comma.

Rewrite It!   In the recent past in an obscure kingdom among the Alps, a decorous king reigned faithfully. His family line of monarchs stretched back to the Middle Ages.

Read It!	Mark It!	Fix It!
King Morton had inherited the Throne, from his Father nearly three decades before. Like his Father, King Morton ruled fairly and showed **compassion** to all	3 <u>prepositional phrases</u> 2 [main clauses] 2 subject-verb pairs (s v)	3 capitals 2 commas 1 end mark

compassion
deep sympathy for someone else's sorrow or hardship

[King Morton had inherited the ~~T~~hrone, from his ~~F~~ather nearly three decades before]. Like his ~~F~~ather, [King Morton ruled fairly and showed **compassion** to all].

Capitalization	*throne, father, father* lowercase, common noun *Father* is only capitalized when used as a proper noun in place of a person's name. *King* is capitalized because it is a title used directly before the name.
Prep Phrase	*From his father* and *like his father* begin with a preposition and end with a noun, the object of the preposition. The word *his* is a possessive pronoun that functions as an adjective. Whose father? *his* *To all* is a preposition + pronoun. Because a pronoun can take the place of a noun, a prepositional phrase can end with a pronoun. The word *all* is an indefinite pronoun that functions as the object of the preposition.
Ask Students	In the first sentence, why is the word *before* not a preposition? A preposition begins a prepositional phrase. **PATTERN** preposition + noun (no verb) *Before* is an adverb, not a preposition.
S V Pairs	MC *King Morton had inherited* MC *King Morton ruled, showed*
Commas	Do not use a comma in front of a prepositional phrase. Do not use a comma if a prepositional opener has fewer than five words.

Rewrite It!   King Morton had inherited the throne from his father nearly three decades before. Like his father King Morton ruled fairly and showed compassion to all.

Read It!	Mark It!	Fix It!	Day 3

As a kindhearted Ruler, King Morton loved his subjects. The people, of the land **esteemed** him. maribella and dorinda, the King's daughters, lived with him

Mark It!
3 <u>prepositional phrases</u>
3 [main clauses]
3 subject-verb pairs (s v)

Fix It!
4 capitals
1 comma
1 end mark

esteemed
regarded with respect and admiration

prep   *op*   *s*   *v*
<u>As a kindhearted Ruler</u>, [King Morton loved his subjects].

s   *prep*   *op*   *v*   *s*
[The people, <u>of the land</u> **esteemed** him]. [maribella and

s
dorinda, the King's daughters, lived <u>with him</u>].

Capitalization	*ruler* lowercase, common noun *Maribella* uppercase, first word of the sentence, proper noun *Dorinda* uppercase, proper noun *king's* lowercase, common adjective
Prep Phrase	Both *as a kindhearted ruler* and *of the land* begin with a preposition and end with a noun, the object of the preposition. The words between the preposition and its object are article adjectives (a, an, the) or adjectives that describe the noun. What kind of ruler? *kindhearted* *With him* is a preposition + pronoun. The word *him* is an objective case pronoun that functions as the object of the preposition.
S V Pairs	MC *King Morton loved* MC *people esteemed* MC *Maribella, Dorinda lived*
Note	*Daughters* is not the subject. *The king's daughters* is an appositive phrase (noun phrase that renames the noun it follows). Week 11 students will learn about appositives and when they require commas.
Commas	Use a comma if a prepositional opener has five words or more. At times an exact word count misses the purpose of the rule: long phrases need a comma to separate the phrase from the main clause. Use a comma after *As a kindhearted ruler*. Do not use a comma in front of a prepositional phrase.

Rewrite It!   As a kindhearted ruler, King Morton loved his subjects. The people of the land esteemed him. Maribella and Dorinda, the king's daughters, lived with him.

Read It!	Mark It!	Fix It!	Day 4

Everyone in the land admired his **devotion**, to his girls. his younger daughter, however, frustrated him greatly

2 <u>prepositional phrases</u>
2 [main clauses]
2 subject-verb pairs (s v)

1 capital
1 comma
1 end mark

devotion
a feeling of strong love or loyalty

$$
\overset{s}{[\text{Everyone}} \underset{}{\overset{prep}{\underline{\text{in the}}}} \overset{op}{\underline{\text{land}}} \overset{v}{\text{admired}} \text{ his } \textbf{devotion}, \overset{prep}{\underline{\text{to his}}} \overset{op}{\underline{\text{girls}}}].
$$

[Everyone <u>in the land</u> admired his **devotion**, <u>to his girls</u>].

[his younger daughter, however, frustrated him greatly].

Capitalization	*His* uppercase, first word of the sentence
Prep Phrase	*In the land* begins with a preposition and ends with a noun, the object of the preposition. *The* is an article adjective.
	To his girls begins with a preposition and ends with a noun, the object of the preposition. The word *his* is a possessive pronoun that functions as an adjective. Whose girls? *his*
S V Pairs	MC ***Everyone admired*** MC ***daughter frustrated***
Commas	Do not use a comma in front of a prepositional phrase.

Rewrite It!   Everyone in the land admired his devotion to his girls. His younger daughter, however, frustrated him greatly.

Learn It!

Conjunction

A **conjunction** connects words, phrases, or clauses. A **coordinating conjunction** (cc) connects the same type of words, phrases, or clauses. The items must be grammatically the same: two or more adjectives, two or more prepositional phrases, two or more main clauses, and so forth. Use the acronym FANBOYS to remember the coordinating conjunctions.

The staff served King Morton, Princess Dorinda, and Princess Maribella.

And connects three nouns: *King Morton, Princess Dorinda,* and *Princess Maribella.*

❜ Use commas to separate three or more items in a series.
PATTERN a, b, and c

The king lived in the castle with his daughters and with the staff.

And connects two prepositional phrases: *with his daughters* and *with the staff.*

✗ Do not use a comma before a cc when it connects two items in a series unless they are main clauses.
PATTERN a and b

Dorinda raced through the gardens, and Maribella collected daisies.

And connects two main clauses. A subject and verb pair (Dorinda raced) comes before the coordinating conjunction, and a subject and verb pair (Maribella collected) comes after. When a subject and verb pair follows the coordinating conjunction, use a comma.

❜ Use a comma before a cc when it connects two main clauses.
PATTERN MC, cc MC

The **PATTERNS a and b** and **MC cc 2nd verb** are the same when *a* and *b* are verbs. However, the emphasis differs.

The **PATTERN a and b** emphasizes that a cc connects two items.

The **PATTERN MC cc 2nd verb** emphasizes that a subject and verb come before the cc, but only a verb comes after the cc.

A comma is not used in either pattern.

Compare the last sentence to this sentence:

Dorinda raced through the gardens and collected daisies.

And connects two verbs: *raced* and *collected.* A subject and verb (Dorinda raced) come before the coordinating conjunction, but only a verb (collected) comes after. The verbs have the same subject. This is the same pattern as **a and b** when *a* and *b* are verbs.

✗ Do not use a comma before a cc when it connects two verbs.
PATTERN MC cc 2nd verb

Mark It! Write *cc* above each coordinating conjunction.

Fix It! Insert or remove commas. Follow the comma rules.

Ask students to identify the coordinating conjunction and explain what it connects.

And connects three verbs: *ran, smelled, picked.* Use two commas. a, b, and c

But connects two adjectives: *lovely, spoiled.* Do not use a comma. a and b

And connects two main clauses: *Maribella sketched,* and *Dorinda bounced.* Use a comma. MC, cc MC

Yet connects two verbs: *groaned, loved.* Do not use a comma. MC cc 2nd verb

                               cc
Dorinda ran through the gardens, smelled the roses, and picked daisies.

            cc
Dorinda was lovely, but spoiled.

                  cc
Maribella sketched the flowers, and Dorinda bounced a ball.

                      cc
The king groaned at Dorinda's mischief, yet loved her anyway.

Coordinating Conjunctions

Figure out what is wrong with the following sentences.
Consider what the coordinating conjunction is connecting.
Rewrite the sentences correctly.

A coordinating conjunction (cc) connects items that are grammatically the same.

The cc *but* cannot connect a main clause [Dorinda cried out] to an adverb clause (when she pricked her finger ...).

Fix by removing the cc *but*.

Dorinda cried out but when she pricked her finger on the thorn.

Dorinda cried out when she pricked her finger on the thorn.

The adverb *then* is not a cc and cannot connect main clauses.

Fix by adding a comma + cc.

The sisters argued then they reunited.

The sisters argued, but then they reunited.

The cc *and* cannot connect a noun (dress) with a verb (was). The cc cannot connect the two verbs (splattered, was) because *mud* is the subject of only the first verb, not the second. It was the dress that was ruined, not the mud.

Fix by inserting the word *dress* to form two main clauses. Use two periods or a comma + cc.

Mud splattered her dress and was ruined.

Mud splattered her dress. The dress was ruined. OR

Mud splattered her dress, and the dress was ruined.

A comma + cc is a correct way to join two main clauses: MC, cc MC. However, a sentence with more than one of these patterns is not stylish. It feels as if it will never end!

Fix by removing the cc *and*. Form two sentences.

Dorinda teased Maribella, but Maribella laughed, and the sisters argued, yet they hugged each other in the end.

Dorinda teased Maribella, but Maribella laughed. The sisters argued, yet they hugged

each other in the end.

Students complete the passage in this order: Read It! Mark It! Fix It!

Princess Dorinda had been an **obstinate** child, from toddlerhood. As a child, she often escaped from the nursery, and found mischief

obstinate
stubborn; having an unyielding attitude

1 coordinating conjunction (cc)	1 indent
3 prepositional phrases	3 commas
2 [main clauses]	1 end mark
2 subject-verb pairs (s v)	

¶ [Princess Dorinda had been an **obstinate** child, from toddlerhood]. As a child, [she often escaped from the nursery, and found mischief].

This is the last week that a detailed explanation about prepositional phrases is provided.

Indentation	new topic
Prep Phrase	Each prepositional phrase begins with a preposition and ends with a noun, the object of the preposition. Remind students to mentally remove prepositional phrases when looking for subjects and verbs. Neither subjects nor verbs are found inside a prepositional phrase.
Conjunction	***and*** connects two verbs: *escaped* and *found* A subject and verb (she escaped) come before the cc, but only a verb (found) comes after the cc. A comma is not used. MC cc 2nd verb
Ask Students	Why does *and* not connect *nursery* and *found*? A coordinating conjunction (cc) connects items that are grammatically the same. *Nursery* is a noun; *found* is a verb.
S V Pairs	MC ***Princess Dorinda had been*** MC ***she escaped, found***
Commas	Do not use a comma in front of a prepositional phrase. Do not use a comma if a prepositional opener has fewer than five words. Do not use a comma before a cc when it connects two verbs. **PATTERN MC cc 2nd verb**

Rewrite It! Princess Dorinda had been an obstinate child from toddlerhood. As a child she often escaped from the nursery and found mischief.

Read It!	Mark It!	Fix It!	Day 2

She once stole, into the Throne Room swung
on the chandeliers and landed, at the feet of the
scandalized **courtiers**

Mark It!	
1 coordinating conjunction (cc)	
4 <u>prepositional phrases</u>	
1 [main clause]	
1 subject-verb pair (s v)	

Fix It!	
2 capitals	
4 commas	
1 end mark	

courtiers
members of a royal court

                    s   v   *prep*   *op*   *v*
[She once stole, into the ~T~hrone ~R~oom, swung

prep   *op*   *cc*   *v*   *prep*   *op* *prep*
on the chandeliers, and landed, at the feet of the

                              op
scandalized **courtiers**].

Prep Phrase	Each prepositional phrase begins with a preposition and ends with a noun, the object of the preposition. The words between the preposition and its object are article adjectives (a, an, the) or adjectives that describe the noun. What kind of room? *throne* What kind of courtiers? *scandalized*
Conjunction	*and* connects three verbs: *stole, swung,* and *landed* a, b, and c
Ask Students	Why does *and* not connect *chandeliers* and *landed*? A coordinating conjunction (cc) connects items that are grammatically the same. *Chandeliers* is a noun; *landed* is a verb.
S V Pairs MC	**She stole, swung, landed**
Commas	Use commas to separate three or more items in a series connected with a cc. **PATTERN a, b, and c** Because the prepositional phrases modify the verbs they follow, place the commas at the end of the prepositional phrases. Do not use a comma in front of a prepositional phrase.

Rewrite It!   She once stole into the throne room, swung on the chandeliers, and landed at the feet of the
scandalized courtiers.

Read It!	Mark It!	Fix It!	Day 3

On another occasion, she upset the prestigious new chef, and her staff. They were experimenting, with Sturgeon **roe** ice cream

roe
fish eggs

Mark It!

1 coordinating conjunction (cc)
2 prepositional phrases
2 [main clauses]
2 subject-verb pairs (s v)

Fix It!

1 capital
3 commas
1 end mark

prep — *op* — *s* — *v*
On another occasion, [she upset the prestigious new

cc — *s* — *v* — *v* — *prep*
chef, and her staff]. [They were experimenting, with

op
Sturgeon **roe** ice cream].

Capitalization	**sturgeon** lowercase, common noun
	Do not capitalize the common name of animals and plants. Just as you do not capitalize *goldfish*, *tuna*, or *shark*, do not capitalize *sturgeon*.
Prep Phrase	Both prepositional phrases begin with a preposition and end with a noun, the object of the preposition. The words between the preposition and its object are adjectives that describe the noun. Which occasion? *another* What kind of ice cream? *sturgeon roe*
Conjunction	**and** connects two nouns: *chef* and *staff* a and b
S V Pairs	MC **she upset**
	MC **They were experimenting**
Note	A word that ends in -ing functions as a verb only if it follows a helping verb. In the second sentence *experimenting* functions as a verb because it follows the helping verb *were*.
Commas	Do not use a comma if a prepositional opener has fewer than five words.
	Do not use a comma to separate two items connected with a cc. **PATTERN a and b**
	Do not use a comma in front of a prepositional phrase.

Rewrite It!   On another occasion she upset the prestigious new chef and her staff. They were experimenting with sturgeon roe ice cream.

Read It!	Mark It!	Fix It!	Day 4

Dorinda sneaked a taste, and expected a sweet
treat but instead of bits of chocolate the taste
of salty fish eggs first surprised and then **repulsed** her

3 coordinating conjunctions (cc)
3 prepositional phrases
2 [main clauses]
2 subject-verb pairs (s v)

3 commas
1 end mark

repulsed
caused disgust

     s   *v*   *cc*   *v*

[Dorinda sneaked a taste, and expected a sweet

    cc   *prep*   *op* *prep*   *op*   *s*

treat], but instead of bits of chocolate, [the taste

prep   *op*   *v*   *cc*   *v*

of salty fish eggs first surprised and then **repulsed** her].

Prep Phrase	Each prepositional phrase begins with a preposition and ends with a noun, the object of the preposition. The words between the preposition and its object are article adjectives (a, an, the) or adjectives that describe the noun. What kind of eggs? *salty fish*
Conjunction	**and** connects two verbs: *sneaked* and *expected* A subject and verb (Dorinda sneaked) come before the cc, but only a verb (expected) comes after the cc. A comma is not used. MC cc 2nd verb **but** connects two main clauses. A subject and verb pair (Dorinda sneaked, expected) comes before the cc, and a subject and verb pair (taste surprised, repulsed) comes after the cc. A comma is required. MC, cc MC **and** connects two verbs: *surprised* and *repulsed* A subject and verb (taste surprised) come before the cc, but only a verb (repulsed) comes after the cc. A comma is not used. MC cc 2nd verb
S V Pairs	MC ***Dorinda sneaked, expected*** MC ***taste surprised, repulsed***
Commas	Do not use a comma before a cc when it connects two verbs. **PATTERN MC cc 2nd verb** Use a comma to separate main clauses connected with a cc. **PATTERN MC, cc MC** Use a comma if two + prepositional phrases open a sentence. Put the comma after the last phrase.
Note	Although *instead of bits of chocolate* initially appears to be a mid-sentence prepositional phrase, after analyzing the sentence, it is clear that *instead of bits of chocolate* comes before the main clause that it modifies. Do not include *instead of bits of chocolate* in the main clause square brackets. Punctuate it as if it were a prepositional opener.

Rewrite It!   Dorinda sneaked a taste and expected a sweet treat, but instead of bits of chocolate, the taste of
salty fish eggs first surprised and then repulsed her.

Learn It!

Clause

A **clause** is a group of related words that contains both a subject and a verb.

Main Clause

Week 1 you learned that a **main clause** contains a subject and a verb and expresses a complete thought.

     s   *v*

[Dorinda's dress was expensive].

 Every sentence must have a main clause.

    s *v*   *s* *v*

[Dorinda's dress was expensive], and [this frustrated her father].

 Two main clauses can be placed in the same sentence if they are connected with a comma and a coordinating conjunction. **MC, cc MC**

Dependent Clause

A **dependent clause** contains a subject and a verb but does not express a complete thought. It cannot stand alone as a sentence but must have a main clause before or after it. In this book you will mark three types of dependent clauses.

Who/Which Clause

      w/w *s*   *v*

[Dorinda's dress, (which she purchased online), was expensive].

 A ***who/which* clause** is a dependent clause that begins with *who* or *which*. It is an adjective clause because it follows the noun it describes. Use the pronoun *who* when referring to people, personified animals, and pets. Use the pronoun *which* when referring to things, animals, and places.

 The subject of most *who/which* clauses is *who* or *which,* but sometimes the subject is another word in the clause.

 When the first word of either a *who* or a *which* clause functions as an adjective, use *whose. Whose* is a possessive case pronoun, which functions as an adjective to show ownership.

 Place commas around a *who/which* clause if it is nonessential.

Do not place commas around a *who/which* clause if it is essential (changes the meaning of the sentence).

 Weeks 3–6 contain only nonessential *who/which* clauses. They require commas.
 Week 7 you will learn how to determine if a clause is essential or nonessential.

That Clause

       that *s*   *v*

[It frustrated the king] (that Dorinda purchased the dress).

 A ***that* clause** is a dependent clause that begins with the word *that* and contains a subject and a verb. Because *that* clauses are essential to the sentence, they do not take commas.

 That clauses do not take commas.

Side notes

Another name for a main clause is an independent clause.

Clause Overview: Appendix III

For more information about clauses, see pages G-20 to G-22.

Another name for a dependent clause is a subordinate clause.

Ask students to identify the subject and verb in the *who/which* clause and the noun that it describes.

What is the verb? **purchased**

Who purchased? **she**

which she purchased online describes *dress*

This clause is nonessential because it does not change the meaning of the sentence. Without the *which* clause, the dress is still expensive. Use commas.

Ask students to identify the subject and verb in the *that* clause.

What is the verb? **purchased**

Who purchased? **Dorinda**

Do not use commas.

Adverb Clause

    AC   *s*   *v*   *v*
(Although Dorinda did not need another dress), [she

                   AC   *s* *v*
purchased this one] (because it had real gold).

An **adverb clause** is a dependent clause that begins with a www word (a subordinating conjunction) and contains a subject and a verb.

The acronym *www.asia.b* reminds you of the eight most common www words. However, these are not the only words that begin an adverb clause. Other words can function as www words too.

Memorize It!   **when   while   where   as   since   if   although   because   after   before   until   unless   whenever   whereas   than**

A www word must have a subject and verb after it to begin an adverb clause.

Use a comma after an adverb clause that comes before a main clause.
PATTERN AC, MC

Do not use a comma before an adverb clause.
PATTERN MC AC

Mark It! and Fix It!

Recognizing the basic clause and phrase structures in a sentence will help you punctuate sentences properly. Label the subject-verb pairs to determine how many clauses are in each sentence. Focus on the word that begins the clause to determine if it is a dependent clause or a main clause. After you have identified each clause, check its placement in the sentence and follow the comma rules.

Mark It!   Place parentheses around the dependent clause.
                Write *v* above each verb and *s* above each subject.
                Identify the dependent clause by looking at the first word of the clause.
                Write *w/w* above the word *who, which,* or *whose.*
                Write *that* above the word *that.*
                Write *AC* above the *www* word.

Fix It!   Insert or remove commas. Follow the comma rules.

            w/w   *s*   *v*
[King Morton, (whose castle was vast), had lost his crown].

                     that   *s* *v* *v*
[It frustrated the king], (that he had lost his crown).

                     AC   *s* *v* *v*
[The king was irritable], (since he had lost his crown).

Sidebar notes

Ask students to identify the subject and verb in the adverb clause.

What is the verb? *did need*

Who did need? *Dorinda*

What is the verb? *had*

What had? *it*

Use a comma after, not before, an adverb clause.

Week 16 students will learn that subordinating conjunctions can also start adjective clauses When they do, different punctuation rules apply.

For the reader, the ability to recognize clauses results in greater comprehension.

For the writer, the ability to organize and punctuate clauses results in clearer communication.

Students complete the passage in this order: Read It! Mark It! Fix It!

The princess who had earned a reputation for beauty considered herself quite **chic**, because she wore her hair, in a french twist, and had a beauty spot on her cheek

chic
attractive and fashionable; stylish

1 coordinating conjunction (cc)	1 indent
3 prepositional phrases	1 capital
1 [main clause]	5 commas
1 who/which clause (w/w)	1 end mark
1 adverb clause (AC)	
3 subject-verb pairs (s v)	

¶ [The princess, (who had earned a reputation for beauty), considered herself quite **chic**], (because she wore her hair, in a french twist, and had a beauty spot on her cheek).

Indentation	new topic
Capitalization	**French** uppercase, proper adjective
	Capitalize proper adjectives formed from proper nouns. The proper adjective *French* comes from the proper noun *France*, the name of a specific country.
Prep Phrase	*For beauty* is a prepositional phrase. In this sentence *for* functions as a preposition.
	PATTERN preposition + noun (no verb) When *for* functions as a conjunction, it connects equal items and means *since*. A word can perform only one function in a sentence.
Conjunction	***and*** connects two verbs: *wore* and *had* A subject and verb (she wore) come before the cc, but only a verb (had) comes after the cc. A comma is not used. MC cc 2nd verb
S V Pairs MC	***princess considered***
w/w	***who had earned*** The subject of the clause is *who*. The *who* clause describes *princess*, the noun it follows.
AC	*because* **she wore, had**
Ask Students	How do you know *because she wore her hair in a French twist and had a beauty spot on her cheek* is an adverb clause?
	The word group begins with *because* and includes a subject + verb.
Commas	Place commas around a nonessential *who/which* clause.
	Do not put a comma in front of an adverb clause. **PATTERN MC AC**
	Do not put a comma in front of a prepositional phrase.
	Do not use a comma before a cc when it connects two verbs. **PATTERN MC cc 2nd verb**

Rewrite It!   The princess, who had earned a reputation for beauty, considered herself quite chic because she wore her hair in a French twist and had a beauty spot on her cheek.

Read It!	Mark It!	Fix It!	Day 2

Her beauty was flawed by her reputation for **fastidiousness**, and self-centeredness. King Morton hoped, that she would consider several young Suitors

fastidiousness
excessively particular, critical, or demanding

1 coordinating conjunction (cc)
2 prepositional phrases
2 [main clauses]
1 *that* clause (that)
3 subject-verb pairs (s v)

1 indent
1 capital
2 commas
1 end mark

s   v   v   *prep*   *op*   *prep*

[Her beauty was flawed <u>by her reputation</u> for

op   *cc*   *op*   s

<u>**fastidiousness**</u>, and self-centeredness]. ¶ [King Morton

v   *that*   s   *v*   *v*

hoped], (that she would consider several young Suitors).

Indentation	new topic	
Conjunction	**and** connects two nouns: *fastidiousness* and *self-centeredness* Both nouns function as the objects of the preposition *for*. For what? *for fastidiousness* and *(for) self-centeredness* a and b	
S V Pairs	MC	**beauty was flawed**
	MC	**King Morton hoped**
	that	*that* **she would consider**
Ask Students	How do you know *that she would consider consider several young suitors* is a *that* clause? The word group begins with *that* and includes a subject + verb.	
Commas	Do not use a comma to separate two items connected with a cc. **PATTERN a and b** Do not put a comma in front of a *that* clause.	
Note	Compound words can be spelled as one word, one hyphenated word, or two words. If in doubt, consult a dictionary. *self-centeredness*	

Rewrite It!   Her beauty was flawed by her reputation for fastidiousness and self-centeredness.
King Morton hoped that she would consider several young suitors.

Read It!	Mark It!	Fix It! Day 3

Dorinda refused them time after time yet they continued to **court** her. None were wealthy handsome or Titled enough, for her highness

2 coordinating conjunctions (cc)
2 prepositional phrases
3 [main clauses]
3 subject-verb pairs (s v)

1 capital
4 commas
1 end mark

court
try to win the favor of

$\overset{s}{[\text{Dorinda}} \overset{v}{\text{refused}} \text{ them time } \overset{prep}{\underline{\text{after}}} \overset{op}{\underline{\text{time}}}], \overset{cc}{\text{yet}} \overset{s}{[\text{they}}$

$\overset{v}{\text{continued}} \text{ to } \textbf{court} \text{ her}]. \overset{s}{[\text{None}} \overset{v}{\text{were}} \text{ wealthy, handsome,}$

$\overset{cc}{\text{or}} \cancel{T}\text{itled enough,} \overset{prep}{\underline{\text{for}}} \overset{op}{\underline{\text{her highness}}}].$

Conjunction	*yet* connects two main clauses. A subject and verb pair (Dorinda refused) comes before the cc, and a subject and verb pair (they continued) comes after the cc. A comma is required. MC, cc MC *or* connects three adjectives: *wealthy, handsome,* or *titled* a, b, and c
S V Pairs	MC *Dorinda refused* MC *they continued*
Ask Students	How do you know *they continued to court her* is a main clause? The word group includes a subject + verb and expresses a complete thought. It does not begin with a word that starts a dependent clause (who, which, that, www word).
	MC *None were*
Note	The phrase *to court* does not follow the **PATTERN** preposition + noun. When *to* is followed by a verb, it is called an infinitive. Do not mark infinitives as prepositional phrases because they include a verb. Do not mark infinitives as verbs because they do not have a subject. They function as neither a prepositional phrase nor a verb. Infinitives function as adjectives, adverbs, or nouns.
Commas	Use a comma to separate two main clauses connected with a cc. **PATTERN** MC, cc MC Use commas to separate three or more items in a series connected with a cc. **PATTERN** a, b, and c Do not put a comma in front of a prepositional phrase.

Rewrite It! Dorinda refused them time after time, yet they continued to court her. None were wealthy, handsome, or titled enough for her highness.

Read It!	Mark It!	Fix It!	Day 4

King Morton whose patience was **dwindling** shook his head in despair, and sighed deeply when his daughter voiced her desires

dwindling
gradually becoming smaller or less

1 coordinating conjunction (cc)
1 <u>prepositional phrase</u>
1 [main clause]
1 *who/which* clause (w/w)
1 *adverb clause* (AC)
3 subject-verb pairs (s v)

3 commas
1 end mark

$$\overset{s}{[}\text{King Morton}, \overset{w/w}{(}\text{whose patience was } \textbf{dwindling}), \overset{s}{\text{shook}}$$

[King Morton, (whose patience was **dwindling**), shook
  s   w/w   s v

his head in despair, and sighed deeply] (when his
       prep op   cc   v   AC

daughter voiced her desires).
   s   v

Conjunction	*and* connects two verbs: *shook* and *sighed* A subject and verb (King Morton shook) come before the cc, but only a verb (sighed) comes after the cc. A comma is not used. MC cc 2nd verb
S V Pairs	MC ***King Morton shook, sighed***
	w/w *whose **patience was dwindling*** The subject of the clause is *patience*. The word *whose* functions as an adjective. (Whose (King Morton's) patience was dwindling.) The *whose* clause describes *King Morton*, the noun it follows.
Ask Students	How do you know *whose patience was dwindling* is a *who/which* clause? The word group begins with *whose* (a form of *who*) and includes a subject + verb.
Commas	AC *when **daughter voiced*** Place commas around a nonessential *who/which* clause. Do not use a comma before a cc when it connects two verbs. **PATTERN MC cc 2nd verb**

Rewrite It!   King Morton, whose patience was dwindling, shook his head in despair and sighed deeply when his daughter voiced her desires.

Learn It!

Sentence Opener

A **sentence opener** is a descriptive word, phrase, or clause that is added to the beginning of a sentence. Using different sentence openers makes writing more interesting.

#1 Subject Opener

①   s   v

[The tired governess wondered how to teach Dorinda].

   A **#1 subject opener** is a sentence that begins with the subject of the sentence. Sometimes an article or adjective will come before the subject, but the sentence is still a #1 subject opener.

#2 Prepositional Opener

②

Before the queen's unfortunate death, [Constance served the queen].

②

At the encouragement of the king, [Constance cared for the girls].

   A **#2 prepositional opener** is a sentence that begins with a prepositional phrase. The first word in the sentence must be a preposition.

> If a prepositional opener has five words or more, follow it with a comma.
> If two or more prepositional phrases open a sentence, follow the last phrase with a comma.

#3 -ly Adverb Opener

③ -ly

Clearly, [Dorinda embarrassed Lady Constance].

③ -ly

Secretly [Constance enjoyed Dorinda's spunk].

   A **#3 -ly adverb opener** is a sentence that begins with an -ly adverb.

> Use a comma if an -ly adverb opener modifies the sentence.

> Do not use a comma if an -ly adverb opener modifies the verb.

To determine if an -ly adverb modifies the sentence, test it: It was _____ that _____ .
   If this makes sense, the -ly adverb is a sentence adverb. Use a comma.
   If this does not make sense, confirm that the -ly adverb modifies the verb. Do not use a comma.

Sentence Opener List: Appendix III

For more information about sentence openers, see pages G-42 to G-45.

The #1 subject opener always starts with a main clause.

Do not include the opener in the main clause square brackets.

Clearly is a sentence adverb. It modifies the entire sentence: It was clear that Dorinda embarrassed Lady Constance. Use a comma.

Secretly modifies the verb: Constance enjoyed in a secret manner. Do not use a comma.

#5 Clausal Opener

The #5 clausal opener will always have a comma and a main clause after it.

⑤ *AC*   *s*   *v*

(Although Dorinda disregarded regal protocol as a child), [Constance expected more from the princess].

> A **#5 clausal opener** is a sentence that begins with an adverb clause. The #5 clausal opener will always have a comma and a main clause after it.

> ❞ Use a comma after an adverb clause that comes before a main clause.
> **PATTERN AC, MC**

#6 Vss Opener

⑥   *s*   *v*

[Lady Constance needed a miracle].

Although *Lady Constance* is a single name, it is two words.

> A **# 6 vss opener** is a very short sentence. *Very short* means two to five words. *Sentence* means it must have a main clause.

The purpose of the very short sentence is to have a short sentence among longer sentences.

Mark It! and Fix It!

Starting this week, you will mark five of the six sentence openers. Number every sentence opener except questions and quoted sentences.

Students will mark every sentence opener except questions and quoted sentences.

Mark It!   Determine the type of opener that begins the sentence and number it. Number the openers after the passage has been marked and fixed.

Fix It!   Insert or remove commas. Follow the comma rules.

①   *s*   *v*

[The young princess counted the days until her birthday].

②

For her birthday, [Dorinda received a golden ball].

③ *-ly*

Oddly, [Dorinda tried to bounce the precious ball].

⑤ *AC*   *s*   *v*   *v*

(Because the ball was made of gold), [it would not bounce].

⑥   *s*   *v*

[King Morton raged].

For her birthday is shorter than five words. Do not use a comma.

Oddly is a sentence adverb. It was odd that ... Do not use a comma.

The #5 opener always uses a comma.

Sometimes it appears that more than one sentence opener begins a sentence. When this happens, place the comma after the last opener. Number the sentence opener based on the first word of the sentence.

Students number the sentence openers after the passage has been marked and fixed.

Clearly Dorinda annoyed many, in the palace.
Lady Constance who had cared for her since
childhood had virtually stopped training her
young **charge**.

charge
a responsibility entrusted to one

3 prepositional phrases   1 indent
2 [main clauses]   4 commas
1 who/which clause (w/w)
3 subject-verb pairs (s v)
2 openers

③ -ly adverb
           s   v   prep   op
¶ Clearly, [Dorinda annoyed many, in the palace].
① subject
   s   w/w   s   v   v   prep op   prep
[Lady Constance, (who had cared for her since
   op   v   v
childhood), had virtually stopped training her

young **charge**].

This is the last week that students label the function of words in the prepositional phrase.

Indentation	new topic
Ask Students	Why is *since childhood* a prepositional phrase and not an adverb clause? *Since childhood* does not have a verb. It follows the **PATTERN** preposition + noun (no verb).
S V Pairs	MC **Dorinda annoyed**
	MC **Lady Constance had stopped**
	w/w **who had cared** The subject of the clause is *who*. The *who* clause describes *Lady Constance*, the noun it follows.
Note	A word that ends in -ing functions as a verb only if it follows a helping verb. The word *training* functions as a noun because it is the thing that had stopped.
Commas	Use a comma if an -ly adverb opener modifies the sentence. It was clear that Dorinda annoyed many. Do not put a comma in front of a prepositional phrase. Place commas around a nonessential *who/which* clause.

Rewrite It!   Clearly, Dorinda annoyed many in the palace. Lady Constance, who had cared for her since childhood, had virtually stopped training her young charge.

Read It!	Mark It!	Fix It!	Day 2

Although Dorinda had seemed a lovable **tractable** and contented child in her youth many years of indulgence had spoiled her. She complained constantly.

tractable
easily managed or controlled

1 coordinating conjunction (cc)
2 prepositional phrases
2 [main clauses]
1 adverb clause (AC)
3 subject-verb pairs (s v)
2 openers

3 commas

⑤ clausal

AC   s   v   v

(Although Dorinda had seemed a lovable, **tractable,**

cc   prep   op   s   prep

and contented child in her youth), [many years of

                                       ⑥ vss

op   v   v   s   v

indulgence had spoiled her]. [She complained

constantly].

Conjunction	*and* connects three adjectives: *lovable, tractable,* and *contented* a, b, and c	
S V Pairs	AC *Although **Dorinda had seemed***	
	MC ***years had spoiled***	
	MC ***She complained***	
Commas	Use commas to separate three or more items in a series connected with a cc. **PATTERN a, b, and c**	
	Use a comma after an adverb clause. **PATTERN AC, MC**	

Rewrite It!   Although Dorinda had seemed a lovable, tractable, and contented child in her youth, many years of indulgence had spoiled her. She complained constantly.

Unfortunately no expense had been spared to **gratify** the two girls when the girls' Mother was alive. They enjoyed custom dolls with complete wardrobes, and assorted furniture but they always asked for more.

gratify
satisfy or indulge

2 coordinating conjunctions (cc)
2 prepositional phrases
3 [main clauses]
1 adverb clause (AC)
4 subject-verb pairs (s v)
2 openers

1 capital
3 commas

③ -ly adverb

                       s   v   v   v
Unfortunately, [no expense had been spared to **gratify**
                                                    ① subject
            AC   s   v   s
the two girls] (when the girls' Mother was alive). [They

  v   prep   op   cc
enjoyed custom dolls with complete wardrobes, and

      op   cc   s   v   prep   op
assorted furniture], but [they always asked for more].

Conjunction	**and** connects two nouns: *wardrobes* and *furniture* Both nouns function as the objects of the preposition *with*. With what? *with wardrobes* and *(with) furniture* a and b **but** connects two main clauses. A subject and verb pair (They enjoyed) comes before the cc, and a subject and verb pair (they asked) comes after the cc. A comma is required. MC, cc MC
Note	The word *girls* is a plural noun, and the word *girls'* is a possessive adjective. The apostrophe indicates that a word is a possessive adjective. *girl's* = one girl; *girls'* = two or more girls
S V Pairs	MC ***expense had been spared***
Ask Students	Why is *gratify* not a verb? *To* comes before *gratify*. *To gratify* is an infinitive. *To gratify* does not have a subject. Every verb has a subject.
	AC *when **mother was*** The adjective *alive* follows the linking verb and describes the subject. MC ***They enjoyed*** MC ***they asked***
Commas	Use a comma if an -ly adverb opener modifies the sentence. It was unfortunate that no expense had been spared. Do not use a comma to separate two items connected with a cc. PATTERN a and b Use a comma to separate two main clauses connected with a cc. PATTERN MC, cc MC

Rewrite It!   Unfortunately, no expense had been spared to gratify the two girls when the girls' mother was alive. They enjoyed custom dolls with complete wardrobes and assorted furniture, but they always asked for more.

When they were young girls they were disappointed, that their fairy-tale playground did not **resemble** Cinderella's Castle. As a teenager, Dorinda stomped her foot, and pouted, when a new television was delivered.

resemble
be like or similar to

Mark It!
1 coordinating conjunction (cc)
1 prepositional phrase
2 [main clauses]
1 *that* clause (that)
2 adverb clauses (AC)
5 subject-verb pairs (s v)
2 openers

Fix It!
1 capital
5 commas

(5) clausal

AC   s   v   s   v
(When they were young girls), [they were disappointed],

that   s   v   v
(that their fairy-tale playground did not resemble

(2) prepositional
prep   op   s   v
Cinderella's Castle). As a teenager, [Dorinda stomped her

cc   v   AC   s   v   v
foot, and pouted], (when a new television was delivered).

Conjunction		*and* connects two verbs: *stomped* and *pouted* A subject and verb (Dorinda stomped) come before the cc, but only a verb (pouted) comes after the cc. A comma is not used. MC cc 2nd verb
S V Pairs	AC	*When* **they were**
	MC	**they were** The adjective *disappointed* follows the linking verb and describes the subject.
	that	*that* **playground did resemble**
	MC	**Dorinda stomped, pouted**
	AC	*when* **television was delivered**
Ask Students		Why is *As a teenager* a #2 prepositional opener and not a #5 clausal opener? *As a teenager* does not have a verb. It follows the **PATTERN preposition + noun (no verb)**.
Commas		Use a comma after an adverb clause. **PATTERN AC, MC**
		Do not put a comma in front of a *that* clause.
		Do not use a comma if a prepositional opener has fewer than five words.
		Do not use a comma before a cc when it connects two verbs. **PATTERN MC cc 2nd verb**
		Do not put a comma in front of an adverb clause. **PATTERN MC AC**

Rewrite It!   When they were young girls, they were disappointed that their fairy-tale playground did not resemble Cinderella's castle. As a teenager Dorinda stomped her foot and pouted when a new television was delivered.

Learn It!

Sentence Opener

A **sentence opener** is a descriptive word, phrase, or clause that is added to the beginning of a sentence. Number every sentence opener except questions and quoted sentences.

#4 -ing Opener

④   S   V
Rolling her eyes, [Dorinda ignored her father].

A **#4 -ing opener** begins with a participle, a verb form that ends in -ing. The -ing opener usually includes additional words that form a phrase. *Rolling* is the participle. *Rolling her eyes* is the participial phrase. The entire phrase functions as an adjective. *Rolling her eyes* describes *Dorinda*.

The thing after the comma must be the thing doing the inging. *Dorinda* is the thing (subject of main clause) after the comma. *Dorinda* is doing the *rolling*.

❜ Use a comma after an -ing opener, even if it is short.
PATTERN -ing word/phrase, main clause

Quotation Marks

"My ball rolled away," the princess cried.

Quotation marks indicate words are spoken. The quote is the sentence in quotation marks. The attribution is the person speaking and the speaking verb. If a quote has an attribution, the attribution may precede, interrupt, or follow the quote.

Capitalize the first word of the quote. Capitalize the first word of the attribution if it is the first word of the sentence.

Place quotation marks around the words that are spoken. Separate an attribution from a direct quote with a comma. If a direct quote is a question or exclamation, follow with a ? or !

❜ Use a comma to separate an attribution from a direct quote.

Noun of Direct Address

"Dorinda, [will you toss the ball outdoors]?"

A **noun of direct address** (NDA) is a noun used to directly address someone. It only appears in a quoted sentence. Capitalize a title used as an NDA with the exceptions of *sir* and *madam*. In the example *Dorinda* is the NDA.

❜ Place commas around a noun of direct address.

Apostrophe

The sisters agreed. "Let's sit on Dad's throne!"

An **apostrophe** indicates that letters are missing in a contraction (Let's) or shows ownership with a possessive adjective. To form a singular possessive adjective, add an apostrophe + *s* to a noun: Dad's. To form a plural possessive adjective when the noun ends in *s*, add an apostrophe after the *s*: girls'. If the plural noun does not end in *s*, add an apostrophe + *s*: children's.

Sentence Opener List: Appendix III

For more information about #4 -ing openers, see page G-44.

A comma separates the -ing opener from the main clause.

A main clause follows the comma. If you remove the -ing opener, a sentence will remain.

In the example, *the princess cried* is the attribution. The first word of the attribution is not capitalized because it does not begin the sentence.

Neither the quoted sentence example under Noun of Direct Address nor the one under Apostrophe has an attribution. *The sisters agreed* is a complete thought. A period follows *agreed*.

A noun can perform only one function in a sentence. The NDA is *Dorinda*. The subject is *you*.

Sisters is a plural noun. An apostrophe is not used.

The apostrophe shows where the letter *u* has been removed from the phrase *Let us*.

The apostrophe + *s* indicates that *Dad's* is a possessive adjective, not a plural noun.

Verb

Every verb has a subject. A verb acts alone or in phrases to perform different actions.

Action Verb

Dorinda had a golden ball. She tossed it into the air.

An **action verb** (av) shows action or ownership.

Had shows ownership. *Tossed* shows action.

Linking Verb

Dorinda was a princess. She appeared spoiled.

A **linking verb** (lv) links the subject to a noun or to an adjective.

Was is a linking verb that links the subject *Dorinda* to the noun *princess*. The noun *princess* follows the linking verb and renames the subject, the word *Dorinda*.

Appeared is a linking verb that links the subject *She* to the adjective *spoiled*. The adjective *spoiled* follows the linking verb and describes the subject, the word *she*.

Helping Verb

Dorinda had tossed the ball. She could appear spoiled.

A **helping verb** (hv) helps an action verb or a linking verb. The helping verb and the verb it helps (action or linking) form a verb phrase.

Had is a helping verb that helps the action verb *tossed*. You know *had* is a helping verb because a verb follows it. The verb phrase *had tossed* shows action.

Could is a helping verb that helps the linking verb *appear*. You know *could* is a helping verb because a verb follows it. The verb phrase *could appear* links the subject *She* to the adjective *spoiled*.

> The noun (or pronoun) that follows an action verb is called a direct object.

> The noun (or pronoun) that follows a linking verb is called a predicate noun.

> The adjective that follows a linking verb is called a predicate adjective.

> Both predicate nouns and predicate adjectives are called subject complements.

> A helping verb does not function alone. One or more verbs will follow a helping verb and form a verb phrase.

> A verb phrase shows action or links the subject to a noun or an adjective.

Mark It! Mark every verb as an action verb (*av*), linking verb (*lv*), or helping verb (*hv*).

```
       s    v            v       s   v
            hv           av          lv
The gold ball would not bounce. It was too heavy.
```

Think About It!

Be verbs can be linking verbs or helping verbs. If a *be* verb has a noun or an adjective after it, it is a linking verb. If a *be* verb has another verb after it, it is a helping verb.

The round gold object was (lv) a ball (n). It was (lv) heavy (adj).
The ball was (hv) thrown (av) into the air.

Many linking verbs can be linking or action verbs. If you can substitute *is* for the verb, it is a linking verb. If you cannot, it is an action verb.

Ice cream tasted sweet. Substitute *is*: Ice cream is sweet. *Tasted* is a linking verb.
She tasted the ice cream. Substitute *is*: She is the ice cream. *Tasted* is an action verb.

Many helping verbs can be helping or action verbs. If a verb on the helping verb list has a verb after it, the first verb is a helping verb. If it does not, it is an action verb.

Dorinda had (av) a golden ball. A verb does not follow *had*.
Dorinda had (hv) tossed (av) the ball. *Tossed* follows *had*.

Students continue to underline the prepositional phrases. However, they no longer need to mark *prep* and *op*.
Students number the sentence openers after the passage has been marked and fixed.

Declaring it **minuscule** she demanded a theater room with sound lighting and comfort. Although Lady Constance did not approve she met Dorindas demands, because she did not want to argue with her.

minuscule
very small

1 coordinating conjunction (cc)   5 commas
2 prepositional phrases   1 apostrophe
2 [main clauses]
2 adverb clauses (AC)
4 subject-verb pairs (s v)
2 openers

④ -ing

　　　　　　　　　　　　s　　　v
　　　　　　　　　　　　　　av

Declaring it **minuscule,** [she demanded a theater

　　　　　　　　　　　　　　　　　⑤ clausal
　　　　　　　　　cc　　　　　　AC

room with sound, lighting, and comfort]. (Although

　s　　　　　　v　　　　v　　　　s　　v
　　　　　hv　　　　av　　　　　　av

Lady Constance did not approve), [she met Dorinda's

　　　　　　　　s　　v　　　　v
　　　AC　　　　　hv　　　av

demands], (because she did not want to argue with her).

This is the only week that an explanation about apostrophes is provided.

Conjunction	**and** connects three nouns: *sound, lighting,* and *comfort* These nouns function as the objects of the preposition *with*. With what? *with sound, (with) lighting,* and *(with) comfort* a, b, and c
S V Pairs	MC **she demanded** (action)
	AC Although **Lady Constance did approve** (action) *Did* is a helping verb. *Did approve* is the verb phrase.
	MC **she met** (action)
	AC because **she did want** (action) *Did* is a helping verb. *Did want* is the verb phrase.
Commas	Use a comma after an -ing opener. **PATTERN -ing word/phrase, main clause** The thing after the comma must be the thing doing the inging. *She* is doing the *declaring*.
	Use commas to separate three or more items in a series connected with a cc. **PATTERN a, b, and c**
	Use a comma after an adverb clause. **PATTERN AC, MC**
	Do not put a comma in front of an adverb clause. **PATTERN MC AC**
Apostrophes	*Dorinda's* is a possessive adjective, not a plural noun. Use an apostrophe to show ownership.

Rewrite It!   Declaring it minuscule, she demanded a theater room with sound, lighting, and comfort. Although Lady Constance did not approve, she met Dorinda's demands because she did not want to argue with her.

Read It!	Mark It!	Fix It!	Day 2

On a crisp spring morning Princess Dorinda played, with her latest plaything which was a golden ball. Tossing it up she wandered among the plant's in the **conservatory**.

conservatory
a greenhouse

4 prepositional phrases
2 [main clauses]
1 *who/which* clause (w/w)
3 subject-verb pairs (s v)
2 openers

1 indent
4 commas
1 apostrophe

② prepositional

¶ On a crisp spring morning, [Princess Dorinda played,
with her latest plaything], (which was a golden ball).
④ -ing
Tossing it up, [she wandered among the plant's

in the **conservatory**].

Indentation	new topic
S V Pairs	MC ***Princess Dorinda played*** (action)
	w/w ***which was*** (linking) The noun *ball* follows the linking verb and renames the subject, the word *which*. The *which* clause describes *plaything*, the noun it follows.
	MC ***she wandered*** (action)
Commas	Use a comma if a prepositional opener has five words or more.
	Do not put a comma in front of a prepositional phrase.
	Place commas around a nonessential *who/which* clause.
	Use a comma after an -ing opener. **PATTERN** -ing word/phrase, main clause
	The thing after the comma must be the thing doing the inging. *She* is doing the *tossing*.
Apostrophes	*Plants* is a plural noun, not a possessive adjective. Do not use an apostrophe.

Rewrite It!   On a crisp spring morning, Princess Dorinda played with her latest plaything, which was a golden ball. Tossing it up, she wandered among the plants in the conservatory.

Read It!	Mark It!	Fix It! Day 3

From a distance, the King observed his daughter, and her golden ball. **Eyeing** the glass windows he suggested Dorinda why dont you toss that ball in the garden.

eyeing
looking at something closely and carefully

1 coordinating conjunction (cc)
2 prepositional phrases
3 [main clauses]
3 subject-verb pairs (s v)
2 openers

1 indent
1 capital
5 commas
1 end mark
2 quotation marks
1 apostrophe

② prepositional

                                    s   v
                                              av   cc
¶ From a distance, [the King observed his daughter, and
                    ④ -ing   s   v
                                                                            av
her golden ball]. **Eyeing** the glass windows, [he suggested],
            v   s   v
            hv   av
"Dorinda, [why don't you toss that ball in the garden].?"

Indentation	new speaker
End Marks	Use a question mark when a quote asks a question. **PATTERN** Attribution, "Quote?"
Conjunction	**and** connects two nouns: *daughter* and *ball* a and b
S V Pairs	MC **king observed** (action)
	MC **he suggested** (action)
	MC **you do toss** (action) The contraction *don't* includes both a helping verb (do) and an adverb (not). *Do toss* is the verb phrase.
Ask Students	Why is *that ball in the garden* not a *that* clause? The word group does not have a subject + verb. *That* is an adjective. Which ball? *that*
Note	Dorinda is the noun of direct address (NDA). Because a noun can perform only one function in a sentence, a noun of direct address is never the subject of the sentence.
Commas	Do not use a comma if a prepositional opener has fewer than five words.
	Do not use a comma to separate two items connected with a cc. **PATTERN a and b**
	Use a comma after an -ing opener. **PATTERN -ing word/phrase, main clause** The thing after the comma must be the thing doing the inging. *He* is doing the *eyeing*.
	Use a comma to separate an attribution from a direct quote. **PATTERN Attribution, "Quote?"**
	Place commas around a noun of direct address (NDA). **Dorinda,**
Apostrophes	*Don't* is a contraction. Use an apostrophe to show where letters have been removed.

Rewrite It!   From a distance the king observed his daughter and her golden ball. Eyeing the glass windows, he suggested, "Dorinda, why don't you toss that ball in the garden?"

Read It!	Mark It!	Fix It!	Day 4

Dorinda rolled her eyes. Crossly, she grabbed her stylish boots, and jacket, and went outside. With her ball in hand the Princess **roamed** through the expansive castle gardens.

roamed
walked without a purpose or direction

2 coordinating conjunctions (cc)
3 prepositional phrases
3 [main clauses]
3 subject-verb pairs (s v)
3 openers

1 indent
1 capital
4 commas

⑥ vss

                    s   v
                                        av

¶ [Dorinda rolled her eyes]. Crossly, [she grabbed her

③ -ly adverb   s   v
                               av

                                              ② prepositional
         cc   cc   av
                         v

stylish boots, and jacket, and went outside]. With her

         s
                       v
                      av

ball in hand, [the Princess **roamed** through the

expansive castle gardens].

Indentation	new topic
Conjunction	**and** connects two nouns: *boots* and *jacket* a and b **and** connects two verbs: *grabbed* and *went* A subject and verb (she grabbed) come before the cc, but only a verb (went) comes after the cc. A comma is not used. MC cc 2nd verb
Ask Students	In the second sentence, why is the word *outside* not a preposition? A preposition begins a prepositional phrase. **PATTERN preposition + noun (no verb)** *Outside* is an adverb, not a preposition.
S V Pairs	MC **Dorinda rolled** (action) MC **she grabbed** (action), **went** (action) The single subject *she* is followed by two verbs. The first verb in the clause is *grabbed*. The second verb in this clause is *went*. Both show action. MC **princess roamed** (action)
Commas	Do not use a comma if an -ly adverb opener modifies the verb(s). She grabbed and went in a cross manner. Do not use a comma to separate two items connected with a cc. **PATTERN a and b** Do not use a comma before a cc when it connects two verbs. **PATTERN MC cc 2nd verb** Use a comma if two + prepositional phrases open a sentence. Put the comma after the last phrase.

Rewrite It!   Dorinda rolled her eyes. Crossly she grabbed her stylish boots and jacket and went outside. With her ball in hand, the princess roamed through the expansive castle gardens.

Learn It!

Adjective

An **adjective** describes a noun or a pronoun. It can come before the noun it describes (*charming* princess), or it can follow a linking verb and describe the subject of the clause (princess was *charming*).

Often, two or more adjectives come before a noun. If the consecutive adjectives are cumulative adjectives, do not use a comma. If they are coordinate adjectives, use a comma.

Adjectives can be grouped into categories.

Categories	Some Examples		
quantity	two	several	few
opinion	careless	unfortunate	spoiled
size	deep	heavy	narrow
age	new	young	ancient
shape	round	angular	square
color	red	blue	brunette
origin	European	Catholic	imperial
material	gold	stone	cotton
purpose	frying (pan)	throne (room)	shade (tree)

Cumulative Adjectives

     adj   *adj*   *n*
The heavy gold ball did not bounce.

Cumulative adjectives build on each other. The first adjective describes the second adjective and the noun that follows. Cumulative adjectives are arranged in a specific order: quantity, opinion, size, age, shape, color, origin, material, purpose. You cannot reverse their order or add *and* between them.

The first adjective (heavy) describes the second adjective and the noun together (gold ball).

It is a gold ball that is heavy. Both the "gold heavy ball" and the "heavy and gold ball" sound strange. *Heavy* and *gold* are cumulative adjectives and do not need a comma.

Do not use a comma to separate cumulative adjectives.

Coordinate Adjectives

       adj   *adj*   *n*
Dorinda was often a careless, spoiled princess.

Coordinate adjectives independently describe the noun that follows. The adjectives belong in the same category. You can reverse their order or add *and* between them.

Dorinda was both a careless princess and a spoiled princess. Each adjective independently describes the noun.

Both the "spoiled careless princess" and the "careless and spoiled princess" sound correct. *Careless* and *spoiled* are coordinate adjectives and need a comma.

 Use a comma to separate coordinate adjectives.

For more information about cumulative and coordinate adjectives, see page G-14.

The chart is a tool. Some adjectives can be classified in more than one category. *Gold* may describe an age (golden years), color (golden blonde), or material (gold ball).

Use the tests on the next page. Consider context and use the definitions.

Cumulative adjectives build on each other. Do not use a comma.

Coordinate adjectives work independently. Use a comma.

Cumulative or Coordinate?

Two tests help determine whether consecutive adjectives before a noun are cumulative or coordinate.

Can you reverse their order?

Can you add *and* between them?

If you answer no, the adjectives are cumulative. Do not use a comma.

If you answer yes, the adjectives are coordinate. Use a comma.

Fix It!   Remove the comma between cumulative adjectives.

Add a comma between coordinate adjectives.

The new, round ball rolled into the deep, narrow well.

Read each sentence and decide if the two adjectives are cumulative or coordinate.

Circle the correct answer.

Insert a comma if the adjectives are coordinate.

In the city lived a skillful, popular toymaker.

cumulative   **(coordinate)**

After observing the princesses, he had a strange, wonderful idea.

cumulative   **(coordinate)**

He would design a solid gold ball fit for royalty.

(cumulative)   coordinate

It would be a unique, expensive toy.

cumulative   **(coordinate)**

Of course, it would feel like heavy lead weights.

(cumulative)   coordinate

However, the girls would enjoy rolling it down a smooth brick path.

(cumulative)   coordinate

He never imagined that the ball would roll into the deep, dark well.

cumulative   **(coordinate)**

Sidebar:

When two adjectives come before a noun, have students test them by reversing their order and by adding *and* between them. If yes to the tests, yes to a comma. If no to the tests, no to a comma.

The first three are modeled for you.

Reverse order: the popular skillful toymaker. Yes, you can reverse the order.

Add *and*: the skillful and popular toymaker. Yes, you can add *and*.

These are coordinate adjectives. They need a comma.

Reverse order: the wonderful strange idea. Yes, you can reverse the order.

Add *and*: the strange and wonderful idea. Yes, you can add *and*.

These are coordinate adjectives. They need a comma.

Reverse order: the gold solid ball. No, you cannot reverse the order.

Add *and*: the solid and gold ball. No, you cannot add *and*.

These are cumulative adjectives. They do not need a comma.

Read It!	Mark It!	Fix It!	Day 1

Meandering aimlessly through the **stately**, imperial garden's princess Dorinda repeatedly tossed her ball up, and down, and caught it with slick confidence.

stately
majestic; very impressive in appearance and size

2 coordinating conjunctions (cc)
2 <u>prepositional phrases</u>
1 [main clause]
1 subject-verb pair (s v)
1 opener

1 capital
4 commas
1 apostrophe

④ -ing

Meandering aimlessly <u>through the **stately**, imperial</u>
                                          s   v
                                                                              av
<u>garden's</u>, [princess Dorinda repeatedly tossed her ball
    cc   cc   v
                                    av
up, and down, and caught it <u>with slick confidence</u>].

Conjunction	***and*** connects two adverbs: *up* and *down* a and b ***and*** connects two verbs: *tossed* and *caught* A subject and verb (Dorinda tossed) come before the cc, but only a verb (caught) comes after the cc. A comma is not used. MC cc 2nd verb
Adjective	The first adjective (stately) describes the second adjective and the noun together (imperial gardens). These adjectives are cumulative. Do not use a comma.
Ask Students	The adjectives *stately* and *imperial* belong in which categories? See page 31. *Stately* is an adjective of opinion; *imperial* is an adjective of origin.
S V Pairs MC	***Princess Dorinda tossed*** (action), ***caught*** (action) The single subject *Princess Dorinda* is followed by two verbs. The first verb in the clause is *tossed*. The second verb in this clause is *caught*. Both show action.
Commas	Use a comma after an -ing opener. **PATTERN -ing word/phrase, main clause** The thing after the comma must be the thing doing the inging. *Princess Dorinda* is doing the *meandering*. Do not use a comma to separate cumulative adjectives (stately imperial gardens). Do not use a comma to separate two items connected with a cc. **PATTERN a and b** Do not use a comma before a cc when it connects two verbs. **PATTERN MC cc 2nd verb**

Rewrite It!   Meandering aimlessly through the stately imperial gardens, Princess Dorinda repeatedly tossed her ball up and down and caught it with slick confidence.

Read It!	Mark It!	Fix It!	Day 2

At the corner of the well a most **regrettable** event occurred. Carelessly, she tossed her precious, golden ball too high and down it fell, with a splash. Dorinda gasped.

regrettable
causing sadness or disappointment

1 coordinating conjunction (cc)
3 prepositional phrases
4 [main clauses]
4 subject-verb pairs (s v)
3 openers

5 commas

② prepositional

                                                                          s

At the corner of the well, [a most **regrettable** event

         v   ③ -ly adverb   s   v
        av   av

occurred]. Carelessly, [she tossed her precious, golden

                              s   v
               cc   av

ball too high], and [down it fell, with a splash].

⑥ vss   s   v
                   av

[Dorinda gasped].

Conjunction	*and* connects two main clauses. A subject and verb pair (she tossed) comes before the cc, and a subject and verb pair (it fell) comes after the cc. A comma is required. MC, cc MC
Adjective	The first adjective (precious) describes the second adjective and the noun together (golden ball). These adjectives are cumulative. Do not use a comma.
S V Pairs	MC *event occurred* (action) MC *she tossed* (action) MC *it fell* (action) MC *Dorinda gasped* (action)
Commas	Use a comma if two + prepositional phrases open a sentence. Put the comma after the last phrase. Do not use a comma if an -ly adverb opener modifies the verb. She tossed in a careless manner. Do not use a comma to separate cumulative adjectives (precious golden ball). Use a comma to separate two main clauses connected with a cc. **PATTERN MC, cc MC** Do not put a comma in front of a prepositional phrase.

Rewrite It!   At the corner of the well, a most regrettable event occurred. Carelessly she tossed her precious golden ball too high, and down it fell with a splash. Dorinda gasped.

Read It!	Mark It!	Fix It!	Day 3

The heavy ball sank to the bottom of the deep dark well. Angry salty tears flowed and Dorinda who was **inconsolable** stomped her foot, in frustration.

inconsolable
not able to be comforted

Mark It!

1 coordinating conjunction (cc)
3 prepositional phrases
3 [main clauses]
1 *who/which* clause (w/w)
4 subject-verb pairs (s v)
2 openers

5 commas

(1) subject

               s   v
                 av

[The heavy ball sank to the bottom of the deep, dark

(1) subject   s   v   cc   s   w/w   s
                     av

well]. [Angry salty tears flowed], and [Dorinda, (who

v   v
lv   av

was **inconsolable**), stomped her foot, in frustration].

Conjunction	*and* connects two main clauses. A subject and verb pair (tears flowed) comes before the cc, and a subject and verb pair (Dorinda stomped) comes after the cc. A comma is required. MC, cc MC
Adjective	The ball sank to the bottom of a well that was both a deep well and a dark well. These adjectives are coordinate. Use a comma.
	The first adjective (angry) describes the second adjective and the noun together (salty tears). These adjectives are cumulative. Do not use a comma.
S V Pairs	MC **ball sank** (action)
	MC **tears flowed** (action)
	MC **Dorinda stomped** (action)
	w/w **who was** (linking) The adjective *inconsolable* follows the linking verb and describes the subject, the word *who*. The *who* clause describes *Dorinda*, the noun it follows.
Commas	Use a comma to separate coordinate adjectives (deep, dark well).
	Use a comma to separate two main clauses connected with a cc. **PATTERN MC, cc MC**
	Place commas around a nonessential *who/which* clause.
	Do not put a comma in front of a prepositional phrase.

Rewrite It!   The heavy ball sank to the bottom of the deep, dark well. Angry salty tears flowed, and Dorinda, who was inconsolable, stomped her foot in frustration.

Read It!	Mark It!	Fix It!	Day 4

Ive lost my golden baaall Dorinda wailed.
I would reward my **benefactor** handsomely,
if only I could have my ball back

	3 [main clauses]	1 indent
	1 adverb clause (AC)	1 comma
	4 subject-verb pairs (s v)	2 end marks
		4 quotation marks
		1 apostrophe

benefactor
a kindly helper

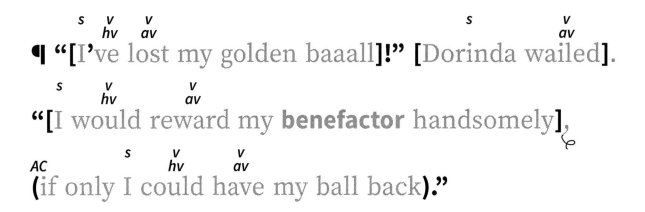

¶ "[I've lost my golden baaall]!" [Dorinda wailed].

"[I would reward my **benefactor** handsomely],

(if only I could have my ball back)."

Indentation	new speaker
Adjective	The first adjective (my) describes the second adjective and the noun together (golden baaall). These adjectives are cumulative. Do not use a comma.
Ask Students	Why is *baaall* misspelled? *Ball* is deliberately misspelled to mimic Dorinda's speech, emphasizing her overreaction.
End Marks	Use an exclamation mark when a quote expresses strong emotion. **PATTERN** "Quote!" attribution. Use a period when a quote makes a statement. Place it inside the closing quotation mark.
S V Pairs	MC ***I've lost*** (action) The contraction *I've* includes both a subject (*I*) and a helping verb (*have*). *Have lost* is the verb phrase.
	MC ***Dorinda wailed*** (action)
	MC ***I would reward*** (action) *Would* is a helping verb. *Would reward* is the verb phrase.
	AC *if **I could have*** (action) *Could* is a helping verb. *Could have* is the verb phrase.
Note	In the first sentence, *have* (' ve) functions as a helping verb because it it is followed by another verb (*lost*). In the second sentence, *have* is an action verb because it does not have a verb after it. See *Think About It!* on page 26.
Commas	Do not put a comma in front of an adverb clause. **PATTERN MC AC**

Rewrite It!   "I've lost my golden baaall!" Dorinda wailed. "I would reward my benefactor handsomely if only I could have my ball back."

Learn It!

Transitional Prepositional Phrases

Of course, Dorinda didn't hear since she was distracted.

Dorinda didn't hear, of course, since she was distracted.

Dorinda was distracted, of course.

Week 1 you learned that short prepositional openers do not take commas. You also learned that you should not place commas in front of prepositional phrases. Transitions, however, do take commas. Therefore, when a prepositional phrase functions as a transition, use commas regardless of where the transitional prepositional phrase appears in the sentence.

❟Place commas around a transitional prepositional phrase.

> Prepositional phrases that function as transitions require commas.
>
> in fact
> in addition
> by the way
> by contrast
> for example
> for instance
> of course
> on the other hand

Interjection

Wow! It weighs a ton. Oh, it's not that heavy.

An **interjection** expresses an emotion. When it expresses a strong emotion, use an exclamation mark and capitalize the word that follows. When it does not express a strong emotion, use a comma.

Interrogative Pronoun

      s   v
[What happened to the ball]?

An **interrogative pronoun** is used to ask a question. The most common interrogative pronouns are *what, whatever, which, whichever, who, whoever, whom, whose.*

> For more information about interrogative pronouns, see page G-6.

Think About It!

When the pronouns *who, whom, whose,* and *which* function as interrogative pronouns, they ask a question. The question is a main clause and expresses a complete thought.

  [Who will find it]?

When the pronouns *who, whom, whose,* and *which* function as relative pronouns, they begin a *who/which* clause. The *who/which* clause is a dependent clause and describes the noun it follows.

  [Dorinda's benefactor will be the person] (who will find it).

Quality Adjective and -ly Adverb

A quality adjective and an -ly adverb are two different ways to dress up writing. Like the strong verb, these stylistic devices create a strong image and feeling. A **quality adjective** is more specific than a weak adjective. A weak adjective is overused, boring, or vague. An **-ly adverb** is used to enhance the meaning of the verb, adjective, or adverb that it modifies.

Look for quality adjectives and -ly adverbs in this book and write them on the collection pages found in Appendix II.

Who/Which Clause

Week 3 you began marking *who/which* clauses. There are two types of *who/which* clauses: nonessential and essential.

Nonessential *Who/Which* Clause

Frogs, which normally do not speak, enjoy damp places.

A **nonessential *who/which* clause** adds information to a sentence, but the clause is not needed for the rest of the sentence to make sense.

Use commas to show that the added information can be removed from the sentence. The nonessential clause may convey important information, but it will not change the meaning of the rest of the sentence if it is removed.

, Place commas around a *who/which* clause if it is nonessential.

Frogs, ~~which normally do not speak~~, enjoy damp places.

Without the *which* clause, the reader still knows that frogs enjoy damp places.

Essential *Who/Which* Clause

The frog who spoke English was unusual.

An **essential *who/which* clause** defines the noun it follows (in the example, frog).

Do not use commas because the essential information about the noun cannot be removed from the sentence. If the essential information about the noun were removed, the overall meaning of the sentence would change.

✗ Do not place commas around a *who/which* clause if it is essential (changes the meaning of the sentence).

The frog ~~who spoke English~~ was unusual.

Without the *who* clause the sentence says the frog was unusual. The reader no longer knows which frog is meant. Removing the clause changes the meaning of the sentence.

Nonessential or Essential?

To determine if a *who/which* clause is essential, remove it from the sentence.

Does the meaning of the sentence change?

If you answer no, the *who/which* clause is nonessential. Use commas.

If you answer yes, the *who/which* clause is essential. Do not use commas.

Fix It!   Add commas to nonessential *who/which* clauses.

Remove commas from essential *who/which* clauses.

       w/w s   v

Dorinda, (who was the youngest grandchild), was spoiled.

       w/w s   v

The grandchild, (who was born first), was also spoiled.

For more information about nonessential and essential clauses, see page G-26.

A *who/which* clause is an adjective clause that begins with *who* or *which*.

Week 16 students will learn that the concept of nonessential and essential applies to all adjective clauses.

Animals in the wild take *which*, but animals (like Frederick) who are characters in stories take *who*.

Ask students to determine if the *who/which* clause is nonessential or essential.

Who was the youngest grandchild is a nonessential *w/w* clause. When a *who/which* clause follows a name, the clause is nonessential. The name identifies who is meant, so the clause simply adds information. Use commas.

Who was born first is an essential *w/w* clause because it defines which grandchild was spoiled. Removing it from the sentence changes the meaning. Do not use commas.

Read It!	Mark It!	Fix It!	Day 1

I would be **honored** to assist you a throaty
voice offered. Instantly, Dorindas tear's dried, as
she looked around for the person who was speaking.
In fact she could turn her tears on and off on a whim.

honored
privileged

1 coordinating conjunction (cc)
3 prepositional phrases
4 [main clauses]
1 *who/which* clause (w/w)
1 adverb clause (AC)
6 subject-verb pairs (s v)
2 openers

2 indents
4 commas
2 quotation marks
2 apostrophes

¶ "[I would be **honored** to assist you]," [a throaty
voice offered]. ¶ Instantly, [Dorinda's tear's dried], (as
she looked around for the person) (who was speaking).
In fact, [she could turn her tears on and off on a whim].

Indentation	new speaker; new topic
Conjunction	***and*** connects two adverbs: *on* and *off* a and b
S V Pairs	MC ***I would be*** (linking) *Would* is a helping verb. *Would be* is the verb phrase. The adjective *honored* follows the linking verb and describes the subject.
	MC ***voice offered*** (action)
	MC ***tears dried*** (action)
	AC *as* ***she looked*** (action)
	w/w ***who was speaking*** (action) The subject of the clause is *who*. *Was* is the helping verb. *Was speaking* is the verb phrase.
Ask Students	Why is *who was speaking* an essential *who* clause? The *who* clause describes *person*, the noun it follows. The *who* clause is essential to the sentence because it defines which person she looked for. Removing it from the sentence changes the meaning.
	MC ***she could turn*** (action) *Could* is the helping verb. *Could turn* is the verb phrase.
Commas	Use a comma to separate an attribution from a direct quote. **PATTERN** "Quote," attribution.
	Do not use a comma if an -ly adverb opener modifies the verb. Tears dried in an instant manner.
	Do not put a comma in front of an adverb clause. **PATTERN MC AC**
	Use a comma if a prepositional opener functions as a transition. ***In fact,***

Rewrite It!   "I would be honored to assist you," a throaty voice offered.

Instantly Dorinda's tears dried as she looked around for the person who was speaking. In fact, she could turn her tears on and off on a whim.

Seeing no one, Dorinda asked oh who has
proposed such a generous thoughtful offer
Hopping toward her on the rim of the well
an amphibian croaked It was I

proposed
suggested

3 <u>prepositional phrases</u>	1 indent
4 [main clauses]	2 capitals
4 subject-verb pairs (s v)	4 commas
2 openers	3 end marks
	4 quotation marks

④ -ing

$\overset{s}{\text{Seeing no one, }} [\overset{s}{\text{Dorinda}} \overset{v}{\underset{av}{\text{asked}}}], \text{``}\overset{}{\underline{\underline{\text{oh}}}}! [\overset{s}{\underline{\underline{\text{who}}}} \overset{v}{\underset{hv}{\text{has}}}$

$\overset{v}{\underset{av}{\textbf{proposed}}} \text{ such a generous, thoughtful offer}]?\text{''}$

④ -ing

¶ Hopping <u>toward her</u> <u>on the rim</u> <u>of the well</u>,

$[\text{an } \overset{s}{\text{amphibian}} \overset{v}{\underset{av}{\text{croaked}}}], \text{``}[\overset{s}{\text{It}} \overset{v}{\underset{lv}{\text{was}}} \overset{}{\text{I}}].\text{''}$

Indentation	new speaker
Interjection	***Oh!*** is an interjection that expresses a strong emotion. Use an exclamation mark and capitalize *Who*.
Adjective	The offer was both a generous offer and a thoughtful offer. These adjectives are coordinate. Use a comma.
S V Pairs MC	***Dorinda asked*** (action)
MC	***Who has proposed*** (action) *Has* is a helping verb. *Has proposed* is the verb phrase.
Ask Students	Why is *Who has proposed* ... not a *who/which* clause? *Who* is an interrogative pronoun that begins a question. *Who has proposed* ... does not follow a noun and describe it.
MC	***amphibian croaked*** (action)
MC	***It was*** (linking) The pronoun *I* follows the linking verb and renames the subject. It is correct to use a subjective case pronoun after a linking verb. It is incorrect to write *It was me* because *me* is an objective case pronoun. Subjective case pronouns follow linking verbs.
Commas	Use a comma to separate an attribution from a direct quote. **PATTERN** Attribution, "Quote?"
	Use a comma to separate coordinate adjectives (generous, thoughtful offer).
	Use a comma after an -ing opener. **PATTERN** -ing word/phrase, main clause
	The thing after the comma must be the thing doing the inging. An *amphibian* is doing the *hopping*.
	Use a comma to separate an attribution from a direct quote. **PATTERN** Attribution, "Quote."

Rewrite It!   Seeing no one, Dorinda asked, "Oh! Who has proposed such a generous,
            thoughtful offer?"
                    Hopping toward her on the rim of the well, an amphibian croaked, "It was I."

Read It!	Mark It!	Fix It!	Day 3

Read It!

As she let loose a spine-tingling shriek Dorinda started to run. Of course her **inquisitiveness** got the better of her and she turned back to the frog. How can you talk Mr. Frog

inquisitiveness
curiosity

Mark It!

1 coordinating conjunction (cc)
3 prepositional phrases
4 [main clauses]
1 adverb clause (AC)
5 subject-verb pairs (s v)
2 openers

Fix It!

1 indent
4 commas
1 end mark
2 quotation marks

⑤ clausal

     s   v   s
           av

¶ (As she let loose a spine-tingling shriek), [Dorinda

  v   ② prepositional   s   v
av   av

started to run]. Of course, [her **inquisitiveness** got the

                       s   v
        cc   av

better of her], and [she turned back to the frog].

     v   s   v
     hv   av

"[How can you talk], Mr. Frog?"

Indentation	new speaker
Conjunction	**and** connects two main clauses. A subject and verb pair (inquisitiveness got) comes before the cc, and a subject and verb pair (she turned) comes after the cc. A comma is required. MC, cc MC
S V Pairs AC	*As **she let** (action)*
MC	***Dorinda started** (action)*
MC	***inquisitiveness got** (action)*
MC	***she turned** (action)*
MC	***you can talk** (action) Can is a helping verb. Can talk is the verb phrase. You is the subject of this sentence. Mr. Frog is the noun of direct address. A noun of direct address is never the subject of a sentence.*
Note	An attribution always has a speaking verb setting up the quotation. *Of course, her inquisitiveness got the better of her, and she turned back to the frog* is a complete thought, not an attribution. For this reason, this sentence requires a period.
Commas	Use a comma after an adverb clause. **PATTERN AC, MC**
	Use a comma if a prepositional opener functions as a transition. ***Of course,***
	Use a comma to separate two main clauses connected with a cc. **PATTERN MC, cc MC**
	Place commas around a noun of direct address (NDA). **, *Mr. Frog***

Rewrite It!   As she let loose a spine-tingling shriek, Dorinda started to run. Of course, her inquisitiveness got the better of her, and she turned back to the frog. "How can you talk, Mr. Frog?"

Read It!	Mark It!	Fix It!	Day 4

Its a long dull story but I might tell it to you
in the future. Would you like me to find your ball
Yes I would appreciate that Ill gladly do it
with one unique **stipulation** the frog responded.

stipulation
a condition that is required as part of an agreement

1 coordinating conjunction (cc)
3 prepositional phrases
6 [main clauses]
6 subject-verb pairs (s v)

3 indents
4 commas
2 end marks
6 quotation marks
2 apostrophes

¶ "[It's a long, dull story], but [I might tell it to you
in the future]. [Would you like me to find your ball]?"

¶ "Yes, [I would appreciate that]." ¶ "[I'll gladly do it
with one unique **stipulation**]," [the frog responded].

Indentation	new speaker; new speaker; new speaker
Adjective	The story was both a long story and a dull story. These adjectives are coordinate. Use a comma.
	The first adjective (one) describes the second adjective and the noun together (unique stipulation). These adjectives are cumulative. Do not use a comma.
Conjunction	**but** connects two main clauses. A subject and verb pair (It's) comes before the cc, and a subject and verb pair (I might tell) comes after the cc. A comma is required. MC, cc MC
Interjection	**Yes,** is an interjection that expresses a mild emotion.
S V Pairs MC	**It's** (linking) The contraction *It's* includes both a subject (It) and a linking verb (is). The noun *story* follows the linking verb and renames the subject.
MC	**I might tell** (action) *Might* is the helping verb. *Might tell* is the verb phrase.
MC	**you Would like** (action) *Would* is a helping verb. *Would like* is the verb phrase.
MC	**I would appreciate** (action) *Would* is the helping verb. *Would appreciate* is the verb phrase.
MC	**I'll do** (action) The contraction *I'll* includes both a subject (I) and a helping verb (will). *Will do* is the verb phrase.
MC	**frog responded** (action)
Commas	Use a comma to separate coordinate adjectives (long, dull story).
	Use a comma to separate two main clauses connected with a cc. **PATTERN MC, cc MC**
	Use a comma after an interjection that does not express strong emotion. **Yes,**
	Use a comma to separate an attribution from a direct quote. **PATTERN "Quote," attribution.**

Rewrite It!	"It's a long, dull story, but I might tell it to you in the future. Would you like me to find your ball?"
	"Yes, I would appreciate that."
	"I'll gladly do it with one unique stipulation," the frog responded.

Learn It!

Participial Phrase

A **participial phrase** is a phrase that begins with a present participle, an -ing word. Week 5 you learned that a #4 -ing opener is a sentence that begins with a participial (-ing) phrase. Like a *who/which* clause, a participial phrase is an adjective because the entire phrase describes a noun in the sentence.

④

Searching for her lost ball, Dorinda stared into the well.

> *Searching* is the -ing word, the present participle. *Searching for her lost ball* is the participial (-ing) phrase.

> When a participial phrase begins a sentence (#4 -ing opener), the entire phrase describes the subject of the sentence. This is why the thing (subject of main clause) after the comma must be the thing doing the inging.

Participial (-ing) phrases do not have to begin a sentence. When a participial phrase comes at the end of a sentence, the entire phrase describes a noun in the sentence. If the noun is the word directly before the -ing phrase, do not use a comma.

Dorinda saw her ball *sitting at the bottom of the well.*

> *Sitting* is the -ing word, the present participle. *Sitting at the bottom of the well* is the participial (-ing) phrase. It describes *ball,* the word directly before it. Do not use a comma.

Dorinda stared into the well, *searching for her lost ball.*

> *Searching* is the -ing word, the present participle. *Searching for her lost ball* is the participial (-ing) phrase. It describes *Dorinda,* not the word directly before it. Use a comma.

❟ Use a comma when a participial (-ing) phrase comes at the end of a sentence and describes a noun other than the word it follows.

✗ Do not use a comma when a participial (-ing) phrase comes at the end of a sentence and describes the word it follows.

Think About It!

The placement of a comma can change the meaning of a sentence.

> The king watched the visitors sitting on his bench.

>> Without a comma this sentence means that the visitors were sitting on the king's bench when the king watched them.

> The king watched the visitors, sitting on his bench.

>> With a comma this sentence means that the king was sitting on his bench when he watched the visitors.

Because both a *who/which* clause and a participial phrase function as adjectives, it is easy to convert one to the other.

> Dorinda saw her ball sitting at the bottom of the well.

> Dorinda saw her ball, which was sitting at the bottom of the well.

Sidebar:

Phrase Overview: Appendix III

For more information about #4 -ing openers, see page G-44.

For more information about participial phrases, see page G-19.

When a participial (-ing) phrase is embedded in a sentence, use commas unless essential.

This concept is taught in Level 6.

Ask students to find the -ing phrase and determine what noun it describes.

Sitting at the bottom of the well describes *ball.* Do not use a comma.

Searching for her lost ball describes *Dorinda.* Use a comma.

Commas or No Commas?

Read each sentence and decide if the *who/which* clause is nonessential or essential.

> If the clause adds information, it is nonessential. Use commas.
> > *Nonessential: Need commas*
>
> If the clause defines the noun it follows, it is essential. Do not use commas.
> > *Essential: Eliminate commas*

The gardens opened to a park, which stretched to the city center.

(**nonessential**)   essential

In the early morning teenagers who enjoyed rowing visited the lake.

nonessential   (**essential**)

White mulberry trees, which attracted silk worms, lined the perimeter.

(**nonessential**)   essential

Stone benches, which sat throughout the garden, welcomed visitors.

(**nonessential**)   essential

Some children who wanted to see the king approached a guard.

nonessential   (**essential**)

Read each sentence and decide if the participial phrase at the end of the sentence describes the word if follows.

> If the -ing phrase describes a noun other than the word it follows, use a comma.
> If the -ing phrase describes the word it follows, do not use a comma.

The king's guard talked to the children wishing to see the king.

Some gardeners were near the lake, planting fresh flowers.

Near the lake were some gardeners planting fresh flowers.

They talked to a young girl playing with a jump rope.

She saw her mother and left, waving as she walked away.

Which stretched to the city center is a nonessential *w/w* clause. Removing it from the sentence does not change the meaning. Use commas.

Who enjoyed rowing is an essential *w/w* clause because it defines which teenagers visited the lake. Removing it from the sentence changes the meaning. Do not use commas.

Which attracted silk worms is a nonessential *w/w* clause because all white mulberry trees attract silk worms. Use commas.

Which sat throughout the garden is a nonessential *w/w* clause. Use commas.

Who wanted to see the king is an essential *w/w* clause because it defines which children approached a guard. Do not use commas.

Wishing to see the king describes *children.* Do not use a comma.

Planting fresh flowers describes *gardeners.* Use a comma for the first sentence. Do not use a comma for the second sentence.

Playing with a jump rope describes *girl.* Do not use a comma.

Waving as she walked away describes *She.* Use a comma.

Ill do anything, that you want! My dad will
kill me, if I lose that ball which cost him a royal
fortune she replied. You must jump in, and
retrieve my ball sitting at the bottom of the well

retrieve
recover or regain

1 coordinating conjunction (cc)
2 <u>prepositional phrases</u>
4 [main clauses]
1 *who/which* clause (w/w)
1 *that* clause (that)
1 adverb clause (AC)
7 subject-verb pairs (s v)

1 indent
5 commas
1 end mark
4 quotation marks
1 apostrophe

¶ "[I'll do anything], (that you want)! [My dad will kill me], (if I lose that ball), (which cost him a royal fortune)," [she replied]. "[You must jump in, and retrieve my ball] sitting at the bottom of the well."

Indentation		new speaker
Conjunction		**and** connects two verbs: *must jump* and *retrieve* A subject and verb (You must jump) come before the cc, but only a verb (retrieve) comes after the cc. A comma is not used. MC cc 2nd verb
Participial		*Sitting at the bottom of the well* describes *ball*, the word directly before it. Do not use a comma.
S V Pairs	MC	**I'll do** (action) The contraction *I'll* includes both a subject (I) and a helping verb (will). *Will do* is the verb phrase.
	that	*that **you want*** (action)
	MC	**dad will kill** (action) *Will* is a helping verb. *Will kill* is the verb phrase.
	AC	*if **I lose*** (action)
	w/w	**which cost** (action) The subject of the clause is *which*. The *which* clause describes *ball*, the noun it follows. It is nonessential because it does not change the meaning of the sentence. Without the *which* clause her dad will still kill her (be mad) if she loses that ball.
	MC	**she replied** (action)
	MC	**You must jump** (action), **retrieve** (action) *Must* is a helping verb. *Must jump* is the verb phrase. The single subject *You* is followed by two verbs: *must jump* and *retrieve*. Both show action.
Note		The word *that* often begins a *that* clause **PATTERN that + subject + verb**. The word *that* can also function as an adjective as in *if I lose that ball*. Which ball? *that*
Commas		Do not put a comma in front of a *that* clause.
		Do not put a comma in front of an adverb clause. **PATTERN MC AC**
		Place commas around a nonessential *who/which* clause.
		Use a comma to separate an attribution from a direct quote. **PATTERN "Quote," attribution.**
		Do not use a comma before a cc when it connects two verbs. **PATTERN MC cc 2nd verb**

Rewrite It!   "I'll do anything that you want! My dad will kill me if I lose that ball, which cost him a royal fortune," she replied. "You must jump in and retrieve my ball sitting at the bottom of the well."

Read It!	Mark It!	Fix It!	Day 2

I'll **salvage** your ball if youll allow me to stay for one night in the palace feasting at your, fancy table, and eating, from your own plate

1 coordinating conjunction (cc)	1 indent
4 prepositional phrases	3 commas
1 [main clause]	1 end mark
1 adverb clause (AC)	2 quotation marks
2 subject-verb pairs (s v)	1 apostrophe

salvage
save something from loss or danger

¶ ["I'll **salvage** your ball] (if you'll allow me to stay for one night in the palace), feasting at your, fancy table, and eating, from your own plate."

(With markings above: s v / hv, v / av over "I'll salvage"; v / av over "your ball"; AC over "if"; s, v / hv, v / av over "you'll allow"; cc over "and")

Indentation	new speaker
Adjective	The first adjective (your) describes the second adjective and the noun together (fancy table). These adjectives are cumulative. Do not use a comma.
	The first adjective (your) describes the second adjective and the noun together (own plate). These adjectives are cumulative. Do not use a comma.
Conjunction	**and** connects two participial (-ing) phrases: *feasting at your fancy table* and *eating from your own plate*. a and b
Participial	*Feasting at your fancy table* and *eating from your own plate* describe *me* (the frog), not *palace*, the word directly before *feasting*. Use a comma.
S V Pairs MC	***I'll salvage*** (action) The contraction *I'll* includes both a subject (I) and a helping verb (will). *Will salvage* is the verb phrase.
AC	*if **you'll allow*** (action) The contraction *you'll* includes both a subject (you) and a helping verb (will). *Will allow* is the verb phrase.
Note	The words *stay, feasting,* and *eating* are not verbs. Remind students that they cannot mark a word as a verb unless it has a subject. *To stay* is an infinitive. *Feasting* and *eating* are participles.
Commas	Use a comma when a -ing phrase at the end of a sentence describes a noun other than the word it follows.
	Do not use a comma to separate cumulative adjectives (your fancy table; your own plate).
	Do not use a comma to separate two items connected with a cc. **PATTERN a and b**
	Do not put a comma in front of a prepositional phrase.

Rewrite It!   "I'll salvage your ball if you'll allow me to stay for one night in the palace, feasting at your fancy table and eating from your own plate."

Read It! **Mark It!** **Fix It!**

Well of course Dorinda responded **hastily**.
The frog hopped into the water disappeared for a few
moments and returned holding Dorindas treasure.
Gleefully, Dorinda snatched the wet slippery ball.

1 coordinating conjunction (cc)	2 indents
3 prepositional phrases	7 commas
3 [main clauses]	2 quotation marks
3 subject-verb pairs (s v)	1 apostrophe
2 openers	

hastily
with unnecessarily quick action that
can result in mistakes

¶ "Well, of course," [Dorinda responded **hastily**].
  ① subject s   v av

¶ [The frog hopped into the water, disappeared for a few
  moments, and returned], holding Dorinda's treasure.

③ -ly adverb   s   v av

Gleefully, [Dorinda snatched the wet, slippery ball].

Indentation	new speaker; new topic
Interjection	**Well,** is an interjection that expresses a mild emotion.
Conjunction	**and** connects three verbs: *hopped, disappeared,* and *returned* a, b, and c
Participial	*holding Dorinda's treasure* describes *frog*, not the word directly before it. Use a comma.
Adjective	The ball was both a wet ball and a slippery ball. These adjectives are coordinate. Use a comma.
S V Pairs	MC **Dorinda responded** (action)
	MC **frog hopped**, (action) **disappeared**, (action) **returned** (action) The single subject *frog* is followed by three verbs. All three show action.
	MC **Dorinda snatched** (action)
Commas	Use a comma after an interjection that does not expresses strong emotion. **Well,**
	Place commas around a transitional prepositional phrase. **, of course,**
	Use a comma to separate an attribution from a direct quote. PATTERN "Quote," attribution.
	Use commas to separate three or more items in a series connected with a cc. PATTERN a, b, and c
	Use a comma when a -ing phrase at the end of a sentence describes a noun other than the word it follows.
	Do not use a comma if an -ly adverb opener modifies the verb. Dorinda snatched in a gleeful manner.
	Use a comma to separate coordinate adjectives (wet, slippery ball).

Rewrite It!
"Well, of course," Dorinda responded hastily.

The frog hopped into the water, disappeared for a few moments, and returned, holding

Dorinda's treasure. Gleefully Dorinda snatched the wet, slippery ball.

Read It!	Mark It!	Fix It!	Day 4

Its solid gold he finally **wheezed**. Skipping back to the palace Princess Dorinda didnt hear him pattering behind her. The exhausted amphibian hoped, that Princess Dorindas word was trustworthy.

wheezed
breathed with difficulty and with a whistling sound

2 prepositional phrases
4 [main clauses]
1 *that* clause (that)
5 subject-verb pairs (s v)
2 openers

1 indent
3 commas
2 quotation marks
3 apostrophes

¶ ["It's solid gold]," [he finally **wheezed**]. Skipping

back to the palace, [Princess Dorinda didn't hear him]

pattering behind her. [The exhausted amphibian hoped],

that
(that Princess Dorinda's word was trustworthy).

Indentation	new speaker
Participial	*Skipping back to the palace* begins the sentence. Use a comma.
	Pattering behind her describes *him* (frog), the word directly before it. Do not use a comma.
S V Pairs	MC ***It's*** (linking) The contraction *It's* includes both a subject (It) and a linking verb (is). The noun *gold* follows the linking verb and renames the subject.
	MC ***he wheezed*** (action)
	MC ***Princess Dorinda did hear*** (action) The contraction *didn't* includes both a helping verb (did) and an adverb (not). *Did hear* is the verb phrase.
	MC ***amphibian hoped*** (action)
	that *that **word** was* (linking) The adjective *trustworthy* follows the linking verb and describes the subject.
Commas	Use a comma to separate an attribution from a direct quote. PATTERN "Quote," attribution.
	Use a comma after an -ing opener. PATTERN -ing word/phrase, main clause
	The thing after the comma must be the thing doing the inging. *Princess Dorinda* is doing the *skipping*.
	Do not put a comma in front of a *that* clause.

Rewrite It! "It's solid gold," he finally wheezed. Skipping back to the palace, Princess Dorinda didn't hear him pattering behind her. The exhausted amphibian hoped that Princess Dorinda's word was trustworthy.

Review It!

Commas

There is always a reason a comma is necessary. Follow the comma rules.

When two comma rules contradict, follow the rule that says to use a comma.

❞ The key to adding commas is to think about parts of speech and the structure of your sentences.

Coordinating Conjunction
Use a comma before a cc when it connects two main clauses. **MC, cc MC**
Use commas to separate three or more items in a series. **a, b, and c**

Who/Which Clause
Use commas unless essential.
    Essential means it changes the meaning of the sentence.

Participial (-ing) Phrase
Mid-sentence use commas unless essential.
End-sentence use a comma when it describes a noun other than the word directly before it.

Adjectives
Use a comma to separate coordinate adjectives.
    Coordinate means you can reverse their order or add *and* between them.

Interjection
Use a comma after an interjection that does not expresses strong emotion.

Noun of Direct Address (NDA)
Use commas.

Quotations
Use a comma to separate an attribution from a direct quote.
    "Quote," attribution.
    Attribution, "Quote."
    "Quote," attribution, "rest of quoted sentence."

Sentence Openers

② prepositional	Use a comma if 5 + words or transition.	
	preposition + noun (no verb)	
③ -ly adverb	Use a comma if an -ly adverb modifies the sentence.	
	It was ____ that ____.	
④ -ing	Use a comma after the phrase.	
	-ing word/phrase, main clause	
⑤ clausal	Use a comma after the clause. **AC, MC**	
	www word + subject + verb,	

✕ Do not use unnecessary commas.

This Fix It! book empowers students to use commas correctly. There is always a reason a comma is necessary.

Do not resort to fickle reasoning such as "It sounds right" or "I want to pause."

Unnecessary Comma Rules

You have now learned several places where commas are unnecessary.

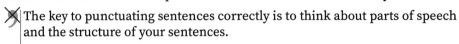 The key to punctuating sentences correctly is to think about parts of speech and the structure of your sentences.

Subject-Verb Pair

    Do not put a comma between a subject and its verb.

Coordinating Conjunction

    Do not use a comma before a cc when it connects two items in a series (unless main clauses). **a and b**
    Do not use a comma before a cc when it connects two verbs. **MC cc 2nd verb**

Prepositional Phrase

    Do not put a comma in front of a prepositional phrase (unless transition).

Who/Which Clause

    Do not use commas when a *who/which* clause is essential.
        Essential means it changes the meaning of the sentence.

Participial (-ing) Phrase

    Mid-sentence do not use commas when an -ing phrase is essential.
    End-sentence do not use a comma when it describes the word directly before it.

Adverb Clause

    Do not use a comma before an adverb clause that follows a main clause. **MC AC**

That Clause

    Do not use a comma before a *that* clause.

Adjectives

    Do not use a comma to separate cumulative adjectives.
        Cumulative means the adjectives must be arranged in a specific order.
        You cannot reverse their order or add *and* between them.

Interjection

    Do not use a comma after an interjection that expresses strong emotion.
        Use an exclamation mark instead.

Quotations

    Do not use a comma after a quoted question or quoted exclamation.
    The question mark or exclamation mark replaces the comma.
        "Quote?" attribution.   **"Quote!" attribution.**

Sentence Openers

    (2) **prepositional**   Do not use a comma if fewer than 5 words.
    (3) **-ly adverb**   Do not use a comma if an -ly adverb modifies the verb.

There is always a reason a comma is necessary.
Follow the comma rules.

While the royal family dined **sumptuously** they heard a faint tap, at the castle door. Within moment's, a footman appeared, and delivered a message to Princess Dorinda.

sumptuously
richly; lavishly

Mark It!	Fix It!
1 coordinating conjunction (cc)	1 indent
3 prepositional phrases	4 commas
2 [main clauses]	1 apostrophe
1 adverb clause (AC)	
3 subject-verb pairs (s v)	
2 openers	

⑤ clausal

AC

� (While the royal family dined **sumptuously**),

[they heard a faint tap, at the castle door]. Within

② prepositional

moment's, [a footman appeared, and delivered a

message to Princess Dorinda].

This is the last week that a detailed explanation about coordinate and cumulative adjectives is provided.

Indentation	new topic
Conjunction	**and** connects two verbs: *appeared* and *delivered* A subject and verb (footman appeared) come before the cc, but only a verb (delivered) comes after the cc. A comma is not used. MC cc 2nd verb
S V Pairs AC	*While **family dined** (action)*
MC	***they heard** (action)*
Ask Students	Why is *tap* not a verb? *Tap* is a noun, the thing they heard. The article *a* signals a noun is coming. The adjective *faint* describes the noun *tap*.
MC	***footman appeared** (action), **delivered** (action)* The single subject *footman* is followed by two verbs. Both show action.
Commas	Use a comma after an adverb clause. **PATTERN AC, MC**
	Do not put a comma in front of a prepositional phrase.
	Do not use a comma if a prepositional opener has fewer than five words.
	Do not use a comma before a cc when it connects two verbs. **PATTERN MC cc 2nd verb**

Rewrite It!   While the royal family dined sumptuously, they heard a faint tap at the castle door. Within moments a footman appeared and delivered a message to Princess Dorinda.

princess he began You have a visitor at the
door. Excusing herself from the table Dorinda
hastened away. She hoped, that the visitor was her
new friend for she was eager to eat dessert with her.

hastened
hurried

1 coordinating conjunction (cc)
3 prepositional phrases
5 [main clauses]
1 *that* clause (that)
6 subject-verb pairs (s v)
2 openers

2 indents
2 capitals
5 commas
4 quotation marks

¶ "princess," [he began], "[You have a visitor at the

door]." ¶ Excusing herself from the table, [Dorinda

hastened away]. [She hoped], (that the visitor was her

new friend), for [she was eager to eat dessert with her].

Indentation	new speaker; new topic
Capitalization	The attribution *he began* interrupts the first quoted sentence. The word *you* is not capitalized. **PATTERN "Quote," attribution, "rest of quoted sentence."**
Participial	*Excusing herself from the table* begins the sentence. Use a comma.
Conjunction	*for* connects two main clauses. A subject and verb pair (she hoped) comes before the cc, and a subject and verb pair (she was) comes after the cc. A comma is required. MC, cc MC
S V Pairs	MC *he began* (action)
	MC *you have* (action) *Have* functions as a helping verb if it is followed by another verb. In this sentence *have* is an action verb. See the bottom of page 26.
	MC *Dorinda hastened* (action)
	MC *She hoped* (action)
	that *that visitor was* (linking) The noun *friend* follows the linking verb and renames the subject.
	MC *she was* (linking) The adjective *eager* follows the linking verb and describes the subject.
Commas	Place commas around a noun of direct address (NDA). ***Princess,***
	Use a comma to separate an attribution from a direct quote. **PATTERN "Quote," attribution, "rest of quoted sentence."**
	Use a comma after an -ing opener. **PATTERN -ing word/phrase, main clause** The thing after the comma must be the thing doing the inging. *Dorinda* is doing the *excusing*.
	Do not put a comma in front of a *that* clause.
	Use a comma to separate two main clauses connected with a cc. **PATTERN MC, cc MC**

Rewrite It! "Princess," he began, "you have a visitor at the door."

Excusing herself from the table, Dorinda hastened away. She hoped that the visitor was her new friend, for she was eager to eat dessert with her.

Read It!　　　　　　　　　　　　**Mark It!**　　　　　**Fix It!**

When she opened the door blood drained from her face. There sat the frog squatting, and looking at Dorinda with sad, huge eye's. You forgot your pledge to treat me **hospitably** he croaked.

hospitably
with a warm, friendly, and generous reception

1 coordinating conjunction (cc)
3 prepositional phrases
4 [main clauses]
1 adverb clause (AC)
5 subject-verb pairs (s v)
2 openers

2 indents
5 commas
2 quotation marks
1 apostrophe

⑤ clausal

　　　　　　s　　　v
　AC　　　　　av
¶ (When she opened the door), [blood drained from

　　　　① subject　v　　　s
　　　　　　　av
her face]. [There sat the frog] squatting, and looking

　　　　　　　　　　　　　　　　　　　　cc

　　　　　　　　　　　　　　s　　v
　　　　　　　　　　　　　　　　av
at Dorinda with sad, huge eye's. ¶ ["You forgot your

　　　　　　　　　　　　　s　　v
　　　　　　　　　　　　　　　av
pledge to treat me **hospitably**]," [he croaked].

Indentation	new place; new speaker
Conjunction	**and** connects two participial (-ing) phrases: *squatting* and *looking* a and b
Participial	*Squatting* and *looking at Dorinda with sad huge eyes* describe *frog*, the word directly before. Do not use a comma.
Adjective	The first adjective (sad) describes the second adjective and the noun together (huge eyes). These adjectives are cumulative. Do not use a comma.
Ask Students	The adjectives *sad* and *huge* belong in which categories? See page 31. *Sad* is an adjective of opinion; *huge* is an adjective of size.
S V Pairs	AC *When* **she opened** (action)
	MC **blood drained** (action)
	MC **frog sat** (action) Students often assume *there* is the subject. However, the subject-verb pair must work together. Who sat? *frog* There is an adverb that tells where.
	MC **You forgot** (action)
	MC **he croaked** (action)
Note	There sat the frog begins with the main clause. It is technically not a subject opener because it does not begin with the subject of the sentence. It is an inverted main clause: the verb comes before the subject.
Commas	Use a comma after an adverb clause that comes before a main clause. **PATTERN AC, MC**
	Do not use a comma to separate two items connected with a cc. **PATTERN a and b**
	Do not use a comma to separate cumulative adjectives (sad huge eyes).
	Use a comma to separate an attribution from a direct quote. **PATTERN "Quote," attribution.**

Rewrite It!　　　　When she opened the door, blood drained from her face. There sat the frog squatting and looking at Dorinda with sad huge eyes.

　　　　　　　"You forgot your pledge to treat me hospitably," he croaked.

Read It!	Mark It!	Fix It!	Day 4

Dorinda slammed the door. Truthfully she hoped that the **audacious** annoying amphibian would leave forget her promise and never return. Dorinda who knocked King Morton inquired, when she returned.

audacious
extremely bold or daring

Mark It!
1 coordinating conjunction (cc)
4 [main clauses]
1 *that* clause (that)
1 adverb clause (AC)
6 subject-verb pairs (s v)
2 openers

Fix It!
2 indents
6 commas
1 end mark
2 quotation marks

⑥ vss   ③ -ly adverb

¶ [Dorinda slammed the door]. Truthfully, [she hoped]

(that the **audacious**, annoying amphibian would leave,

forget her promise, and never return). ¶ "Dorinda, [who

knocked]?" [King Morton inquired], (when she returned).

Indentation	new topic; new speaker
Adjective	The amphibian was both an audacious amphibian and an annoying amphibian. These adjectives are coordinate. Use a comma.
Conjunction	***and*** connects three verbs: *would leave*, *forget*, and *return* a, b, and c
S V Pairs	MC ***Dorinda slammed*** (action)
	MC ***she hoped*** (action)
	that *that* ***amphibian would*** (helping) ***leave*** (action), ***forget*** (action), ***return*** (action) The single subject *amphibian* is followed by three verbs.
	MC ***who knocked*** (action) *Who* is an interrogative pronoun that begins a question. *Who knocked* does not follow a noun and describe it, so it is a main clause, not a dependent clause.
	MC ***King Morton inquired*** (action)
	AC *when* ***she returned*** (action)
Commas	Use a comma if an -ly adverb opener modifies the sentence. It was truthful that Dorinda hoped that the frog would leave.
	Use a comma to separate coordinate adjectives (audacious, annoying amphibian).
	Use commas to separate three or more items in a series connected with a cc. **PATTERN a, b, and c**
	Place commas around a noun of direct address (NDA). ***Dorinda,***
	Do not put a comma in front of an adverb clause. **PATTERN MC AC**

Rewrite It!   Dorinda slammed the door. Truthfully, she hoped that the audacious, annoying amphibian would leave, forget her promise, and never return.

"Dorinda, who knocked?" King Morton inquired when she returned.

Learn It!

Run-On

A **run-on** occurs when a sentence has main clauses that are not connected properly. There are two types of run-ons: fused sentence and comma splice.

A frog sat on the steps Dorinda looked horrified.

> A **fused sentence** is two main clauses placed in one sentence without any punctuation between them.

Dorinda was furious, she slammed the door.

Dorinda told what happened, the king was displeased.

> A **comma splice** is two main clauses placed in one sentence with only a comma between them.

There are three simple ways to fix a run-on.

Period

A frog sat on the steps. Dorinda looked horrified.

> A sentence is an expression of one idea, so if the main clauses are separate ideas, they belong in two separate sentences. Place a period at the end of each main clause. This is the simplest way to fix a run-on.

Semicolon

Dorinda was furious; she slammed the door.

> A semicolon can fix a run-on. However, it cannot always join main clauses. It should only be used when the two main clauses express a single idea and are similar in length or construction. Use a semicolon sparingly.

Comma + CC

Dorinda told what happened, **and** the king was displeased.

> When a coordinating conjunction (cc) best expresses the relationship between the two main clauses, connect the main clauses with a comma and a coordinating conjunction (for, and, nor, but, or, yet, so).

Dorinda told what happened and the king was displeased.

> This is grammatically wrong. If you connect two main clauses with a coordinating conjunction, you must place a comma before the coordinating conjunction. The comma without the cc is a comma splice. The coordinating conjunction without a comma is a comma error.

Fix It! Fix run-on sentences with the best method.

Dorinda knew she was in trouble. the staff remained silent.
≡

The butler smirked; a footman sighed.

Two footmen removed the salad, and two more served the entrée.

This week's Fix It! provides specific directions for fixing run-on sentences.

Sidebar:

For more information about run-ons, see page G-17.

There are often several effective ways to fix a run-on. Students will learn a fourth way Week 21.

Where the frog sat and how Dorinda looked are separate ideas. Form two sentences.

Slamming the door was how Dorinda expressed her anger, so both MCs express a single idea. The MCs are similar in length. Use a semicolon.

And links two sentences when there is a continuation of events or one event causes the other. The second sentence follows from the first. Use a comma + cc.

A cc alone is not strong enough to hold two MCs together. Use a comma + cc.

What Dorinda knew and how the staff remained are separate ideas. Form two sentences.

Both the butler and the footman are responding to Dorinda's attitude, so their responses express a single idea. The MCs are similar in length and construction. Use a semicolon.

Two more footmen served the entrée after two removed the salad. The second sentence follows from the first. Use a comma + cc.

For more information about quotation marks, see pages G-27 and G-32.

Quote and Attribution

"I will not serve the frog."

> A **quote** is the sentence in quotation marks. Quotation marks surround the quote to show that these are the speaker's exact words.
>
> A quote may be one or more sentences long and must be punctuated correctly with capital letters and end marks. Commas and periods always go inside closing quotation marks. Exclamation marks and question marks go inside closing quotation marks when they are part of the quoted material.

the princess said

> An **attribution** is the person speaking and the speaking verb. Although the attribution contains a main clause (subject and verb), it does not express a complete thought. What did the princess say? The quote which tells what the princess said must be in the same sentence as the attribution in order for the sentence to make sense.
>
> An attribution sets up a direct quote. It may may precede, interrupt, or follow the quote. The first word of the attribution is capitalized when the attribution begins the sentence.

Attribution, "Quote."

MC   *MC*

[The princess said]**,** "[I will not serve the frog]."

> This example contains two clauses: a main clause and a main clause. However, because the quote is *what* the person said, it is a necessary part of the attribution. If you insert a period after *said*, the sentence does not make sense.
> What did the princess say? The quote must be in the same sentence in order to make sense. With this pattern, a comma correctly separates the attribution (a main clause) from the quote (a main clause).

"Quote," attribution, "rest of quoted sentence."

"Quote," attribution.

MC   *MC*

"[Must I serve the frog]**?**" [the princess asked].

> When a quoted sentence asks a question or expresses a strong emotion, a question mark or exclamation mark replaces the comma. The attribution is not capitalized when the attribution interrupts or follows the quote because the attribution belongs in the same sentence as the quote.

Attribution, "Quote?"

"Quote?" attribution.

Attribution, "Quote!"

MC   *MC*

[The princess wailed for several minutes]. "[I will not serve the frog]."

> This example contains two clauses: a main clause and a main clause. Because *Dorinda wailed for several minutes* expresses a complete thought, it is not an attribution. Both main clauses require end marks.

"Quote!" attribution.

MC   *that*

[The princess said] (that she would not serve the frog).

> This example contains two clauses: a main clause and a *that* clause. Together the two clauses express a complete thought. Because *that she would not serve the frog* is not the speaker's direct words but an indirect quote, quotation marks are not used. An indirect quote is a paraphrase of what someone said and uses third-person pronouns and past tense verbs.

When *that* sets up words that someone said, it is known as an indirect quote. It does not use quotation marks or first-person pronouns. The same sentence using a direct quote: The princess said, "I will not serve the frog."

Read It!	Mark It!	Fix It!	Day 1

Despite her **deficiencies**, Dorinda truthfully answered her father it was a frog. King Mortons eyes widened and he inquired what did he want

deficiencies
faults in someone

Mark It!
1 coordinating conjunction (cc)
1 <u>prepositional phrase</u>
5 [main clauses]
5 subject-verb pairs (s v)
2 openers

Fix It!
2 indents
2 capitals
3 commas
2 end marks
4 quotation marks
1 apostrophe
(fix run-on with period)

②　prepositional

¶ <u>Despite her **deficiencies**</u>, [Dorinda truthfully
　　　　 v
　　　　av
answered her father]. "[it was a frog]." ¶ [King
　　s
①　subject
　　　s　　　 v
　　　　　　 av　　　 cc　　 s　　　 v
　　　　　　　　　　　　　　　　　 av
Morton's eyes widened], and [he inquired], "[what
　v　　s　　v
　hv　　　 av
did he want]?"

Indentation	new speaker; new speaker
Conjunction	**and** connects two main clauses. A subject and verb pair (eyes widened) comes before the cc, and a subject and verb pair (he inquired) comes after the cc. A comma is required. MC, cc MC
S V Pairs	MC **Dorinda answered** (action)
	MC **It was** (linking) The noun *frog* follows the linking verb and renames the subject.
	MC **eyes widened** (action)
	MC **he inquired** (action)
	MC **he did want** (action) *Did* is a helping verb. *Did want* is the verb phrase.
Run-On	Use a period to fix the run-on (fused sentence). The first two main clauses are separate ideas and belong in separate sentences.
Note	Compare these two main clauses.
	The MC *Dorinda truthfully answered her father* is a complete thought, not an attribution. It requires a period.
	The MC *he inquired* ends with the speaking verb and begs for more information. It is an attribution and belongs in the same sentence as the direct quote. PATTERN Attribution, "Quote?"
Commas	Do not use a comma if a prepositional opener has fewer than five words.
	Use a comma to separate two main clauses connected with a cc. PATTERN MC, cc MC
	Use a comma to separate an attribution from a direct quote. PATTERN Attribution, "Quote?"

Rewrite It!　　Despite her deficiencies Dorinda truthfully answered her father. "It was a frog."
　　　　　　　　　King Morton's eyes widened, and he inquired, "What did he want?"

Read It!	Mark It!	Fix It!	Day 2

Read It!

Crying yet again Dorinda sobbed the story
of the frogs considerate rescue, and of her foolish
promise she miserably wailed I will not touch
that ugly **despicable** thing

despicable
regarded with distaste, disgust, or disdain

Mark It!

1 coordinating conjunction (cc)
2 prepositional phrases
3 [main clauses]
3 subject-verb pairs (s v)
2 openers

Fix It!

1 indent
1 capital
4 commas
2 end marks
2 quotation marks
1 apostrophe
(fix run-on with period)

(4) -ing

                                    s   v
                                               av

¶ Crying yet again, [Dorinda sobbed the story

                                              cc
of the frog's considerate rescue, and of her foolish
         s   v   s   v   v
    (1) subject   av   hv   av
promise]. [she miserably wailed], "[I will not touch

that ugly, **despicable** thing]!"

Indentation	new topic (or speaker)
Conjunction	***and*** connects two prepositional phrases: *of the … rescue* and *of her foolish promise*. **a and b** In this sentence *yet* functions as an adverb, not a conjunction. When *yet* functions as a conjunction, it connects equal items. A word will only perform one function at a time.
Ask Students	The adjectives *ugly* and *despicable* belong in which category? See page 31. Both are adjectives of opinion. Because they are in the same category, they are coordinate adjectives.
S V Pairs	MC ***Dorinda sobbed*** (action) MC ***She wailed*** (action) MC ***I will touch*** (action) *Will* is a helping verb. *Will touch* is the verb phrase.
Note	The word *that* often begins a that clause **PATTERN that + subject + verb**. The word *that* can also function as an adjective as in *that ugly, despicable thing*. Which thing? *that*
Run-On	Use a period to fix the run-on (fused sentence). The first two main clauses are separate ideas and belong in separate sentences.
Note	*She miserably wailed* is an attribution and belongs in the same sentence as the direct quote. **PATTERN Attribution, "Quote!"**
Commas	Use a comma after an -ing opener. **PATTERN -ing word/phrase, main clause** The thing after the comma must be the thing doing the inging. *Dorinda* is doing the *crying*. Do not use a comma to separate two items connected with a cc. **PATTERN a and b** Use a comma to separate an attribution from a direct quote. **PATTERN Attribution, "Quote!"** Use a comma to separate coordinate adjectives (ugly, despicable thing).

Rewrite It!   Crying yet again, Dorinda sobbed the story of the frog's considerate rescue and of her foolish promise. She miserably wailed, "I will not touch that ugly, despicable thing!"

Read It!	Mark It!	Fix It!	Day 3

Read It!

Dorindas **theatrics** frustrated her father her tear's annoyed him. Daughter he urged you are a royal princess, your word must be trustworthy

theatrics
exaggerated mannerisms, actions, or words

Mark It!

5 [main clauses]

5 subject-verb pairs (s v)

1 opener

Fix It!

1 indent

1 capital

3 commas

2 end marks

1 semicolon

4 quotation marks

2 apostrophes

(fix run-ons with semicolon and period)

①	subject

               s   v   s

¶ [Dorinda's **theatrics** frustrated her father]; [her tear's

v
av
annoyed him]. "Daughter," [he urged], "[you are a royal

s	v	v
hv	lv
princess],. [your word must be trustworthy]."

Indentation	new topic (or speaker)
S V Pairs	MC ***theatrics frustrated*** (action)
	MC ***tears annoyed*** (action)
	MC ***he urged*** (action)
	MC ***you are*** (linking) The noun *princess* follows the linking verb and renames the subject.
	MC ***word must be*** (linking) *Must* is a helping verb. *Must be* is the verb phrase. The adjective *trustworthy* follows the linking verb and describes the subject.
Run-On	Use a semicolon to fix the first run-on (fused sentence). The first two main clauses express a single idea and are similar in length and construction.
	Use a period to fix the second run-on (comma splice). The quotation includes two main clauses. They are separate ideas and belong in separate sentences.
Note	The attribution *he urged* interrupts the first quoted sentence. It is correct that *you* is not capitalized. **PATTERN "Quote," attribution, "rest of quoted sentence."**
Commas	Place commas around a noun of direct address (NDA). ***Daughter,***
	Use a comma to separate an attribution from a direct quote. **PATTERN "Quote," attribution, "rest of quoted sentence."**
	Do not use a comma to separate two main clauses. Use a period. MC, MC is always wrong.

Rewrite It!	Dorinda's theatrics frustrated her father; her tears annoyed him. "Daughter," he urged, "you are a royal princess. Your word must be trustworthy."

Read It!	Mark It!	Fix It!	Day 4

Reluctantly, Princess Dorinda slunk to the door,
she opened it just wide enough, for the frog to squeeze
through you may enter she sighed **audibly**.

audibly
loud enough to be heard

2 <u>prepositional phrases</u>
4 [main clauses]
4 subject-verb pairs (s v)
2 openers

1 indent
2 capitals
4 commas
2 end marks
2 quotation marks
(fix run-ons with periods)

③ -ly adverb

¶ Reluctantly, [Princess Dorinda slunk <u>to the door</u>],.
① subject
[she opened it just wide enough, <u>for the frog</u> to squeeze through]. "[you may enter]," [she sighed **audibly**].

Indentation	new topic (or speaker)
Ask Students	In the second sentence, why is the word *through* not a preposition? A preposition begins a prepositional phrase. **PATTERN preposition + noun (no verb)** *Through* is an adverb, not a preposition.
S V Pairs	MC ***Princess Dorinda slunk*** (action) MC ***She opened*** (action) MC ***You may enter*** (action) *May* is a helping verb. *May enter* is the verb phrase. MC ***she sighed*** (action)
Run-On	Use a period to fix the first run-on (comma splice). The first two main clauses are separate ideas and belong in separate sentences. Use a period to fix the second run-on (fused sentence). The second and third main clauses are separate ideas and belong in separate sentences.
Note	*She sighed audibly* is an attribution and belongs in the same sentence as the direct quote. **PATTERN "Quote," attribution.**
Commas	Do not use a comma if an -ly adverb opener modifies the verb. Dorinda slunk in a reluctant manner. Do not use a comma to separate two main clauses. Use a period. MC, MC is always wrong. Do not put a comma in front of a prepositional phrase. Use a comma to separate an attribution from a direct quote. **PATTERN "Quote," attribution.**

Rewrite It! Reluctantly Princess Dorinda slunk to the door. She opened it just wide enough for the frog to squeeze through. "You may enter," she sighed audibly.

Learn It!

Noun and Pronoun Functions

A **noun** names a person, place, thing, or idea. A **pronoun** replaces a noun in order to avoid repetition. Both nouns and pronouns perform many functions (jobs) in a sentence.

sn   av   do   op   nda   sp lv   pn

The king showed hospitality to the frog. "Frederick, I am King Morton."

For more information about noun and pronoun functions (jobs), see page G-7.

This book explains six noun jobs: subject, object of the preposition, noun of direct address, direct object, predicate noun, appositive. It does not explain indirect objects or object complements.

When the sentence is a command, the subject, *you*, is implied.

Subject

Week 1 you learned that a **subject** is a noun or pronoun that performs a verb action. It tells who or what the clause is about.

What is the verb? *showed.* Who showed? *king. King* is the subject noun (sn) because it tell who the first clause is about.

What is the verb? *am.* Who am? *I. I* is the subject pronoun (sp) because it tells who the second clause is about.

Object of the Preposition

Week 1 you learned that an **object of the preposition** is a noun or pronoun at the end of a prepositional phrase. PATTERN preposition + noun (no verb)

To the frog begins with a preposition (to), ends with a noun (frog), and has no verb in between. The noun *frog* is the object of the preposition (op) because it is the noun at the end of the prepositional phrase.

Noun of Direct Address

Week 5 you learned that a **noun of direct address** is a noun used to directly address someone. It only appears in a quoted sentence.

The noun *Frederick* is a noun of direct address (nda) because it is the noun the king uses to directly address the frog.

An NDA is never the subject of the sentence. A noun can do only one job at a time.

The next two jobs are similar. Find both by asking *subject verb what?* or *subject verb whom?*

Direct Object

A **direct object** is a noun or pronoun that follows an action verb and answers the question *what* or *whom.* A direct object receives the verb's action. That means it completes the verb's meaning.

King showed what? *hospitality.* The noun *hospitality* follows the action verb and functions as the direct object (do) because *hospitality* tells what the *king showed.*

The noun (or pronoun) that follows an action verb is called a direct object.

Predicate Noun

A **predicate noun** is a noun or pronoun that follows a linking verb and answers the question *what* or *whom.* A predicate noun renames the subject. The subject and predicate noun are different names for the same person, place, thing, or idea.

I am whom? *King Morton.* The noun *King Morton* follows the linking verb and functions as the predicate noun (pn) because *King Morton* is another name for *I.*

The noun (or pronoun) that follows a linking verb is called a predicate noun (or pronoun).

Mark It!   Continue to mark every verb as *av*, *lv*, or *hv*.

Mark every subject noun (*sn*), subject pronoun (*sp*), object of the preposition (*op*), noun of direct address (*nda*), direct object (*do*), predicate noun (*pn*), and appositive (*app*).

Both a predicate noun and a predicate adjective are types of subject complements. See page G-7.

Appositives are on the next page.

Who/Which Clause

Week 7 you learned that a ***who/which* clause** is a dependent clause that describes the noun it follows. A *who/which* clause is easy to recognize because it begins with the word *who* or *which*.

w/w

[King Morton ruled the land], (which was an obscure kingdom).

Invisible *Who/Which* Clause

An **invisible *who/which* clause** occurs when the *who* or *which* and the verb are removed from the clause. They become invisible.

w/w

[King Morton ruled the land], (which was an obscure kingdom).

If a *who/which* clause contains a *be* verb, the *who* or *which* and the *be* verb can be removed to form an invisible *who/which* clause.

which was   app

[King Morton ruled the land], (an obscure kingdom).

In this example, the words *which was* are implied. They are not written in the sentence. When the words "which was" are removed, the words that remain are called an appositive phrase.

An **appositive** (app) is a noun or noun phrase that renames the noun it follows. The noun and the appositive are different names for the same person, place, thing, or idea. *Kingdom* is another name for *land*.

An appositive often includes words that describe it. In the example *kingdom* is the noun that functions as an appositive. *An obscure kingdom* is the appositive phrase.

Follow the same comma rules for the invisible *who/which* clause (the appositive phrase) that you follow for the regular *who/which* clause.

> Place commas around a *who/which* clause if it is nonessential.

> Do not place commas around a *who/which* clause if it is essential (changes the meaning of the sentence).

Mark It! Mentally insert *who* or *which* and the *be* verb. Place parentheses around the invisible *who/which* clause. Write **app** above the appositive.

w/w   app

[I am King Morton], ((who is) ruler of this land).

Run-On

Fix It! no longer tells you how to fix the run-on sentence. You must determine yourself if a run-on exists and how to eliminate it. If the passage contains two or more main clauses in one sentence, look for a run-on.

Remember, there are three simple ways to fix a run-on:

- Place a period at the end of each main clause. This is the simplest fix.

- ; Fix It! will indicate if a semicolon is the best option.

- , cc If a coordinating conjunction (cc) connects two main clauses, confirm that a comma is in front of the cc. The cc without a comma is a comma error.

Sidebar:

An invisible *who/which* clause is an appositive phrase. See page G-7.

Because the comma rules for the *who/which* clause and the appositive phrase are the same, students can mentally insert *who* or *which* and the *be* verb to determine if the appositive phrase requires commas.

A predicate noun and an appositive both rename a noun.

A predicate noun follows a linking verb and renames the subject noun.

An appositive immediately follows the noun it renames.

Phrase Overview: Appendix III

When students mentally insert *who is*, the appositive phrase *ruler of this land* becomes a *who* clause: who is ruler of this land.

This is why the comma rules for the *who/which* clause and appositive phrase are the same!

hopping behind her the frog followed Dorinda,
to the elaborate dining hall, I appreciate your
hospitality **sire** Im Frederick the frog volunteered.

sire
a respectful term of address to a man of rank or authority

10 noun/pronoun jobs
2 prepositional phrases
4 [main clauses]
4 subject-verb pairs (s v)
1 opener

1 indent
2 capitals
5 commas
2 end marks
2 quotation marks
1 apostrophe

④ -ing

¶ hopping behind her, [the frog followed Dorinda,
to the elaborate dining hall]. "[I appreciate your
hospitality], **sire**. [I'm Frederick]," [the frog volunteered].

This is the only week that an explanation for every direct object and predicate noun is given.

Indentation		new topic (or speaker)
Capitalization		*Sire* Capitalize a title used as an NDA with the exceptions of *sir* and *madam*.
S V Pairs	MC	*frog followed* (action) Followed whom? *Dorinda* The noun *Dorinda* follows the action verb (AV) and functions as the direct object.
	MC	*I appreciate* (action) Appreciate what? *hospitality* The noun *hospitality* follows the action verb (AV) and functions as the direct object.
	MC	*I'm* (linking) The contraction *I'm* includes both a subject (I) and a linking verb (am). I'm who? *Frederick* The noun *Frederick* follows the linking verb (LV) and renames the subject. *Frederick* functions as a predicate noun.
	MC	*frog volunteered* (action)
Note		The first main clause is a complete thought, not an attribution. It requires a period.
		The quotation includes two main clauses. Both require a period.
		The frog volunteered is an attribution and belongs in the same sentence as the second quoted sentence. **PATTERN "Quote," attribution.**
Commas		Use a comma after an -ing opener. **PATTERN -ing word/phrase, main clause** The thing after the comma must be the thing doing the inging. The *frog* is doing the *hopping*.
		Do not put a comma in front of a prepositional phrase.
		Do not use a comma to separate two main clauses. Use a period. MC, MC is always wrong.
		Place commas around a noun of direct address (NDA). **, Sire**
		Use a comma to separate an attribution from a direct quote. **PATTERN "Quote," attribution.**

Rewrite It!   Hopping behind her, the frog followed Dorinda to the elaborate dining hall. "I appreciate your hospitality, Sire. I'm Frederick," the frog volunteered.

Read It!	Mark It!	Fix It!	Day 2

Dorinda pick up Frederick her father commanded and feed him from your golden plate. yuck then I wont touch another bite she **whined**

whined
complained in an annoying way

Mark It!
8 noun/pronoun jobs
1 coordinating conjunction (cc)
1 prepositional phrase
4 [main clauses]
4 subject-verb pairs (s v)

Fix It!
2 indents
2 capitals
4 commas
2 end marks
6 quotation marks
1 apostrophe

¶ "Dorinda, [(you) pick up Frederick," [her father commanded], "and feed him from your golden plate]." ¶ "yuck! [then I won't touch another bite]," [she whined].

Indentation	new speaker; new speaker
Conjunction	**and** connects two verbs: *pick* and *feed* A subject and verb ((you) pick) come before the cc, but only a verb (feed) comes after the cc. A comma is not used. MC cc 2nd verb The comma after *commanded* is for the attribution.
Interjection	**Yuck!** is an interjection that expresses a strong emotion. Use an exclamation mark and capitalize *Then*.
S V Pairs	MC **(you) pick up** (action), **feed** (action) The noun *Dorinda* is an NDA. The subject of an imperative sentence is always *you*. The single subject *you* is followed by two verbs. Pick up whom? *Frederick* The noun *Frederick* follows the AV and functions as the direct object. Feed whom? *him* The pronoun *him* follows the AV and functions as the direct object.
	MC **father commanded** (action)
	MC **I won't touch** (action) The contraction *won't* includes both a helping verb (will) and an adverb (not). Touch what? *bite* The noun *bite* follows the AV and functions as the direct object.
	MC **she whined** (action)
Note	The attribution *her father commanded* interrupts the first quoted sentence. It is correct that *and* is not capitalized. **PATTERN** "Quote," attribution, "rest of quoted sentence." *She whined* is an attribution and belongs in the same sentence as the direct quote. **PATTERN** "Quote," attribution.
Commas	Place commas around a noun of direct address (NDA). **Dorinda,** Use a comma to separate an attribution from a direct quote.

Rewrite It!   "Dorinda, pick up Frederick," her father commanded, "and feed him from your golden plate."

"Yuck! Then I won't touch another bite," she whined.

patiently King Morton who valued **integrity**
explained that "a promise was a promise," additionally
he reminded Dorinda about her royal duties and the
expectations of the people the nation's citizens.

integrity
the quality of being honest and fair

③ -ly adverb

11 noun/pronoun jobs
1 coordinating conjunction (cc)
2 prepositional phrases
2 [main clauses]
1 *who/which* clause (w/w)
1 *that* clause (that)
4 subject-verb pairs (s v)
1 invisible *who/which* clause (w/w)
2 openers

1 indent
2 capitals
5 commas
1 end mark
2 quotation marks

¶ patiently [King Morton, (who valued **integrity**), explained] (that "a promise was a promise),". additionally, [he reminded Dorinda about her royal duties and the expectations of the people], ((who were) the nation's citizens).

Indentation	new topic
Quotations	Do not use quotation marks around an indirect quote. The same sentence using a direct quote: Patiently King Morton, who valued integrity, explained, "A promise is a promise."
Conjunction	**and** connects two nouns (objects of the preposition): *duties* and *expectations* a and b
S V Pairs MC	**King Morton explained** (action) Do not use quotations with an indirect quote (after *that*).
w/w	**who valued** (action) The subject of the clause is *who*. The *who* clause describes *King Morton*, the noun it follows. Valued what? *integrity* The noun *integrity* follows the AV and functions as the direct object.
that	*that* **promise was** (linking) Was what? *promise* The noun *promise* follows the linking verb and renames the subject. *Promise* functions as a predicate noun.
MC	**he reminded** (action) Reminded whom? *Dorinda* The noun *Dorinda* follows the AV and functions as the direct object.
Invisible w/w	*(who were) the nation's citizens* is an invisible *who* clause. With the words *who were* removed, the noun *citizens* follows the noun *people* and renames it. *Citizens* functions as an appositive.
Note	Use a period to fix the run-on (comma splice). The main clauses are separate ideas and belong in separate sentences. The *that* clause belongs with the first main clause.
Commas	Place commas around a nonessential *who/which* clause.
	Do not use a comma to separate two main clauses. Use a period. MC, MC is always wrong.
	Use a comma if an -ly adverb opener modifies the sentence. It was additional that he reminded Dorinda.
	Place commas around a nonessential invisible *who/which* clause (appositive phrase).

Rewrite It!   Patiently King Morton, who valued integrity, explained that a promise was a promise.
Additionally, he reminded Dorinda about her royal duties and the expectations of the people,
the nation's citizens.

Read It!	Mark It!	Fix It!	Day 4

Dorinda **complied**, because she would not touch the frog, with her own precious finger's she held her napkin between her thumb, and first finger.

complied
obeyed

8 noun/pronoun jobs
1 coordinating conjunction (cc)
2 prepositional phrases
2 [main clauses]
1 adverb clause (AC)
3 subject-verb pairs (s v)
2 openers

1 indent
1 capital
4 commas
1 apostrophe

⑥ vss   ⑤ clausal

s   *v*   *s*   *v*   *v*
sn   *av*   *AC*   *sp*   *hv*   *av*

¶ [Dorinda **complied**]. (because she would not touch

do   *op*   *s*   *v*
                                     sp   *av*

the frog, with her own precious finger's), [she held her

do   *op*   *cc*   *op*

napkin between her thumb, and first finger].

Indentation	new topic
Conjunction	**and** connects two nouns (objects of the preposition): *thumb* and *finger* a and b
S V Pairs MC	**Dorinda complied** (action)
AC	*because* **she would touch** (action) *Would* is a helping verb. *Would touch* is the verb phrase. Would touch what? *frog* The noun *frog* follows the AV and functions as the direct object.
MC	**she held** (action) She held what? *napkin* The noun *napkin* follows the AV and functions as the direct object.
Note	Use a period to fix the run-on (comma splice). The structure of this passage is MC. AC, MC. The main clauses are separate ideas and belong in separate sentences.
Ask Students	Why does the adverb clause belong with the second main clause? The *because* clause tells why she held her napkin the way she did. It does not tell why she complied.
Commas	Do not use a comma to separate two main clauses. Use a period. MC, MC is always wrong.
	Do not put a comma in front of a prepositional phrase.
	Use a comma after an adverb clause that comes before a main clause. **PATTERN AC, MC**
	Do not use a comma to separate two items connected with a cc. **PATTERN a and b**

Rewrite It!   Dorinda complied. Because she would not touch the frog with her own precious fingers, she held her napkin between her thumb and first finger.

Learn It!

For more information about pronouns, see pages G-6 and G-7.

Pronoun

A **pronoun** takes the place of a noun. Without pronouns, a passage would sound monotonous, even strange. An **antecedent** is the word the pronoun refers to. If the antecedent is not mentioned or if it is unclear, confusion occurs.

She laughed and yelled, "Give him that!"

Who is she? Who is him? What is that? These sentences are confusing because the pronouns are missing antecedents.

Dorinda gave Maribella toast with sturgeon roe. She wrinkled her face.

Who wrinkled her face, Dorinda or Maribella? The antecedent is unclear.

Pronoun Case

Pronouns function like nouns. However, specific pronouns do only certain jobs.

Subjective case pronouns do the job of subject nouns and predicate nouns.

sn   *sp*
Frederick knocked at the door. Who knocked at the door?

Who knocked? *Frederick, subject noun*
Who knocked? *Who, subject pronoun*

lv pn   *lv pn*
The prince is a frog. The prince is he.

Prince is who? *frog* The noun *frog* follows the linking verb and renames the subject.
Prince is who? *he* The pronoun *he* follows the linking verb and renames the subject.

Objective case pronouns do the job of direct objects and objects of a preposition.

av   do   *av   do*
The frog followed Dorinda. The frog followed her.

Followed whom? *Dorinda* The noun *Dorinda* follows the action verb.
Followed whom? *her* The pronoun *her* follows the action verb.

op   *op*
You will sit with the frog. I must sit with whom?

The noun *frog* follows the preposition.
The pronoun *whom* follows the preposition.

Possessive case pronouns do the job of adjectives and predicate nouns.

adj   *adj*
The frog ate from Dorinda's plate. The frog ate from her plate.

From whose plate? *Dorinda's*
From whose plate? *her*

pn   *pn*
The delicious dinner was Dorinda's food. The dinner was hers.

Was what? *food* The noun *food* follows the linking verb and renames the subject.
Was what? *hers* The pronoun *hers* follows the linking verb and renames the subject.

Subjective Case
subject predicate pronoun
I
you
he, she, it
we
you
they
who

Objective Case
direct object object of preposition
me
you
him, her, it
us
you
them
whom

Possessive Case	
adjective	predicate pronoun
my	mine
your	yours
his, her, its	his, hers, its
our	ours
your	yours
their	theirs
whose	whose

Think About It!

Fill in the blanks with a word from the word bank. Use each word one time.

Word Bank

he
her
his
it
its
me
mine
theirs
them
they
us
we
whom
whose
you
you

Case	Subjective			Objective			Possessive				
Function (job)	subject predicate pronoun			direct object object of prep			adjective			predicate pronoun	
	I			*me*			my			*mine*	
	you			*you*			your			yours	
he	she	*it*	him	*her*	it	*his*	her	*its*	his	hers	its
	we			us			our			ours	
	you			you			your			yours	
	they			them			their			*theirs*	
	who			*whom*			*whose*				

What Is It and Why?

Read each sentence and determine if the underlined pronoun is a subjective case, an objective case, or a possessive case pronoun.

Write the type of pronoun in the blank and explain why.

Dorinda was bored. She and Maribella went to town.

__subjective case__ Why? __She is the subject of the clause.__

Dorinda spotted the frog, who sat near a store.

__subjective case__ Why? __**Who** is the subject of the clause.__

"Oh no! It is he!"

__subjective case__ Why? __**He** is a predicate pronoun (follows LV).__

Maribella kindly greeted him.

__objective case__ Why? __**Him** is a direct object (follows AV).__

"Would you come into the store with us?"

__objective case__ Why? __**Us** is the object of the preposition.__

He saw the store. Its door was closed.

__possessive case__ Why? __Whose door? **Its** is an adjective.__

Maribella started to open the door, but Frederick stopped her.

__objective case__ Why? __**Her** is a direct object (follows AV).__

Read It!	Mark It!	Fix It!	Day 1

Unceremoniously, she grabbed one of Fredericks hind legs and deposited him on the table, beside her plate he was a revolting, green amphibian, promptly she receded into her chair.

unceremoniously
hastily and rudely

10 noun/pronoun jobs	4 commas
1 coordinating conjunction (cc)	2 end marks
4 <u>prepositional phrases</u>	1 apostrophe
3 [main clauses]	
3 subject-verb pairs (s v)	
3 openers	

③ -ly adverb

          s   *v*
          sp   *av*   *do*

Unceremoniously, [she grabbed one of Frederick's hind

                  v
op   *cc*   *av*   *do*   *op*   *op*

legs and deposited him on the table, beside her plate].

① subject
s   *v*
sp   *lv*   *pn*   ③ -ly adverb

[he was a revolting, green amphibian]. promptly

  s   *v*
 sp   *av*   *op*

[she receded into her chair].

Conjunction	**and** connects two verbs: *grabbed* and *deposited* MC cc 2nd verb
Ask Students	The adjectives *revolting* and *green* belong in which categories? See page 31. *Revolting* is an adjective of opinion; *green* is an adjective of color. The first adjective (revolting) describes the second adjective and the noun together (green amphibian).
S V Pairs	MC **she grabbed, deposited** (action) The single subject *she* is followed by two verbs. Both show action.
	MC **he was** (linking) The noun *amphibian* follows the linking verb and renames the subject.
	MC **she receded** (action)
Note	This passage includes three main clauses. The main clauses are separate ideas and belong in separate sentences.
Commas	Do not use a comma if an -ly adverb opener modifies the verb. Dorinda grabbed in an unceremonious manner.
	Do not put a comma in front of a prepositional phrase.
	Do not use a comma to separate cumulative adjectives (revolting green amphibian).
	Do not use a comma to separate two main clauses. Use a period. MC, MC is always wrong.

Rewrite It!   Unceremoniously she grabbed one of Frederick's hind legs and deposited him on the table beside her plate. He was a revolting green amphibian. Promptly she receded into her chair.

Read It!	Mark It!	Fix It!	Day 2

After supper, King Morton invited Frederick, to the Guest Room which was a splendid suite. Velvet carpeted the floor, silk blanketed the bed. Frederick knew, that he would **relish** his palace stay.

relish
enjoy; take pleasure in

Mark It!
- 13 noun/pronoun jobs
- 2 <u>prepositional phrases</u>
- 4 [main clauses]
- 1 *who/which* clause (w/w)
- 1 *that* clause (that)
- 6 subject-verb pairs (s v)
- 3 openers

Fix It!
- 1 indent
- 2 capitals
- 5 commas
- 1 semicolon

② prepositional

                         op   s sn   v av   do

¶ After supper, [King Morton invited Frederick, to the

op   w/w   s sp   v lv   pn   ① subject s sn

Guest Room], (which was a splendid suite). [Velvet

v av   do   s sn   v av   do   ① subject s sn

carpeted the floor],; [silk blanketed the bed]. [Frederick

v av   that   s sp   v hv   v av   do

knew], (that he would **relish** his palace stay).

Indentation		new time (or place)
S V Pairs	MC	***King Morton invited*** (action)
	w/w	***which was*** (linking) The *which* clause describes *guest room*, the noun it follows. The noun *suite* follows the linking verb and renames the subject, the word *which*. It is nonessential because it does not change the meaning of the sentence. Without the *which* clause, King Morton still invited Frederick to the guest room.
	MC	***velvet carpeted*** (action)
	MC	***silk blanketed*** (action)
	MC	***Frederick knew*** (action)
	that	*that **he would relish*** (action) *Would* is a helping verb. *Would relish* is the verb phrase.
Ask Students		What is the best way to fix the run-on (comma splice)? Use a semicolon. Both main clauses, *velvet carpeted the floor* and *silk blanketed the bed*, express a single idea and are similar in length and construction.
Commas		Do not use a comma if a prepositional opener has fewer than five words.
		Do not put a comma in front of a prepositional phrase.
		Place commas around a nonessential *who/which* clause.
		Do not use a comma to separate two main clauses. Use a period or semicolon. MC, MC is always wrong.
		Do not put a comma in front of a *that* clause.

Rewrite It!   After supper King Morton invited Frederick to the guest room, which was a splendid suite. Velvet carpeted the floor; silk blanketed the bed. Frederick knew that he would relish his palace stay.

Read It!	Mark It!	Fix It!	

Read It!

Evidently Dorinda Maribella and King Morton had not **deduced** the frog's true identity, Frederick was not a lowly frog, but a royal prince.

deduced
concluded using logic or reason

Mark It!

7 noun/pronoun jobs
2 coordinating conjunctions (cc)
2 [main clauses]
2 subject-verb pairs (s v)
2 openers

Fix It!

1 indent
5 commas

③ -ly adverb

             s   s   s
             sn   sn   cc   sn

¶ Evidently, [Dorinda, Maribella, and King Morton

(hv) (av) ... do ... ① subject sn

had not **deduced** the frog's true identity], [Frederick

(lv) ... pn ... cc ... pn

was not a lowly frog, but a royal prince].

Indentation	new topic	
Conjunction	**and** connects three nouns (subjects): *Dorinda, Maribella,* and *King Morton* a, b, and c	
	but connects two nouns (predicate nouns): *frog* but *prince* a and b	
S V Pairs	MC	**Dorinda, Maribella, King Morton had deduced** (action) *Had* is a helping verb. *Had deduced* is the verb phrase.
	MC	**Frederick was** (linking) The nouns *frog, prince* follow the linking verb and rename the subject.
Ask Students	What is the best way to fix the run-on (comma splice)? Use a period. *What had not been deduced* and *who Frederick was* are separate ideas. Form two sentences.	
Commas	Use a comma if an -ly adverb opener modifies the sentence. It was evident that Dorinda, Maribella, and King Morton had not deduced the frog's true identity.	
	Use commas to separate three or more items in a series connected with a cc. **PATTERN a, b, and c**	
	Do not use a comma to separate two main clauses. Use a period. MC, MC is always wrong.	
	Do not use a comma to separate two items connected with a cc. **PATTERN a and b**	

Rewrite It!   Evidently, Dorinda, Maribella, and King Morton had not deduced the frog's true identity. Frederick was not a lowly frog but a royal prince.

Read It!	Mark It!	Fix It!	Day 4

Read It!

When he had lived at his fathers castle Frederick had been a swollen-headed **pretentious** teenager on a humid afternoon in July young Frederick had been riding his horse a strong thoroughbred through a forest in his father's, vast Kingdom.

pretentious
characterized by an exaggerated assumption of dignity or importance

Mark It!

11 noun/pronoun jobs
5 prepositional phrases
2 [main clauses]
1 adverb clause (AC)
3 subject-verb pairs (s v)
1 invisible *who/which* clause (w/w)
2 openers

Fix It!

1 indent
1 capital
6 commas
1 end mark
1 apostrophe

⑤ clausal

        s   *v*   *v*   *op*   *s*
AC   *sp* *hv*   *av*   *sn*

(When he had lived at his father's castle), [Frederick

   v   *v*   *pn*
  hv   *lv*

had been a swollen-headed, pretentious teenager].

     ② prepositional   *s*   *v*
               op   *op*   *sn*   *hv*

¶ on a humid afternoon in July, [young Frederick had

 v   *v*   *do*   *w/w*   *app*
hv   *av*

been riding his horse, (*(which was)* a strong thoroughbred),

         op   *op*

through a forest in his father's, vast Kingdom].

Indentation	new time
S V Pairs	AC *When **he had lived*** (action) *Had* is a helping verb. *Had lived* is the verb phrase.
	MC ***Frederick had been*** (linking) *Had* is a helping verb. *Had been* is the verb phrase. Had been what? *teenager* The noun *teenager* follows the linking verb and renames the subject. *Teenager* functions as a predicate noun.
	MC ***Frederick had been riding*** (action) *Had* and *been* are helping verbs. *Had been riding* is the verb phrase. Had been riding what? *horse* The noun *horse* follows the AV and functions as the direct object.
Invisible w/w	*(which was) a strong thoroughbred* is an invisible *which* clause. With the words *which was* removed, the noun *thoroughbred* follows the noun *horse* and renames it. *Thoroughbred* functions as an appositive because the subject and the verb (which was) are not in the phrase.
Note	This passage includes two main clauses. Both require a period.
Commas	Use a comma after an adverb clause that comes before a main clause. **PATTERN AC, MC**
	Use a comma to separate coordinate adjectives (swollen-headed, pretentious teenager).
	If two or more prepositional phrases open a sentence, follow the last phrase with a comma.
	Place commas around a nonessential invisible *who/which* clause (appositive phrase).
	Do not use a comma to separate cumulative adjectives (father's vast kingdom).

Rewrite It!   When he had lived at his father's castle, Frederick had been a swollen-headed, pretentious teenager.

              On a humid afternoon in July, young Frederick had been riding his horse, a strong thoroughbred, through a forest in his father's vast kingdom.

Learn It!

Pronoun Types

There are more than one hundred pronouns in the English language. Grammarians organize pronouns in various ways. One way to organize pronouns is by type.

Some pronouns appear in more than one category. For example, when *who* begins a dependent clause (a *who/which* clause) it is classified as a relative pronoun. When *who* begins a question, it is classified as an interrogative pronoun.

A **personal pronoun** refers to a specific person, place, or thing recently mentioned. In English there are three persons: first, second, and third.

> The chef had served a new dessert. Dorinda looked at Maribella.

> "*I* see that *you* did not eat the ice cream that *she* made."

The antecedent for *I*, the first-person pronoun, is Dorinda, the person speaking.

The antecedent for *you*, the second-person pronoun, is Maribella, the person spoken to.

The antecedent for *she*, the third-person pronoun, is the chef, the person spoken about.

A **reflexive pronoun** ends in -*self* or -*selves*, functions as an object, and reflects the subject of the same clause.

> The king mumbled to *himself*.

The pronoun *himself* is the object of the preposition *to* and reflects (refers to) the subject of the clause. The antecedent for the pronoun *himself* is the subject of the clause, the noun *king*.

An **intensive pronoun** ends in -*self* or -*selves*, functions as an appositive, and intensifies the noun or pronoun it refers to. Intensive pronouns can be removed from the sentence.

> The frog *himself* spoke to the king.

The pronoun *himself* emphasizes the noun *frog*. The antecedent for the pronoun *himself* is the noun *frog*, and the intensive pronoun can be removed from the sentence: *The frog spoke to the king.*

A **relative pronoun** begins a dependent adjective clause (a *who/which* clause) and refers to the noun the entire clause describes.

> The frog, *who* used to be a prince, spoke respectfully yet boldly.

The *who* clause describes *frog*, the noun it follows. The antecedent for the pronoun *who* is the noun *frog*. *The frog used to be a prince.*

> The king, *whom* the frog addressed, listened intently.

The *who* clause describes *king*, the noun it follows. The antecedent for the pronoun *whom* is the noun *king*. *The frog addressed the king.*

An **interrogative pronoun** begins a question. The antecedent is the answer to the question.

> *What* was the frog's name?

The pronoun *what* begins a question. The antecedent for the pronoun *what* is the answer to the question: *Frederick was the frog's name.*

For more information about pronouns, see pages G-6 and G-7.

Personal

1st
I, me, my, mine, we, us, our, ours

2nd
you, your, yours

3rd
he, him, his, she, her, hers, it, its, they, them, their, theirs

Reflexive and Intensive

---

same words, different uses

myself, yourself, himself, herself, itself, ourselves, yourselves, themselves

Relative

---

who, whom, whose, which, that

Interrogative

---

what, whatever, which, whichever, who, whoever, whom, whose

Demonstrative

Demonstrative

this, that, these, those

Indefinite

all, another, any, anybody, anyone, anything, anywhere, both, each, either, everybody, everyone, everything, everywhere, few, more, most, much, neither, no one, nobody, none, nothing, nowhere, one, other, others, own, several, some, somebody, someone, something, somewhere

Most indefinite pronouns are either singular or plural.

A few can be both, depending on the noun they replace.

These are the most common indefinite pronouns that can be singular and plural: all, any, more, most, none, some.

Some (singular) of this chocolate is broken.

Some (plural) of these desserts smell good.

A **demonstrative pronoun** points to a particular person or thing. *This* and *that* refer to singular items. *These* and *those* refer to plural items.

This was an unusual frog.

The antecedent for the pronoun *this* is the noun *frog*.

An **indefinite pronoun** is not specific. Indefinite pronouns do not refer to a particular person, place, or thing and will not have a defined antecedent.

Everything on the table smelled good.

The reader can only assume it was food that smelled good because the pronoun *everything* does not have an antecedent.

Mark It! Continue to mark every verb as **av**, **lv**, or **hv**.

Continue to mark every subject noun (**sn**), subject pronoun (**sp**), object of the preposition (**op**), noun of direct address (**nda**), direct object (**do**), predicate noun (**pn**), and appositive (**app**).

Think About It!

Demonstrative pronouns, indefinite pronouns, and possessive case pronouns function as adjectives when they come before a noun.

This was an unusual amphibian. This frog spoke.

In the first sentence *This* is a demonstrative pronoun and functions as the subject of the clause. The antecedent of the pronoun *this* is *frog*.

In the second sentence *This* comes before the noun *frog* and tells which frog. It functions as an adjective.

Reflexive pronouns and objective case pronouns function as objects. When the object refers to the subject of the clause, a reflexive pronoun is used. Think of the *reflexive* pronoun as a pronoun *reflecting* its subject.

First Dorinda served herself. Then Dorinda served her.

In the first sentence the direct object *herself* refers to the subject *Dorinda*. *Herself* is a reflexive pronoun reflecting its subject.

In the second sentence Dorinda served another girl. We know this because the direct object is the objective case pronoun *her*.

Reflexive pronouns and intensive pronouns are the same pronouns with different uses. A reflexive pronoun functions as an object and is a necessary part of the sentence. An intensive pronoun functions as an appositive to show emphasis and can be removed from the sentence.

The frog thought to himself about how Dorinda herself might help him.

Himself is a reflexive pronoun because it is the object of the preposition *to* and refers to (reflects) the subject *frog*. It is a necessary part of the sentence because without it, *to* would not have an object.

Herself is an intensive pronoun because it is an appositive that emphasizes *Dorinda*, the noun it follows.

Read It!	Mark It!	Fix It!	Day 1
	12 noun/pronoun jobs	1 indent	
	3 prepositional phrases	3 capitals	
	4 [main clauses]	7 commas	
	2 adverb clauses (AC)	2 end marks	
	6 subject-verb pairs (s v)	4 quotation marks	
	1 opener	1 apostrophe	

Read It!

After he had ridden for several miles his horse reared up, because a thin, young boy stood in the path. please Sir Ive lost my way the boy explained, can I have a ride out of this **daunting** forest

daunting
causing fear or discouragement

(5) clausal

```
        s   v      v                                          s
AC      sp  hv     av                                 op      sn
(After he had ridden for several miles), [his horse

 v                    AC                       s      v
 av                                            sn     av
reared up], (because a thin, young boy stood in the

 op                          nda  sp hv av    do        sn
                             s  v  v
path). ¶ "please, Sir, [I've lost my way]," [the boy

 v              v  s  v      do                    op
 av             hv sp av
explained], . "[can I have a ride out of this daunting forest]?"
```

Indentation	new speaker
Capitalization	*sir* Capitalize a title used as an NDA with the exceptions of *sir* and *madam*.
S V Pairs	AC *After* **he had ridden** (action) *Had* is a helping verb. *Had ridden* is the verb phrase.
	MC **horse reared** (action)
	AC *because* **boy stood** (action)
	MC **I've lost** (action) The contraction *I've* includes both a subject (I) and a helping verb (have). *Have lost* is the verb phrase.
	MC **boy explained** (action)
	MC **I Can have** (action) *Can* is a helping verb. *Can have* is the verb phrase.
Direct Objects	Remind students that a direct object is a noun or pronoun that follows an AV and answers the question *subject verb what?* or *subject verb whom?*
Note	The first main clause includes two adverb clauses and requires a period.
	The boy exclaimed is an attribution and belongs in the same sentence as the quote that precedes it. **PATTERN "Quote," attribution.**
	The second quoted sentence asks a question and requires a question mark.
Commas	Use a comma after an adverb clause. **PATTERN AC, MC**
	Do not put a comma in front of an adverb clause. **PATTERN MC AC**
	Do not use a comma to separate cumulative adjectives (thin young boy).
	Place commas around a noun of direct address (NDA). **, sir,**
	Use a comma to separate an attribution from a direct quote. **PATTERN "Quote," attribution.**
	Do not use a comma to separate two main clauses. Use a period. MC, MC is always wrong.

Rewrite It!

After he had ridden for several miles, his horse reared up because a thin young boy stood in the path.

"Please, sir, I've lost my way," the boy explained. "Can I have a ride out of this daunting forest?"

Read It!	Mark It!	Fix It!	Day 2

Get out of my way Peasant the rude thoughtless prince retorted he was **oblivious**, that the boy was a "wizard" in disguise.

oblivious
not aware

7 noun/pronoun jobs
2 <u>prepositional phrases</u>
3 [main clauses]
1 *that* clause (that)
4 subject-verb pairs (s v)
1 opener

1 indent
2 capitals
4 commas
1 end mark
4 quotation marks

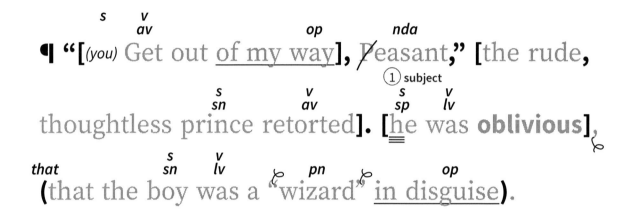

Indentation	new speaker
Capitalization	***peasant*** This NDA is neither a title nor a proper noun.
Quotations	Do not use quotation marks around *wizard*. This is not a direct quote.
Ask Students	Why does *wizard* not belong in quotation marks? This is not a direct quote.
S V Pairs MC	***(you) Get*** (action) The noun *peasant* is an NDA. The subject of an imperative sentence is always *you*.
MC	***prince retorted*** (action)
MC	***he was*** (linking) The adjective *oblivious* follows the linking verb and describes the subject.
that	*that* ***boy was*** (linking) The noun *wizard* follows the linking verb and renames the subject.
Predicate Noun	Remind students that a predicate noun is a noun or pronoun that follows a linking verb and renames the subject. Like the direct object, it answers the the question *subject verb what?* or *subject verb whom?*
Note	This passage contains three main clauses. Use two periods.
	The attribution belongs in the same sentence as the direct quote.
Commas	Place commas around a noun of direct address (NDA). **, *peasant,***
	Use a comma to separate an attribution from a direct quote. **PATTERN "Quote," attribution.**
	Use a comma to separate coordinate adjectives (rude, thoughtless prince).
	Do not put a comma in front of a *that* clause.

Rewrite It!   "Get out of my way, peasant," the rude, thoughtless prince retorted. He was oblivious that the boy was a wizard in disguise.

Read It!	Mark It!	Fix It!	Day 3

instantly the boys voice thundered for your
lack of compassion and **decency** you must spend
your day's as a frog a worthless creature

decency
polite, moral, and honest behavior

Mark It!
8 noun/pronoun jobs
1 coordinating conjunction (cc)
3 prepositional phrases
2 [main clauses]
2 subject-verb pairs (s v)
1 invisible who/which clause (w/w)
1 opener

Fix It!
1 indent
2 capitals
3 commas
1 end mark
2 quotation marks
2 apostrophes

③ -ly adverb

¶ instantly [the boy's voice thundered], "for your lack of compassion and **decency**, [you must spend your day's as a frog], ((which is) a worthless creature)."

Indentation	new speaker
Conjunction	**and** connects two nouns (objects of the preposition): *compassion* and *decency* a and b
S V Pairs	MC **voice thundered** (action)
	MC **you must spend** (action) *Must* is a helping verb. *Must spend* is the verb phrase.
Invisible w/w	(which is) a worthless creature is an invisible *which* clause. With the words *which is* removed, the noun *creature* follows the noun *frog* and renames it. *Creature* functions as an appositive because the subject and the verb (which is) are not in the phrase.
Note	The attribution belongs in the same sentence as the direct quote.
Commas	Use a comma to separate an attribution from a direct quote. **PATTERN Attribution, "Quote."**
	If two or more prepositional phrases open a sentence, follow the last phrase with a comma.
	Place commas around a nonessential invisible who/which clause (appositive phrase).

Rewrite It!   Instantly the boy's voice thundered, "For your lack of compassion and decency, you must spend your days as a frog, a worthless creature."

Read It!	Mark It!	Fix It!	Day 4

Staring reproachfully the boy zapped the air and the Prince found himself hopping off the saddle, and **plummeting**, to the ground

plummeting
falling suddenly straight down

6 noun/pronoun jobs
2 coordinating conjunctions (cc)
2 prepositional phrases
2 [main clauses]
2 subject-verb pairs (s v)
1 opener

1 capital
4 commas
1 end mark

(4) -ing

Staring reproachfully, [the boy zapped the air],
s *v* *do*
sn *av*

cc
and [the Prince found himself] hopping off the
s *v* *do*
sn *av*

op *cc* *op*
saddle, and **plummeting**, to the ground.

Participial	*Staring reproachfully* begins the sentence. Use a comma. *Hopping off the saddle* and *plummeting to the ground* describe *himself* (prince), the word directly before. Do not use a comma.
Conjunction	**and** connects two main clauses. A subject and verb pair (boy zapped) comes before the cc, and a subject and verb pair (prince found) comes after the cc. A comma is required. MC, cc MC **and** connects two participial (-ing) phrases: *hopping off the saddle* and *plummeting to the ground.* a and b
Pronoun	The reflexive pronoun *himself* is used because it refers to the subject of the clause.
S V Pairs	MC **boy zapped** (action) MC **prince found** (action)
Note	This passage contains two main clauses connected with a comma + cc. Use one period.
Commas	Use a comma after an -ing opener. **PATTERN** -ing word/phrase, main clause The thing after the comma must be the thing doing the inging. *Boy* is doing the *staring.* Use a comma to separate two main clauses connected with a cc. **PATTERN MC, cc MC** Do not use a comma to separate two items connected with a cc. **PATTERN a and b** Do not put a comma in front of a prepositional phrase.

Rewrite It! Staring reproachfully, the boy zapped the air, and the prince found himself hopping off the saddle and plummeting to the ground.

Learn It!

Usage Errors

You no longer need to label verb types or noun and pronoun functions. However, from now on you must identify and fix common usage errors. These errors will include homophones, subject-verb agreement, verb tense, and pronouns.

For more information about homophones and usage, see page G-35.

Fix It!   Place a line through the incorrect word and write the correct word above it.

Frederick loved horses. One year his father had given his brother

and ~~he~~ *him* beautiful stallions. Prince Frederick ~~spends~~ *spent* many hours

cleaning and brushing ~~there~~ *their* horses so that they could ride

through the countryside.

Invisible Prepositions

A **prepositional phrase** begins with a preposition and ends with a noun or pronoun, which is called the object of the preposition. When a prepositional phrase begins a sentence, label it as a #2 sentence opener.

For more information about prepositions, see page G-8.

Maribella hosted a dinner ~~on~~ Monday.

She celebrated her birthday ~~on~~ the first of April.

> The preposition *on* can be dropped when the prepositional phrase refers to time. In the sentence *Maribella hosted a dinner Monday*, the preposition *on* is implied, not written. *Monday* is the object of the unwritten or invisible preposition.

Maribella hosted a dinner ~~on~~ last Monday.

Maribella will host a book club ~~on~~ next week.

> Prepositions of time are always dropped before the adjectives *last, next, this, that, some, every*. The phrase ends with a noun. The words between the unwritten or invisible preposition and the noun are adjectives, never verbs.

Invisible #2 Prepositional Opener

An **invisible #2 prepositional opener** is formed when a word or phrase indicating time is followed by a main clause. The preposition *on* or *during* is implied.

For more information about the #2 prepositional opener, see page G-42.

(during) That afternoon [Dorinda went shopping].

> The preposition *during* is implied. You can confirm that this is a prepositional opener by inserting a preposition and making sure the phrase follows the PATTERN preposition + noun (no verb).

Mark It!   Underline the invisible prepositional phrase and write *on* or *during* where the preposition could be inserted.

②

(on) Last Friday [she bought a diamond tiara].

After students mark the main clause, two words remain: Last Friday. Ask students if they refer to time and if they could follow the prepositional pattern.

Insert *(on)*.

The phrase begins with a preposition and ends with a noun (Friday). It has an adjective, but no verb.

For more information about *that* clauses, see Noun Clause on pages G-22 and G-41.

Invisible *That* Clause

An **invisible *that* clause** occurs when the word *that* is implied, not stated directly. The word *that* is invisible.

$$s \quad v \qquad\qquad s \quad v \qquad v$$
Frederick knew a royal kiss could restore him.

This sentence has two subject-verb pairs and appears to have two main clauses.

$$s \quad v \qquad\qquad s \quad v \qquad v$$
Frederick knew. A royal kiss could restore him.

If you insert a period, the sentences do not make sense. A main clause must express a complete thought. What did Frederick know? These words must be in the same sentence in order to make sense.

$$s \qquad v \quad that \qquad\qquad s \quad v \qquad v$$
[Frederick knew] (a royal kiss could restore him).

The word *that* is implied, not written in the sentence. The second clause is a dependent *that* clause. You can confirm this by inserting the word *that* into the sentence: Frederick knew (that) a royal kiss could restore him.

Mark It! Place parentheses around the invisible *that* clause and write ***that*** where the word *that* could be inserted. Write *v* above each verb and *s* above each subject.

$$s \qquad v \quad that \quad s \quad v \qquad v$$
He realized ((*that)* he must befriend a princess).

If what appears to be a main clause does not express a complete thought, have students insert the word *that* to see if the clause is an invisible *that* clause.

The subject-verb pairs are **He realized** and **he must befriend**. *He realized* does not express a complete thought without the rest of the sentence. You can insert *that* after *realized*: He realized (that) he must befriend the princess. This is an invisible *that* clause.

Number Words/Numerals

Use words for numbers expressed in one or two words and ordinal numbers.

twenty	fifty-three	three hundred
first	second	third

Use numerals for numbers that use three or more words, for numbers mixed with symbols, and for dates.

123	204
$500	40%

December 25, not December 25th

Read It!	Mark It!	Fix It!	Day 1

The wizard continued as a frog, you might learn **humility**, and gratitude for simple kindnesses, which people offer yourself, you will be restored to normal, if a princess kisses you in true kindheartedness.

humility
the quality of not being proud or arrogant

1 coordinating conjunction (cc)	2 capitals	
4 prepositional phrases	6 commas	
3 [main clauses]	1 end mark	
1 who/which clause (w/w)	1 quotation mark	
1 adverb clause (AC)	1 usage	
5 subject-verb pairs (s v)		
1 opener		

① subject

 S   V   S   V   V
[The wizard continued], "as a frog, [you might learn

                                    cc   w/w
humility, and gratitude for simple kindnesses], (which

  S   V   you   S   V   V   V
people offer yourself). [you will be restored to normal],

AC   S   V
(if a princess kisses you in true kindheartedness).

No closing quotation mark because quote continues.

Conjunction		**and** connects two nouns (direct objects): *humility* and *gratitude* a and b
S V Pairs	MC	**wizard continued**
	MC	**you might learn**
	w/w	*which* **people offer** The *which* clause describes *kindnesses*, the noun it follows. It is essential because it defines the type of kindnesses that will teach the frog humility and gratitude. Removing it from the sentence changes the meaning.
	MC	**You will be restored**
	AC	*if* **princess kisses**
Note		*The wizard continued* is an attribution and belongs in the same sentence as the first quoted sentence.
		Use a period to fix the run-on (comma splice). The quoted sentence contains two main clauses. The first sentence includes the attribution, a main clause, and a *which* clause. The second sentence includes a main clause and an adverb clause.
Commas		Use a comma to separate an attribution from a direct quote. PATTERN Attribution, "Quote."
		Do not use a comma if a prepositional opener has fewer than five words.
		Do not use a comma to separate two items connected with a cc. PATTERN a and b
		Do not place commas around an essential *who/which* clause.
		Do not use a comma to separate two main clauses. Use a period. MC, MC is always wrong.
		Do not put a comma in front of an adverb clause. PATTERN MC AC
Usage		Change the pronoun *yourself* (reflexive) to *you* (objective). Use a reflexive pronoun only when the pronoun following the verb refers to the subject.

Rewrite It! The wizard continued, "As a frog you might learn humility and gratitude for simple kindnesses which people offer you. You will be restored to normal if a princess kisses you in true kindheartedness.

Read It!	Mark It!	Fix It!	Day 2

If you ever confess, that you are a prince you will be **fated** to froghood forever. The frog had kept his secret for 6, long years hoping, he would eventually return too normal.

fated
destined; inevitably predetermined

2 [main clauses]
2 *that* clauses (that)
1 adverb clause (AC)
5 subject-verb pairs (s v)
1 opener

1 indent
5 commas
1 quotation mark
1 number
1 usage

No opening quotation mark because quote continues.

AC **s** **v** *that* **s** **v** **s**
(If you ever confess), (that you are a prince), [you

① subject
v **v** **v** **s** **v**
will be **fated** to froghood forever]." ¶ [The frog had

v *six* *that* **s**
kept his secret for 6, long years], hoping, ((that) he

v **v** *to*
would eventually return too normal).

Indentation	new time
Participial	*Hoping he would eventually return to normal* describes *frog*, not the word directly before it. Use a comma.
S V Pairs	AC *If **you confess*** that *that **you are*** MC ***you will be fated*** MC ***frog had kept*** that *(that) **he would return*** This is an invisible *that* clause. It does not express a complete thought.
Commas	Use a comma after an adverb clause that comes before a main clause. **PATTERN AC, MC** There is no comma after *confess* because the *that* clause is essential to the AC. Do not put a comma in front of a *that* clause. Do not use a comma to separate cumulative adjectives (six long years). Use a comma when a -ing phrase at the end of a sentence describes a noun other than the word it follows. There is no comma after *hoping* because the *that* clause is essential to the participial (-ing) phrase. Do not put a comma in front of a *that* clause.
Ask Students	What is the difference between *to*, *two*, and *too*? *To* is a preposition or an infinitive marker. *Two* is a number. *Too* is an adverb meaning also or to an excessive degree.
Number	Spell out numbers that can be expressed in one or two words.
Usage	Change *too* (adverb) to *to* (preposition).

Rewrite It! If you ever confess that you are a prince, you will be fated to froghood forever."
The frog had kept his secret for six long years, hoping he would eventually return to normal.

Read It!	Mark It!	Fix It!	Day 3

Frederick had resided as a frog in King Mortons **sequestered** expansive garden and he had wished, one of the princesses who frequently spent time in the garden would be his friend

sequestered
private; secluded

Mark It!	Fix It!
1 coordinating conjunction (cc)	4 commas
4 <u>prepositional phrases</u>	1 end mark
2 [main clauses]	1 apostrophe
1 *who/which* clause (w/w)	
1 *that* clause (that)	
4 subject-verb pairs (s v)	
1 opener	

①subject

                S   V   V
[Frederick had resided as a frog in King Morton's

                                                cc   s   V   V
sequestered expansive garden], and [he had wished],

that   s   w/w s   V
((that) one of the princesses, (who frequently spent

                              V   V
time in the garden), would be his friend).

Conjunction	**and** connects two main clauses. A subject and verb pair (Frederick had resided) comes before the cc, and a subject and verb pair (he had wished) comes after the cc. A comma is required. MC, cc MC
S V Pairs	MC **Frederick had resided**
	MC **he had wished**
	that *(that)* **one would be** This is an invisible *that* clause. It does not express a complete thought.
	w/w **who spent** The *who* clause describes *princesses*, the noun it follows. This *who* clause could be either essential or nonessential. With commas it is saying that all princesses (in this case, Maribella and Dorinda) spent time in the garden. Without commas it is saying that Frederick wanted to be friends only with the princesses who spent time in the garden, not with those who did not spend time in the garden.
Note	This passage contains two main clauses connected with a comma + cc. Use one period.
Commas	Use a comma to separate two main clauses connected with a cc. **PATTERN MC, cc MC**
	Do not put a comma in front of a *that* clause.
	Place commas around a nonessential *who/which* clause.

Rewrite It!   Frederick had resided as a frog in King Morton's sequestered expansive garden, and he had wished one of the princesses, who frequently spent time in the garden, would be his friend.

Read It!	Mark It!	Fix It!	Day 4

Unfortunately for him he had met Dorinda, before he had met Maribella, that evening, he assessed the situation, and **conjectured** how to charm Dorinda the younger princess.

conjectured
formed a theory; guessed

1 coordinating conjunction (cc)
2 prepositional phrases
2 [main clauses]
1 adverb clause (AC)
3 subject-verb pairs (s v)
1 invisible *who/which* clause (w/w)
2 openers

1 indent
1 capital
6 commas
1 end mark

③ -ly adverb

Unfortunately for him, [he had met Dorinda], (before he had met Maribella). ¶ *(during)* that evening, [he assessed the situation, and **conjectured** how to charm Dorinda], ((who was) the younger princess).

Indentation	new time
Conjunction	*and* connects two verbs: *assessed* and *conjectured* MC cc 2nd verb
S V Pairs	MC *he had met*
	AC *before* **he had met**
	MC **he assessed, conjectured**
Invisible #2	*That* tells which evening and functions as an adjective. *Evening* is a noun, a reference to time. Insert *during*. *(during) That evening* follows the prepositional **PATTERN preposition + noun (no verb)**. *That evening* is not a *that* clause (that + subject + verb) because it does not contain a subject or a verb.
Invisible w/w	*(who was) the younger princess* is an invisible *who* clause. With the words *who was* removed, the noun *princess* follows the noun *Dorinda* and renames it. *Princess* functions as an appositive because the subject and the verb (who was) are not in the phrase.
Note	This passage contains two main clauses. Use two periods. The first sentence includes a main clause and an adverb clause.
Commas	Use a comma if an -ly adverb opener modifies the sentence. It was unfortunate that he had met Dorinda before he had met Maribella. Because the -ly adverb opener is followed by a prepositional phrase, place the comma after *him*.
	Do not put a comma in front of a prepositional phrase.
	When more than one sentence opener begins a sentence, place the comma after the last opener.
	Do not put a comma in front of an adverb clause. **PATTERN MC AC**
	Do not use a comma to separate two main clauses. Use a period. MC, MC is always wrong.
	Do not use a comma if a prepositional opener has fewer than five words.
	Do not use a comma before a cc when it connects two verbs. **PATTERN MC cc 2nd verb**
	Place commas around a nonessential invisible *who/which* clause (appositive phrase).

Rewrite It!   Unfortunately for him, he had met Dorinda before he had met Maribella.

That evening he assessed the situation and conjectured how to charm Dorinda, the younger princess.

Learn It!

Adjective

An **adjective** describes a noun or pronoun. An adjectives tells which one, what kind, how many, or whose.

Adjectives come in three forms.

An adjective can be a single word or word group (phrase or clause).

For more information about phrases, see pages G-18 and G-19.

Single Word Adjectives

An adjective can come before the noun it describes, or it can follow a linking verb and describe the subject of the clause.

    adj   *adj*

The green frog croaked. The frog was green.

    The adjective *green* describes *frog*. Which frog? *green*

Phrasal Adjectives

A **prepositional phrase** begins with a preposition and ends with a noun or pronoun. The entire phrase functions as a single unit. That means while each word in the prepositional phrase has its own job, all the words work together to do the job of an adjective or an adverb.

If a prepositional phrase comes immediately after a noun and describes that noun, the entire phrase does the job of an adjective.

        pp adj

The frog with green skin croaked.

    With green skin is a prepositional phrase. The entire phrase is a phrasal adjective that comes after a noun and describes that noun. Which frog? *with green skin*

Most prepositional phrases are adjectives or adverbs, adding detail to a sentence.

A **participial phrase** begins with a present participle, an -ing word. The entire phrase describes a noun in the sentence and does the job of an adjective.

 -ing adj

Wearing a top hat, the frog croaked.

    -ing adj

The frog, wearing a top hat, croaked.

    Wearing a top hat is a participial (-ing) phrase. The entire phrase is a phrasal adjective that describes a noun in the sentence. Which frog? *wearing a top hat*

A participial phrase is an adjective.

Past participial phrases are taught in Level 6.

If a participial phrase unintentionally modifies the wrong noun in a sentence, it is called a misplaced participle.

Clausal Adjectives

A *who/which* clause is a dependent clause that begins with *who* or *which* and includes a subject and verb. The entire clause describes the noun it follows and does the job of an adjective.

    w/w

The frog, (who wore a top hat), croaked.

    Who wore a top hat is a *who/which* clause. The entire clause is a clausal adjective that describes the noun it follows. Which frog? *who wore a top hat*

For more information about adjective clauses, see page G-21.

This week emphasizes that *who/which* clauses are adjective clauses.

Week 17 students learn about other adjective clauses.

Mark It!   Weeks 15–16 write *adj* above each single word adjective.

              Write *pp adj* above each prepositional phrase that functions as an adjective.

              Write *-ing adj* above each participial phrase.

An adverb can be a single word or word group (phrase or clause).

Adverb

An **adverb** modifies a verb, an adjective, or another adverb. An adverb tells how, when, where, why, to what extent.

Adverbs come in three forms.

Single Word Adverbs

An adverb often ends in -ly. However, many adverbs do not.

adv   *adv*

The frog usually croaked. The frog often croaked.

The adverb *usually* modifies *croaked*. Croaked when? *usually*
The adverb *often* modifies *croaked*. Croaked when? *often*

adv

The frog did not croak.

The words *yes, no, not, too, even, else* function as adverbs.

Phrasal Adverbs

A **prepositional phrase** begins with a preposition and ends with a noun. The entire phrase functions as a single unit. That means while each word in the prepositional phrase has its own job, all the words work together to do the job of an adjective or an adverb.

If a prepositional phrase tells how, when, where, or why, the entire phrase does the job of an adverb.

pp adv

In the morning the frog croaked.

In the morning is a prepositional phrase. The entire phrase is a phrasal adverb that modifies a verb in the sentence. Croaked when? *in the morning*

Clausal Adverbs

For more information about adverb clauses, see page G-21.

An **adverb clause** is a dependent clause that begins with a www word and includes a subject and verb. The entire clause modifies a verb in the sentence and does the job of an adverb.

AC

The frog croaked (as he woke).

As he woke is an adverb clause. The entire clause is a clausal adverb that modifies a verb in the sentence. Croaked when? *as he woke*

Mark It!   Weeks 15–16 write *adv* above each single word adverb.

Write **pp adv** above each prepositional phrase that functions as an adverb.

Quality Adjectives and -ly Adverbs

Like strong verbs, quality adjectives and -ly adverbs create a strong image or feeling. Continue to look for quality adjectives and -ly adverbs in this book and write them on the collection pages in Appendix II. Use these words in your own writing.

Read It!	Mark It!	Fix It!	Day 1

The next morning during a **substantial** breakfast of omelets pastries and fruit King Morton who always treats his guests with generosity graciously insisted, that Frederick stay for a week.

substantial
plentiful

Mark It!		Fix It!
3 adjectives (adj)		1 indent
2 adverbs (adv)		6 commas
1 coordinating conjunction (cc)		1 usage
5 <u>prep phrases</u> (<u>pp adj</u>) or (<u>pp adv</u>)		
1 [main clause]		
1 *who/which* clause (w/w)		
1 *that* clause (that)		
3 subject-verb pairs (s v)		
1 opener		

②　prepositional

　　　pp adv　　　*adj*　　　　　*pp adv*　　　　*adj*
¶ (on) The next morning during a **substantial** breakfast
pp adj　　　　　　　　*cc*　　　　*s*　　*w/w s*
of omelets, pastries, and fruit, [King Morton, (who
　　　　　　　v
adv　　*treated*　*adj*　　　*pp adv*　　　　　*adv*
always ~~treats~~ his guests with generosity), graciously
　v　　　*that*　　*s*　　*v*　*pp adv*
insisted], (that Frederick stay for a week).

This is the last week that a note under S V Pairs is provided.

Indentation	new time (or place)
Conjunction	***and*** connects three nouns (objects of preposition): *omelets, pastries,* and *fruit* **a, b, and c**
Ask Students	Which words and phrases function as adjectives? Which function as adverbs? Use the questions.
	Insisted when? *(on) The next morning* (adverb)　　Which morning? *next* (adjective)
	Insisted when? *during a substantial breakfast* (adverb)
	What kind of breakfast? *of omelets, pastries, and fruit* (adjective)
	What kind of breakfast? *substantial* (adjective)　　Treated when? *always* (adverb)
	Treated how? *with generosity* (adverb)　　Whose guests? *his* (adjective)
	Insisted how? *graciously* (adverb)　　Stay when? *for a week* (adverb)
S V Pairs	MC ***King Morton insisted***
	w/w ***who treated*** The *who* clause describes *King Morton,* the noun it follows. (adjective clause)
	that *that* ***Frederick stay***
Note	This passage includes one main clause. Use one period.
Invisible #2	*The next morning* is a reference to time. Insert *on.* *(on) The next morning* follows the prepositional **PATTERN preposition + noun (no verb).**
Commas	If two or more prepositional phrases open a sentence, follow the last phrase with a comma.
	Use commas to separate three or more items in a series connected with a cc. **PATTERN a, b, and c**
	Place commas around a nonessential *who/which* clause.
	Do not put a comma in front of a *that* clause.
Usage	Change *treats* (present tense) to *treated* (past tense).

Rewrite It!　　The next morning during a substantial breakfast of omelets, pastries, and fruit, King Morton, who always treated his guests with generosity, graciously insisted that Frederick stay for a week.

Read It!	Mark It!	Fix It!	Day 2

Dorinda groaned. Glancing down she noticed that Fredericks hind leg was **inadvertently** touching her omelet ew she cried, as she swept him from her plate, and spitefully hurled him against the wall.

inadvertently
unintentionally

Mark It!

4 adjectives (adj)
3 adverbs (adv)
1 coordinating conjunction (cc)
2 prep phrases (pp adj) or (pp adv)
1 -ing phrase (-ing adj)
3 [main clauses]
1 *that* clause (that)
1 adverb clause (AC)
5 subject-verb pairs (s v)
2 openers

Fix It!

1 indent
1 capital
3 commas
2 end marks
2 quotation marks
1 apostrophe

⑥ vss ④ -ing

s   v   -ing adj   adv   s   v

¶ [Dorinda groaned]. Glancing down, [she noticed]

that   adj   adj   s   v   adv   v

(that Frederick's hind leg was **inadvertently** touching

adj   s   v   AC   s   v   pp adv

her omelet). "ew!" [she cried], (as she swept him from

adj   cc   adv   v   pp adv

her plate, and spitefully hurled him against the wall).

Indentation	new topic
Interjection	***Ew!*** is an interjection that expresses a strong emotion. Use an exclamation mark. Do not capitalize *she* because it is an attribution after the quote.
Conjunction	***and*** connects two verbs: *swept* and *hurled* MC cc 2nd verb
Ask Students	Which words and phrases function as adjectives? Which function as adverbs? Use the questions. *Glancing down* (adjective) describes whom? *she* Glancing where? *down* (adverb) Which leg? *hind* (adjective) Whose hind leg? *Frederick's* (adjective) Was touching how? *inadvertently* (adverb) Whose omelet? *her* (adjective) Swept where? *from her plate* (adverb) Whose plate? *her* (adjective) Hurled how? *spitefully* (adverb) Hurled where? *against the wall* (adverb)
S V Pairs	MC ***Dorinda groaned*** MC ***she noticed*** that *that* ***leg was touching*** MC ***she cried*** AC as ***she swept***, ***hurled*** Cried when? *as she swept him ... and spitefully hurled him ... .* (adverb clause)
Note	This passage includes three main clauses. Use three periods. The participial (-ing) phrase and *that* clause belong with the second main clause. *She cried* is an attribution and belongs in the same sentence as the quote. **PATTERN** "Quote," attribution.
Commas	Use a comma after an -ing opener. **PATTERN** -ing word/phrase, main clause The thing after the comma must be the thing doing the inging. *She* is doing the *glancing*. Do not put a comma in front of an adverb clause. **PATTERN** MC AC Do not use a comma before a cc when it connects two verbs. **PATTERN** MC cc 2nd verb

Rewrite It!   Dorinda groaned. Glancing down, she noticed that Frederick's hind leg was inadvertently touching her omelet. "Ew!" she cried as she swept him from her plate and spitefully hurled him against the wall.

| Read It! | Mark It! | Fix It! | Day 3 |

Ow he grunted I believe my leg is broken Dorinda **feigned** remorse, for her unkind action's mumbling an apology I wish I had broken all, of your legs she muttered pitilessly.

feigned
pretended

Mark It!

5 adjectives (adj)
1 adverb (adv)
2 <u>prep phrases</u> (pp adj) or (pp adv)
1 -ing phrase (-ing adj)
5 [main clauses]
2 *that* clauses (that)
7 subject-verb pairs (s v)
1 opener

Fix It!

2 indents
4 commas
4 end marks
6 quotation marks
1 apostrophe

¶ "Ow!" [he grunted]. "[I believe] (that) my leg is broken)!" ¶ [Dorinda feigned remorse, for her unkind action's], mumbling an apology. "[I wish] (that) I had broken all, of your legs)," [she muttered pitilessly].

Indentation	new speaker; new speaker
Interjection	*Ow!* is an interjection that expresses a strong emotion. Use an exclamation mark. Do not capitalize *he* because it is an attribution after the quote.
Ask Students	Which words and phrases function as adjectives? Which function as adverbs? Use the questions. Whose leg? *my* (adjective) What kind of leg? *broken* (adjective) The adjective follows the linking verb and describes the subject. What kind of remorse? *for her unkind actions* (adjective)　　　What kind of actions? *unkind* (adjective) Whose unkind actions? *her* (adjective) *Mumbling an apology* (adjective) describes whom? *Dorinda*　　　What kind of all? *of your legs* (adjective) Whose legs? *your* (adjective)　　　Muttered how? *pitilessly* (adverb)
S V Pairs	MC ***he grunted***　　　　　　　　　　　　　MC ***I believe***
that	(that) **leg is** This is an invisible *that* clause. It does not express a complete thought.
	MC ***Dorinda feigned***　　　　　　　　　　MC ***I wish***
that	(that) ***I had broken*** This is an invisible *that* clause. The word *broken* is a verb because it expresses the action Dorinda wished to do. This differs from earlier in the passage when *broken* describes the leg.
	MC ***she muttered***
Note	The attribution *he grunted* belongs with the interjection. It is correct that *he* is not capitalized. **PATTERN** "Quote!" attribution. The third main clause is a complete thought, not an attribution. *She muttered* is an attribution and belongs in the same sentence as the second quoted sentence. **PATTERN** "Quote," attribution.
Commas	Do not put a comma in front of a prepositional phrase. Use a comma when a -ing phrase at the end of a sentence describes a noun other than the word it follows. Use a comma to separate an attribution from a direct quote. **PATTERN** "Quote," attribution.

Rewrite It!　　"Ow!" he grunted. "I believe my leg is broken!"

Dorinda feigned remorse for her unkind actions, mumbling an apology. "I wish I had broken all of your legs," she muttered pitilessly.

Read It!	Mark It!	Fix It!	Day 4

Dorindas behavior **mortifies** her father,
King Morton gently lifted the frog placed him
on a silver tray and carried him to the doctor, caring
for the animals. He ordered Dorinda to follow.

mortified
humiliated; shamed

3 adjectives (adj)
1 adverb (adv)
1 coordinating conjunction (cc)
3 prep phrases (pp adj) or (pp adv)
1 -ing phrase (-ing adj)
3 [main clauses]
3 subject-verb pairs (s v)
3 openers

1 indent
4 commas
1 end mark
1 apostrophe
1 usage

⑥ vss
          adj   s   v
                              mortified   adj

¶ [Dorinda's behavior ~~mortifies~~ her father],.

① subject
    s   adv   v   v

[King Morton gently lifted the frog, placed him

pp adv   adj   cc   v   pp adv

on a silver tray, and carried him to the doctor],

                                  ⑥ vss
-ing adj   pp adj   s   v

caring for the animals. [He ordered Dorinda to follow].

Indentation	new topic
Conjunction	***and*** connects three verbs: *lifted, placed,* and *carried*

Ask Students	Which words and phrases function as adjectives? Which function as adverbs? Use the questions.
	Whose behavior? *Dorinda's* (adjective) Whose father? *her* (adjective)
	Lifted how? *gently* (adverb) Placed where? *on a silver tray* (adverb)
	Which tray? *silver* (adjective) Carried where? *to the doctor* (adverb)
	Caring for the animals (adjective) describes whom? *doctor*

S V Pairs	MC ***behavior mortified***
	MC ***King Morton lifted, placed, carried***
	MC ***He ordered***
Note	This passage contains three main clauses. Use three periods.
Commas	Do not use a comma to separate two main clauses. Use a period. MC, MC is always wrong.
	Use commas to separate three or more items in a series connected with a cc. **PATTERN a, b, and c**
	Do not use a comma when a participial phrase at the end of a sentence describes the word it follows.
Usage	Change *mortifies* (present tense) to *mortified* (past tense).

Rewrite It!   Dorinda's behavior mortified her father. King Morton gently lifted the frog, placed him on a silver tray, and carried him to the doctor caring for the animals. He ordered Dorinda to follow.

Learn It!

Clausal Adjectives and Clausal Adverbs

In this book you have looked at the first word of a dependent clause to determine if the dependent clause functions as an adjective or as an adverb.

If a dependent clause begins with a www word, it usually functions as an adverb.

Adverb clauses can appear anywhere in a sentence.

Use a comma after, not before, an adverb clause.

If a dependent clause begins with *who* or *which*, it functions as an adjective.

A *who/which* clause follows a noun and describes it.

Use commas unless essential.

Although the words *when* and *where* are www words, these two words can also begin adjective clauses.

To determine if a dependent clause that begins with *when* or *where* is an adjective clause or an adverb clause, look at its location. If it comes immediately after a noun and describes that noun, it is an adjective clause.

You can test if a dependent clause that begins with *when* or *where* is an adjective clause by inserting *which was* or *which were* before the clause.

Frederick remained in the infirmary, ((*which was*) where he rested).

Where he rested is a dependent clause. It begins with the word *where* and includes a subject and a verb.

The dependent clause follows the noun *infirmary* and describes it.
Which infirmary? *where he rested* It makes sense to say *Frederick remained in the infirmary (which was) where he rested,* so this is an adjective clause.

It is a nonessential because without the clause, Frederick still remained in the infirmary. It requires a comma.

⸲ Place commas around an adjective clause if it is nonessential.

✗ Do not place commas around an adjective clause if it is essential (changes the meaning of the sentence).

Mark It!   Place parentheses around the dependent clause (DC).

Write *v* above each verb and *s* above each subject.

If the dependent clause (DC) begins with *when* or *where,* decide if it is an adjective clause or an adverb clause.

If it is an adjective clause, the test (who was/were or which was/were) works.

If it is an adverb clause, write *AC* above the www word.

Follow the comma rules.

$$\overset{s}{}\qquad\overset{v}{}$$

The vet worked during the day, ((*which was*) when Frederick was awake).

$$\overset{AC}{}\quad\overset{s}{}\ \overset{v}{}$$

Dorinda would apologize, (when she felt like it).

Students place dependent clauses in parentheses to visually see that the dependent clause is a unit.

Distinguishing between clausal adjectives and clausal adverbs helps with punctuation.

Use a comma after an adverb clause, not before.

AC, MC   MC AC

Adjective clauses use commas unless they are essential to the sentence.

Identify adverb clauses by **PATTERN www word + subject + verb.**

First Word:

when, while, where, as, since, if, although, because, after, before, until, unless, whenever, whereas, than

The first word connects the adverb clause to the main clause. The www word is never the subject of the clause.

Identify adjective clauses by looking at location. An adjective clause follows a noun and describes that noun.

First Word:

who, whom, whose, which, when, where, that

The first word is often the subject of the clause.

That **Clause**

A *that* clause can be an adjective clause or a noun clause. While each word in the *that* clause has its own job, all the words work together to do the job of either a noun or an adjective. In this book, most *that* clauses are noun clauses that function as direct objects.

To determine if a *that* clause functions as an adjective or as a noun, look at its location. If it comes immediately after a noun and describes that noun, it is an adjective clause.

You can test if a *that* clause is an adjective clause by replacing *that* with *which*.

> *which*
> The leg (~~that~~ was broken) had to be set.

The *that* clause follows the noun *leg* and describes it. Which leg? *that was broken*

It makes sense to say *The leg ~~that~~ which was broken had to be set.* This *that* clause is an adjective clause.

> Frederick knew (that his leg was broken).

Frederick knew what? *that his leg was broken* This *that* clause is a noun clause that follows the action verb and functions as the direct object.

That clauses that function like nouns and *that* clauses that function like adjectives are essential to the sentence.

 That clauses do not take commas.

Think About It!

Both adjectives and adverbs add detail to a sentence. When a prepositional phrase or a dependent clause tells how, when, where, or why, the entire word group does the job of an adverb. When a prepositional phrase or a dependent clause comes after a noun and describes the noun, the entire word group does the job of an adjective and tells which one, what kind, how many, or whose.

These two sentences contain similar words but have different meanings.

> The veterinarian examined Frederick <u>in the infirmary</u>.

Examined where? *in the infirmary*

In the infirmary comes after the noun *Frederick*, but it does not describe Frederick. It is not an adjective.

In the infirmary tells where the veterinarian examined Frederick, so it is an adverb.

> The veterinarian <u>from the infirmary</u> examined Frederick.

Which veterinarian? *from the infirmary*

From the infirmary comes after the noun *veterinarian* and describes it.

From the infirmary tells which veterinarian examined Frederick, so it is an adjective.

Strong Verb, Quality Adjective, and -ly Adverb

A strong verb, a quality adjective, and an -ly adverb are three different ways to dress up writing. These stylistic devices create a strong image and feeling. A strong verb is an action verb, never a linking or helping verb. A quality adjective is more specific than a weak adjective. A weak adjective is overused, boring, or vague. An -ly adverb is used to enhance the meaning of the verb, adjective, or adverb that it modifies.

Continue to look for strong verbs, quality adjectives, and -ly adverbs in this book and write them on the collection pages found in Appendix II.

Read It!	Mark It!	Fix It!	Day 1

Read It!

In the infirmary the palace vet positioned the frog on the adjustable, exam table where he treated his smallest patients after he examined Frederick he set the broken frog leg which **dangled** oddly.

dangled
hung loosely in a swaying motion

Mark It!

7 adjectives (adj)
1 adverb (adv)
2 prep phrases (pp adj) or (pp adv)
2 [main clauses]
1 who/which clause (w/w)
1 adverb clause (AC)
5 subject-verb pairs (s v)
2 openers

Fix It!

1 indent
1 capital
4 commas
1 end mark

② prepositional

pp adv   adj   s   v
¶ In the infirmary [the palace vet positioned the frog

pp adv   adj   adj   s   v
on the adjustable, exam table], *(which was)* where he treated

⑤ clausal

adj   adj   AC   s   v
his smallest patients). (after he examined Frederick),

s   v   adj   adj   w/w s   v   adv
[he set the broken frog leg], (which **dangled** oddly).

Indentation	new place
Ask Students	Which words and phrases function as adjectives? Which function as adverbs? Use the questions.
	Positioned where? *In the infirmary* (adverb) What kind of vet? *palace* (adjective)
	Positioned where? *on the adjustable exam table* (adverb) Which table? *exam* (adjective)
	What kind of exam table? *adjustable* (adjective) What kind of patients? *smallest* (adjective)
	Whose smallest patients? *his* (adjective) What kind of leg? *frog* (adjective)
	What kind of frog leg? *broken* (adjective) Dangled how? *oddly* (adverb)
S V Pairs MC	**vet positioned**
DC	where **he treated** The *where* clause describes *table*, the noun it follows. (adjective clause)
Ask Students	Why does *where he treated his smallest patients* require a comma?
	It is a nonessential adjective clause. It describes the noun *table*. If you remove it from the sentence, the vet still positioned the frog on that table.
AC	After **he examined** Set when? *After he examined Frederick* (adverb clause)
MC	**he set**
w/w	**which dangled** The *which* clause describes *leg*, the noun it follows. (adjective clause)
Commas	Do not use a comma to separate cumulative adjectives (adjustable exam table).
	Place commas around a nonessential adjective clause.
	Use a comma after an adverb clause that comes before a main clause. **PATTERN AC, MC**
	Place commas around a nonessential *who/which* clause.

Rewrite It!   In the infirmary the palace vet positioned the frog on the adjustable exam table, where he treated his smallest patients. After he examined Frederick, he set the broken frog leg, which dangled oddly.

Read It!	Mark It!	Fix It!	Day 2

Frogs are animal's, which heal slowly so it will be a lengthy **convalescence** the vet informed King Morton, and Dorinda, he will stay in the infirmary, for a month

convalescence
the gradual recovery of health and strength after illness

Mark It!
1 adjective (adj)
1 adverb (adv)
2 coordinating conjunctions (cc)
2 <u>prep phrases</u> (<u>pp adj</u>) or (<u>pp adv</u>)
4 [main clauses]
1 *who/which* clause (w/w)
5 subject-verb pairs (s v)

Fix It!
1 indent
1 capital
6 commas
2 end marks
4 quotation marks
1 apostrophe

¶ "[Frogs are animal's], (which heal slowly), so [it will be a lengthy **convalescence**]," [the vet informed King Morton, and Dorinda]. "[he will stay in the infirmary, for a month]."

Indentation	new speaker	
Conjunction	**so** connects two main clauses. A subject and verb pair (Frogs are) comes before the cc, and a subject and verb pair (it will be) comes after the cc. A comma is required. MC, cc MC **and** connects two nouns (direct objects): *King Morton* and *Dorinda* a and b	
Ask Students	Which words and phrases function as adjectives? Which function as adverbs? Use the questions.	
	Heal how? *slowly* (adverb) Will stay where? *in the infirmary* (adverb)	What kind of convalescence? *lengthy* (adjective) Will stay when? *for a month* (adverb)
S V Pairs	MC *Frogs are*	
	w/w *which heal* The *which* clause describes *animals*, the noun it follows. (adjective clause) The *which* clause is essential to the sentence because it defines which animals heal slowly. Removing it from the sentence changes the meaning.	
	MC *it will be*	
	MC *vet informed*	
	MC *He will stay*	
Commas	Do not place commas around an essential *who/which* clause. The comma after the *which* clause is required because of this rule: Use a comma to separate two main clauses connected with a cc. **PATTERN MC, cc MC** Use a comma to separate an attribution from a direct quote. **PATTERN "Quote," attribution.** Do not use a comma to separate two items connected with a cc. **PATTERN a and b** Do not use a comma to separate two main clauses. Use a period. MC, MC is always wrong. Do not put a comma in front of a prepositional phrase.	

Rewrite It!   "Frogs are animals which heal slowly, so it will be a lengthy convalescence," the vet informed King Morton and Dorinda. "He will stay in the infirmary for a month."

Read It!	Mark It!	Fix It!	Day 3

Hearing the doctors announcement Dorinda became **sullen**. After her father insisted, that she deliver Fredericks meal's she regretted the day, when the accident happened.

4 adjectives (adj)	1 indent	
1 -ing phrase (-ing adj)	4 commas	
2 [main clauses]	3 apostrophes	
1 *that* clause (that)		
1 adverb clause (AC)		
5 subject-verb pairs (s v)		
2 openers		

sullen
showing irritation or ill humor by a gloomy silence

④ -ing
-ing adj   *adj*   *s*

¶ Hearing the doctor's announcement, [Dorinda

⑤ clausal
v   *adj*   *AC*   *adj*   *s*   *v*   *that*   *s*

became **sullen**]. (After her father insisted), (that she

v   *adj*   *s*   *v*

deliver Frederick's meal's), [she regretted the day],

s   *v*

((which was) when the accident happened).

Indentation	new topic
Ask Students	Which words and phrases function as adjectives? Which function as adverbs? Use the questions. *Hearing the doctor's announcement* (adjective) describes whom? *Dorinda* Whose announcement? *doctor's* (adjective) What kind of Dorinda? *sullen* (adjective) It follows the linking verb and describes the subject. Whose father? *her* (adjective) Whose meals? *Frederick's* (adjective)
S V Pairs	MC ***Dorinda became*** AC *After **father insisted*** Regretted when? *After her father insisted* (adverb clause) that *that **she deliver*** Father insisted what? *that she deliver Frederick's meals* This *that* clause functions as a direct object. It does not follow or describe a noun. MC ***she regretted*** DC *when **accident happened*** The *when* clause describes *day*, the noun it follows. (adjective clause)
Ask Students	Why does *when the accident happened* not have a comma? It is an essential adjective clause. It defines the day she regretted.
Commas	Use a comma after an -ing opener. **PATTERN -ing word/phrase, main clause** The thing after the comma must be the thing doing the inging. *Dorinda* is doing the *hearing*. Use a comma after an adverb clause that comes before a main clause. **PATTERN AC, MC** There is no comma after *insisted* because the *that* clause is essential to the AC. Do not put a comma in front of a *that* clause. Do not place commas around an essential adjective clause.

Rewrite It!   Hearing the doctor's announcement, Dorinda became sullen. After her father insisted that she deliver Frederick's meals, she regretted the day when the accident happened.

Read It!	Mark It!	Fix It!	Day 4

Dorinda **resolved** to avoid the infirmary where Frederick now stayed, when the king ordered her to assist Frederick while he recuperated she knew it would be difficult.

resolved
came to a definite decision; determined

1 adjective (adj)
1 adverb (adv)
2 [main clauses]
1 *that* clause (that)
2 adverb clauses (AC)
6 subject-verb pairs (s v)
2 openers

1 capital
3 commas
1 end mark

(1) subject

S   V

[Dorinda **resolved** to avoid the infirmary], ((which was) where

(5) clausal

S   adv   v   AC   S   v

Frederick now stayed). (when the king ordered her

AC   s   v   s   v

to assist Frederick) (while he recuperated), [she knew]

that   s   v   v   adj

((that) it would be difficult).

Ask Students	Which words and phrases function as adjectives? Which function as adverbs? Use the questions. Stayed when? *now* (adverb) What kind of it? *difficult* (adjective) The adjective follows the linking verb and describes the subject.	
S V Pairs	MC	***Dorinda resolved***
	DC	*where* ***Frederick stayed*** The *where* clause describes *infirmary*, the noun it follows. (adjective clause)
Ask Students	Why does *where Frederick now stayed* require a comma? It is a nonessential adjective clause. It describes the noun *infirmary*. If you remove it, Dorinda still resolved to avoid the infirmary.	
	AC	*When* ***king ordered*** Knew when? *when the king ordered her to assist Frederick* (adverb clause)
	AC	*while* ***he recuperated*** Assist when? *while he recuperated* (adverb clause)
	MC	***she knew***
	that	*(that)* ***it would be*** This is an invisible *that* clause. It does not express a complete thought. She knew what? *that it would be difficult* This *that* clause functions as a direct object. It does not follow or describe a noun.
Commas	Place commas around a nonessential adjective clause.	
	Do not use a comma to separate two main clauses. Use a period. MC, MC is always wrong.	
	Use a comma after an adverb clause that comes before a main clause. **PATTERN AC, MC** There is no comma after *Frederick* because *while he recuperated* is essential to the first AC. Do not use a comma before an adverb clause.	

Rewrite It!   Dorinda resolved to avoid the infirmary, where Frederick now stayed. When the king ordered her to assist Frederick while he recuperated, she knew it would be difficult.

Review It!

Clausal Adverb or Clausal Adjective?

The words *when, where,* and *that* begin different types of dependent clauses.

If *when* or *where* begins an adverb clause, use a comma after, not before. AC, MC MC AC

If *when* or *where* begins an adjective clause, use commas unless essential.

That clauses are always essential and never use commas.

Read each sentence, underline the dependent clause, and identify it.

For adjective clauses, circle the noun that the clause describes. Punctuate correctly.

The king told Dorinda to read (stories) that she loved to Frederick.

adverb   **nonessential adjective**   (**essential adjective**)

The (morning) when the king issued his command was damp and cold.

adverb   **nonessential adjective**   (**essential adjective**)

Frederick was concerned when Dorinda took him from the infirmary.

(**adverb**)   **nonessential adjective**   **essential adjective**

Dorinda knew to take him where her father had told her.

(**adverb**)   **nonessential adjective**   **essential adjective**

They went to the palace (library,) where the imperial collection was kept.

adverb   (**nonessential adjective**)   **essential adjective**

Frederick grimaced when she selected *How to Rid Your Garden of Pests.*

(**adverb**)   **nonessential adjective**   **essential adjective**

He suggested (books) that told engaging stories instead.

adverb   **nonessential adjective**   (**essential adjective**)

She found *Frog and Toad Are Friends* where the children's books were.

(**adverb**)   **nonessential adjective**   **essential adjective**

Frederick noticed *The Frog Prince* on the (shelf) where fairytales resided.

adverb   **nonessential adjective**   (**essential adjective**)

Dorinda read her favorite (part,) where the frog becomes a prince.

adverb   (**nonessential adjective**)   **essential adjective**

If students struggle, review pages 91 and 92.

Look at location.

If the dependent clause comes immediately after a noun and describes that noun, it is an adjective clause.

Adverb Clause

use comma after, not before

AC, MC

MC AC

Nonessential Adjective Clause

adds information to the sentence

use commas

Essential Adjective Clause

defines the noun it follows

do not use commas

That Clause

always essential

do not take commas

For more information about writing direct quotes, see page 56.

Direct Quote

A **direct quote** is an exact copy of another person's written or spoken words.

Copy the original source exactly, including capitalization, spelling, and punctuation. If you need to change part of the sentence to make it grammatical, put the changed part in square brackets. Begin and end the the direct quote with quotation marks.

"[The princess] had a golden ball in her hand, which was her favourite play-thing, and she amused herself with tossing it into the air and catching it again as it fell."

The square brackets alert the reader that *The princess* was not used in the original. However, the meaning remains the same.

Although the word *favourite* is spelled differently in modern American English, the quote must be an exact copy of the original.

The Frog-Prince
by Edgar Taylor

ONE fine evening a young princess went into a wood, and sat down by the side of a cool spring of water. She had a golden ball in her hand, which was her favourite play-thing, and she amused herself with tossing it into the air and catching it again as it fell. After a time she threw it up so high that when she stretched out her hand to catch it, the ball bounded away and rolled along upon the ground, till at last it fell into the spring. The princess looked into the spring after her ball; but it was very deep, so deep that she could not see the bottom of it. Then she began to lament her loss, and said, "Alas! if I could only get my ball again, I would give all my fine clothes and jewels, and every thing

1

This *Fix It! Grammar* book is an adaptation of a story first recorded by the German brothers Jacob and Wilhelm Grimm. When Edgar Taylor translated the fairy tale into English, he changed the title to "The Frog-Prince" and altered the ending.

She knew, that she would have to treat him royally but she could be a "royal pain." Dorinda read to Frederick you're favorite stories, in the **imperial** library the King announced, and walked away.

imperial
regal; majestic; grand

2 coordinating conjunctions (cc)	1 indent
2 prepositional phrases	1 capital
4 [main clauses]	6 commas
1 *that* clause (that)	4 quotation marks
5 subject-verb pairs (s v)	1 usage
1 opener	

(1) subject

     s   v   *that*   s   v   v

[She knew], (that she would have to treat him royally),

cc   s   v   v

but [she could be a "royal pain."] ¶ "Dorinda, [(you) read   s   v

        your

to Frederick ~~you're~~ favorite stories, in the **imperial**

      s   v   cc   v

library]," [the King announced, and walked away].

Students no longer mark adjectives and adverbs.

Indentation	new speaker
Quotations	Do not use quotation marks around *royal pain*. This is not a direct quote.
Conjunction	**but** connects two main clauses. A subject and verb pair (She knew) comes before the cc, and a subject and verb pair (she could be) comes after the cc. A comma is required. MC, cc MC **and** connects two verbs: *announced* and *walked*. MC cc 2nd verb
S V Pairs	MC **She knew**
	that *that* **she would have** She knew what? *that she would have to treat him royally* This *that* clause functions as a direct object. It does not follow or describe a noun.
	MC **she could be**
	MC **(you) read** The noun *Dorinda* is an NDA. The subject of an imperative sentence is always *you*.
	MC **king announced, walked**
Commas	Do not put a comma in front of a *that* clause.
	Use a comma to separate two main clauses connected with a cc. **PATTERN MC, cc MC**
	Place commas around a noun of direct address (NDA). ***Dorinda,***
	Do not put a comma in front of a prepositional phrase.
	Use a comma to separate an attribution from a direct quote. **PATTERN "Quote," attribution.**
	Do not use a comma before a cc when it connects two verbs. **PATTERN MC cc 2nd verb**
Usage	Change *you're* (contraction for you are) to *your* (possessive case pronoun). Whose stories? *your*

Rewrite It!   She knew that she would have to treat him royally, but she could be a royal pain.

         "Dorinda, read to Frederick your favorite stories in the imperial library," the king announced and walked away.

Read It!	Mark It!	Fix It!	Day 2

Every day, Dorinda took Frederick to the library, whenever she entered the frog **marveled** at the 100's of colorful books, that covered the walls, from floor to ceiling.

marveled
was filled with wonder and admiration

6 prepositional phrases	1 indent
2 [main clauses]	1 capital
1 *that* clause (that)	5 commas
1 adverb clause (AC)	1 end mark
4 subject-verb pairs (s v)	1 apostrophe
2 openers	1 number
	1 usage

② prepositional

¶ *(On)* Every day, [Dorinda took Frederick to the library].

⑤ clausal
AC   they
(whenever ~~she~~ entered), [the frog **marveled** at the

hundreds
~~100's~~ of colorful books], (that covered the walls,

from floor to ceiling).

Indentation	new time (or place)
S V Pairs MC	*Dorinda took*
AC	*Whenever they entered* Marveled when? *Whenever they entered* (adverb clause)
MC	*frog marveled*
that	*that covered* The *that* clause describes *books*, the noun it follows. (adjective clause)
Invisible #2	*Every day* is a reference to time. Insert on. (on) *Every day* follows the prepositional **PATTERN preposition + noun (no verb).**
Commas	Do not use a comma if a prepositional opener has fewer than five words.
	Do not use a comma to separate two main clauses. Use a period. MC, MC is always wrong.
	Use a comma after an adverb clause that comes before a main clause. **PATTERN AC, MC**
	Do not put a comma in front of a *that* clause.
	Do not put a comma in front of a prepositional phrase.
Ask Students	Why is 100's incorrect? Spell out numbers that can be expressed in one or two words. *Hundreds* is a plural noun, not a possessive adjective. Do not use an apostrophe.
Usage	Change the pronoun *she* (singular) to *them* (plural). The two nouns *Dorinda* and *Frederick* are the antecedent of *they*.

Rewrite It!   Every day Dorinda took Frederick to the library. Whenever they entered, the frog marveled at the hundreds of colorful books that covered the walls from floor to ceiling.

Read It! **Mark It!** **Fix It!**

At last, Frederick has an idea lets play
a game he eagerly **proffered**, as he searched the
row in front of him, Ill read the first line of a story
and you tell me the name of the book

proffered
suggested; proposed

1 coordinating conjunction (cc)	1 indent
5 prepositional phrases	1 capital
5 [main clauses]	4 commas
1 adverb clause (AC)	4 end marks
6 subject-verb pairs (s v)	2 apostrophes
1 opener	1 usage

② prepositional   *s*   *v*   *had*   *s*   *v*

¶ At last, [Frederick ~~has~~ an idea]. "[(you) let's play

     s   *v*   *AC*   *s*   *v*

a game]!" [he eagerly **proffered**], (as he searched the

       s v   *v*

row in front of him). "[I'll read the first line of a story],

cc   *s*   *v*

and [you tell me the name of the book]."

Indentation	new speaker
End Marks	Use an exclamation mark when a quote expresses strong emotion. **PATTERN "Quote!" attribution.** It is correct that *he* is not capitalized. The attribution *he eagerly proffered* is not the first word of the sentence.
Conjunction	**and** connects two main clauses. A subject and verb pair (I'll read) comes before the cc, and a subject and verb pair (you tell) comes after the cc. A comma is required. MC, cc MC
S V Pairs MC	**Frederick had**
MC	**(you) Let** The subject of an imperative sentence is always *you*. The contraction *Let's* includes both a verb (Let) and an objective pronoun (us).
MC	**he proffered**
AC	**as he searched** Proffered when? *as he searched the row in front of him* (adverb clause)
MC	**I'll read** The contraction *I'll* includes both a subject (I) and a helping verb (will).
MC	**you tell**
Note	*(To) play* is an infinitive. It does not function as a verb. The word *to* is implied, not written. Although students might not recognize that this is an infinitive, they should know that they cannot mark a word as a verb unless it has a subject. Every verb has a subject.
Commas	Do not use a comma if a prepositional opener has fewer than five words.
	Do not put a comma in front of an adverb clause. **PATTERN MC AC**
	Do not use a comma to separate two main clauses. Use a period. MC, MC is always wrong.
	Use a comma to separate two main clauses connected with a cc. **PATTERN MC, cc MC**
Usage	Change *has* (present tense) to *had* (past tense).

Rewrite It!   At last Frederick had an idea. "Let's play a game!" he eagerly proffered as he searched the
row in front of him. "I'll read the first line of a story, and you tell me the name of the book."

Agreeing **hesitantly** Dorinda sat beside Frederick
who's scrawny, skeletal fingers opened a book
in the light of the moon a little egg lay on a leaf
read Frederick. Dorinda thought, for a moment.

hesitantly
doubtfully

5 prepositional phrases	1 indent
4 [main clauses]	1 capital
1 *who/which* clause (w/w)	5 commas
5 subject-verb pairs (s v)	1 end mark
2 openers	1 usage

④ -ing
                                    s   v
Agreeing **hesitantly,** [Dorinda sat beside Frederick],

w/w whose   s   v
(~~who's~~ scrawny, skeletal fingers opened a book).

                                        s   v
"in the light of the moon [a little egg lay on a leaf],"
                                ⑥ vss
  v   s   s   v
[read Frederick]. ¶ [Dorinda thought, for a moment].

Indentation		new topic
S V Pairs	MC	*Dorinda sat*
	w/w	*whose fingers opened* The subject of the clause is *fingers*. The word *whose* functions as an adjective. (Whose (Frederick's) scrawny skeletal fingers opened a book.) The *whose* clause describes *Frederick*, the noun it follows. (adjective clause) It is nonessential because it does not change the meaning of the sentence. Without the *whose* clause, Dorinda still sat beside Frederick.
	MC	*egg lay*
	MC	*Frederick read*
	MC	*Dorinda thought*
Commas		Use a comma after an -ing opener. **PATTERN** -ing word/phrase, main clause The thing after the comma must be the thing doing the inging. *Dorinda* is doing the *agreeing*. Place commas around a nonessential *who/which* clause. Do not use a comma to separate cumulative adjectives (scrawny skeletal fingers). Use a comma to separate an attribution from a direct quote. **PATTERN** "Quote," attribution. Do not put a comma in front of a prepositional phrase.
Note		Use the exact words and punctuation of the original. Because *The Very Hungry Caterpillar* by Eric Carle does not have a comma after the long #2 prepositional opener, the quoted sentence does not have a comma after the word *moon*.
Usage		Change *who's* (contraction for who is) to *whose* (possessive case pronoun). Use *who* when the pronoun functions as a subject and *whose* when the pronoun functions as an adjective.

Rewrite It!   Agreeing hesitantly, Dorinda sat beside Frederick, whose scrawny skeletal fingers
                  opened a book. "In the light of the moon a little egg lay on a leaf," read Frederick.
                        Dorinda thought for a moment.

Learn It!

Fix It!

Starting this week, the Fix It! section no longer indicates how many indents, commas, capitals, and end marks are needed in each passage. Make needed fixes based on grammar and punctuation rules. This is what you must do with your own writing too since no one tells you how many indents, commas, capitals, and end marks you need in the paragraphs that you write.

#4 -ing Opener Impostor

Week 5 you learned that a **#4 -ing opener** is a sentence that begins with a participial phrase. However, not every sentence that begins with a word that ends with the letters *ing* is a #4 -ing opener. You must consider what the words are doing in the sentence.

(4) -ing   *S*   *V*

Guessing the title, [Dorinda enjoyed the game].

> When a participial phrase (#4 -ing opener) begins a sentence,
> > a comma separates the -ing opener from the main clause, and
> > the thing after the comma must be the thing doing the inging.
>
> When an -ing word functions as an adjective, it is called a participle.
> *Guessing the title* is a participial phrase because it functions as an adjective that describes the subject of the main clause (Dorinda).

(1) subject
     S   *V*

[Guessing the title entertained Dorinda].

> *Guessing* is the subject of the sentence. What entertained? *Guessing* (subject noun)
>
> When an -ing word functions as a noun, it is called a gerund. Mark it as a #1 subject opener.

(2) prepositional   *S*   *V*

During the game [Dorinda laughed].

> *During* is a preposition, not a participle.
>
> If a sentence begins with the preposition *concerning, according to, regarding,* or *during,* mark it as a #2 prepositional opener.

Literary Titles

Capitalize the first word and the last word of titles and subtitles. Capitalize all other words except articles, coordinating conjunctions, and prepositions.

Dorinda read *Frog and Toad Are Friends* by Arnold Lobel.

> Italicize titles of full-length works: book, magazine, movie, newspaper, website.
> If handwriting, underline because you cannot italicize.

She recited the nursery rhyme "Five Little Speckled Frogs."

> Place titles found within a larger source in quotation marks: article, chapter, short story, poem, speech, webpage.
> Place commas and periods inside closing quotation marks.

Sidebar:

When the subject is an -ing gerund, no comma follows the opening phrase because there should not be a comma between a subject and its verb.

Guessing the title entertained Dorinda. Since the subject (Guessing) includes what they are guessing (the title), putting a comma after the word *title* would separate the subject from its verb.

During is a preposition meaning "at some time in the course of." No one can *dure* because there is no modern verb *to dure* and no participle *during.* Long ago the verb *to dure* meant to endure, but that is now archaic.

According to is always a preposition. As prepositions, *concerning* and *regarding* mean "with regard to" or "about."

Title capitalization rules apply to all titles, including titles for papers and titles for places or people.

A Lamp on the Corner (student paper)

Stratford-upon-Avon (place in England)

House of Representatives (group of people)

For more information about *that* clauses, see pages 13, 80, and 92.

Demonstrative

> this, that, these, those

Adjective Questions

> which one, what kind, how many, whose

That Clause Pattern

> that + subject + verb

That generations had enjoyed is a dependent *that* clause. It follows the pattern that + subject + verb. You can replace *that* with *which*.

Which place? *that* (adjective)

That she could always find a thrilling book is a dependent *that* clause. It follows the **PATTERN** **that + subject + verb.** You can remove *that* and the sentence still makes sense.

Reach what? *that* (pronoun)

The Word *That*

Although the word *that* usually begins a dependent *that* clause, it does not when the word *that* is a demonstrative pronoun or an adjective.

Demonstrative Pronoun

A **pronoun** takes the place of a noun.

> s   op
> That was the best book. I will read more about that.

Like other pronouns, demonstrative pronouns perform a noun function. In the first example, *that* is the subject of the main clause. In the second example, *that* is the object of the preposition *about*.

Adjective

An **adjective** describes a noun or a pronoun. When a demonstrative pronoun comes before a noun, it functions as an adjective.

> adj   adj
> That book was the best book. I will read more about that frog.

That comes before a noun and answers the question which one.
Which book? *that* Which frog? *that*

Confirm that the word *that* functions as an adjective by replacing *that* with *the*:
> ~~That~~ The book was the best book. I will read more about ~~that~~ the frog.

Dependent Clause

A **dependent clause** contains a subject and a verb but does not express a complete thought. A **that clause** is a dependent clause that begins with the word *that*.

> that   s   v
> Dorinda did not recognize the sentence (that he read).

To confirm that the word *that* begins a *that* clause, look for a subject (he) and a verb (read).

When the word *that* begins a *that* clause, you can often remove it from the sentence:
> Dorinda did not recognize the sentence ~~that~~ he read.

If the *that* clause is an adjective clause, you can replace the word *that* with *which*:
> Dorinda did not recognize the sentence ~~that~~ which he read.

What Is It and Why?

Read each sentence and determine if the word *that* begins a dependent *that* clause or if it is a demonstrative pronoun or an adjective.

The library housed stacks of books that generations had enjoyed.

Dorinda had spent hours in that place.

She knew that she could always find a thrilling book.

Pointing to a book, Frederick said, "Can you reach that for me?"

Read It!	Mark It!	Fix It!	Day 1

That has to be The very hungry Caterpillar
she **responded**, she had enjoyed that book
a favorite of hers since she was a young child.

Mark It!

1 <u>prepositional phrase</u>
3 [main clauses]
1 adverb clause (AC)
4 subject-verb pairs (s v)
1 invisible *who/which* clause (w/w)
1 opener

Fix It!	
? indents	0
? capitals	3
? commas	4
? end marks	1
2 quotation marks	

responded
replied; answered

 s   v
"[That has to be <u>The very hungry Caterpillar</u>],"
                              ① subject
 s   v   S   V   V
[she **responded**]. [she had enjoyed that book],

w/w   AC   s   v
(*(which was)* a favorite <u>of hers</u>), (since she was a young child).

Capitalization	The *Very Hungry Caterpillar* is the title of a book. Capitalize the first letter of every word in this title. The title should be italicized if typed and underlined if handwritten.
S V Pairs MC	***That has*** This is a main clause because it expresses a complete thought. The demonstrative pronoun *That* is the subject pronoun.
MC	***she responded***
MC	***She had enjoyed***
AC	*since **she was*** Had enjoyed when? *since she was a young child* (adverb clause)
Invisible w/w	*(which was) a favorite of hers* is an invisible *which* clause. With the words *which was* removed, the noun *favorite* follows the noun *book* and renames it. *Favorite* functions as an appositive because the subject and the verb (*which was*) are not in the phrase.
Commas	Use a comma to separate an attribution from a direct quote. **PATTERN** "Quote," attribution.
	Do not use a comma to separate two main clauses. Use a period. MC, MC is always wrong.
	Place commas around a nonessential invisible *who/which* clause (appositive phrase).
	When two comma rules contradict, follow the rule that says to use a comma. A comma is needed after *hers* because of this rule: Place commas around a nonessential invisible *who/which* clause (appositive phrase). A comma is not needed after *hers* because of this rule: Do not put a comma in front of an adverb clause. **PATTERN MC AC**

Rewrite It!   "That has to be *The Very Hungry Caterpillar*," she responded. She had enjoyed that book, a favorite of hers, since she was a young child.

Note: Students underline book titles when handwriting.

Read It!	Mark It!	Fix It!	Day 2

Playing the game improved her mood. Let me do one she said. There was a boy called Eustace Clarence Scrubb and he almost deserved it, hoping to **stump** Frederick she smirks.

stump
to be too difficult to answer

Mark It!	
1	coordinating conjunction (cc)
6	[main clauses]
6	subject-verb pairs (s v)
2	openers

Fix It!	
? indents	**1**
? capitals	**1**
? commas	**4**
? end marks	**1**
4 quotation marks	
1 usage	

(1) subject

            s   v   s   v

¶ [Playing the game improved her mood]. "[(you) Let me do one,]" [she said]. "[There was a boy called Eustace Clarence Scrubb], and [he almost deserved

(4) -ing

it]," hoping to **stump** Frederick, [she ~~smirks~~ *smirked*].

Indentation		new topic
Conjunction		***and*** connects two main clauses. A subject and verb pair (boy was called) comes before the cc, and a subject and verb pair (he deserved) comes after the cc. A comma is required. MC, cc MC
S V Pairs	MC	***Playing improved*** What improved? *Playing* (subject noun)
	MC	***(you) Let*** The subject of an imperative sentence is always *you*.
	MC	***she said***
	MC	***boy was called*** Students often assume *there* is the subject. However, the subject-verb pair must work together. Who was called? *boy*
	MC	***he deserved***
	MC	***she smirked***
Note		*(To) do* is an infinitive. It does not function as a verb. The word *to* is implied, not written. Although students might not recognize that this is an infinitive, they should know that they cannot mark a word as a verb unless it has a subject. Every verb has a subject.
Commas		Use a comma to separate an attribution from a direct quote. **PATTERN** "Quote," attribution.
		Use a comma to separate two main clauses connected with a cc. **PATTERN MC, cc MC**
		Do not use a comma to separate two main clauses. Use a period. MC, MC is always wrong.
		Use a comma after an -ing opener. **PATTERN -ing word/phrase, main clause** The thing after the comma must be the thing doing the inging. *She* is doing the *hoping*.
Usage		Change *smirks* (present tense) to *smirked* (past tense).

Rewrite It!   Playing the game improved her mood. "Let me do one," she said. "There was a boy called Eustace Clarence Scrubb, and he almost deserved it." Hoping to stump Frederick, she smirked.

Read It!	Mark It!	Fix It!	Day 3

Guessing confidently Frederick answered oh
thats easy its The voyage Of The Dawn Treader,
playing the game amused himself he chose another,
Jennas **reputation** was only as good as her word

reputation
the opinion that people have about someone

Mark It!	
2 <u>prepositional phrases</u>	
6 [main clauses]	
6 subject-verb pairs (s v)	
3 openers	

Fix It!	
? indents	**1**
? capitals	**8**
? commas	**4**
? end marks	**6**
4 quotation marks	
3 apostrophes	
1 usage	

④ -ing

¶ Guessing confidently, [Frederick answered], "oh!

[that's easy]! [it's The voyage Øf Ⱦhe Dawn Treader]!"

⑥ vss   ⑥ vss
[playing the game amused himself]. [he chose another].

"[Jenna's **reputation** was only as good as her word]."

Indentation	new speaker
Capitalization	*The Voyage of the Dawn Treader* is the title of a book. Do not capitalize prepositions (of) or articles (the) unless they are the first or last word in the title. The title should be italicized if typed and underlined if handwritten.
Interjection	*Oh!* is an interjection that expresses a strong emotion. Use an exclamation mark and capitalize *That's.*
S V Pairs	MC *Frederick answered*
	MC *That's* The contraction *That's* includes both a subject (That) and a verb (is). This is a main clause because it expresses a complete thought. The demonstrative pronoun *That* is the subject pronoun.
	MC *It's* The contraction *It's* includes both a subject (It) and a verb (is).
	MC *Playing amused* What amused? *Playing* (subject noun)
	MC *He chose*
	MC *reputation was*
Opener	*Playing the game amused him* begins with the subject. Any sentence that contains 2–5 words is a very short sentence.
Commas	Use a comma after an -ing opener. **PATTERN** -ing word/phrase, main clause The thing after the comma must be the thing doing the inging. *Frederick* is doing the *guessing.* Use a comma to separate an attribution from a direct quote. **PATTERN** Attribution, "Quote." Do not use a comma to separate two main clauses. Use a period. MC, MC is always wrong.
Usage	Change the pronoun *himself* (reflexive) to *him* (objective). Use a reflexive pronoun only when the pronoun following the verb refers to the subject.

Rewrite It!   Guessing confidently, Frederick answered, "Oh! That's easy! It's *The Voyage of the Dawn Treader!*" Playing the game amused him. He chose another. "Jenna's reputation was only as good as her word."

Read It!	Mark It!	Fix It!	Day 4

Dorinda who didnt know walked over to look,
the words on the cover were One good turn deserves
another reading the title made Dorinda **suspicious**,
at that moment she decided, the game was over

suspicious
causing a feeling of doubt or mistrust

Mark It!	
2 <u>prepositional phrases</u>	
4 [main clauses]	
1 *who/which* clause (w/w)	
1 *that* clause (that)	
6 subject-verb pairs (s v)	
4 openers	

Fix It!	
? indents	**1**
? capitals	**7**
? commas	**5**
? end marks	**4**
1 apostrophe	

(1) subject
s   w/w s   v   v   v
¶ [Dorinda, (who didn't know), walked over to look].

(1) subject
s   v
[the words on the cover were One good turn deserves

(1) subject
s   v
another]. [reading the title made Dorinda **suspicious**].

(2) prepositional
s   v   that   s   v
at that moment [she decided], ((that) the game was over).

Indentation		new topic
Capitalization		*One Good Turn Deserves Another* is the title of a book. Capitalize the first letter of every word in this title. The title should be italicized if typed and underlined if handwritten.
S V Pairs	MC	**Dorinda walked**
	w/w	**who did know** The contraction *didn't* includes both a helping verb (did) and an adverb (not). The *who* clause describes *Dorinda*, the noun it follows. (adjective clause) It is nonessential because it does not change the meaning of the sentence. Without the *who* clause, Dorinda still walked over to look.
	MC	**words were**
	MC	**Reading made** What made? *Reading* (subject noun)
	MC	**she decided**
	that	*(that)* **game was** This is an invisible *that* clause. It does not express a complete thought.
Commas		Place commas around a nonessential *who/which* clause.
		Do not use a comma to separate two main clauses. Use a period. MC, MC is always wrong.
		Do not put a comma in front of a *that* clause.

Rewrite It!   Dorinda, who didn't know, walked over to look. The words on the cover were *One Good Turn Deserves Another*. Reading the title made Dorinda suspicious. At that moment she decided the game was over.

Learn It!

Who/Which **Clause**

You have learned that a ***who/which* clause** is a dependent clause that begins with the word *who* or *which* and follows the noun it describes.

The pronoun *who* has three forms: *who, whom, whose*.

The pronoun ***who*** is a subjective case pronoun that functions as a subject.
Use *who* when the subject of a *who* clause is *who*.

w/w   s   v

Dorinda read to Frederick, (who listened eagerly).

    The *who/which* clause describes *Frederick*, the noun it follows.
    He listened eagerly.
    The subject of the *who* clause is *who*.

> *Who*, like *he*, functions as a subject. If you can replace *who* with *he*, it is a subject.
>
> *who (he) listened eagerly*

The pronoun ***whom*** is an objective case pronoun that functions as an object.
Use *whom* when the subject of a *who* clause is not *who*.

w/w   s   v

Dorinda read to Frederick, (whom she initially disliked).

    The *who/which* clause describes *Frederick*, the noun it follows.
    She initially disliked him.
    The subject of the *who* clause is *she*. Begin the clause with *whom*.

> *Whom*, like *him*, functions as an object. If you can replace *whom* with *him*, it is an object.
>
> *she initially disliked whom (him)*

The pronoun ***whose*** is a possessive case pronoun that shows ownership.
Use *whose* when the first word of either a *who* or a *which* clause functions as an adjective.

w/w   s   v

Dorinda read to Frederick, (whose humor made her laugh).

    The *who/which* clause describes *Frederick*, the noun it follows.
    His humor made her laugh. Whose humor? *whose* (Frederick's)
    The first word of the clause functions as an adjective. Begin the clause with *whose*.

> *Whose*, like *his*, functions as an adjective in order to show ownership. If you can replace *whose* with *his*, it is an adjective.
>
> *whose (his) humor made her laugh*

Mark It!   Place parentheses around the *who/which* clause.
                   Write *w/w* above the word *who, whom,* or *whose*.
                   Write *v* above each verb and *s* above each subject.

Fix It!   Place a line through the incorrect pronoun and write the correct word above it.
                   Use *who* when the subject of the *who* clause is *who*.
                   Use *whom* when the subject of the *who* clause is not *who*.
                   Use *whose* when the first word functions as an adjective.

Homophone

A **homophone** is a word that sounds like another word but is spelled differently and has a different meaning. Do not confuse *whose* with *who's*.

    Whose is a possessive pronoun that functions as an adjective.

    Who's is a contraction for *who is*. It includes both a subject (who) and a verb (is).
    You can use *who's* to begin a *who* clause only when the subject of the clause is *who*.

Who, Whom, or Whose?

Week 12 you learned that pronouns have 3 cases: subjective, objective, and possessive. Here is a portion of the chart on page 67.

3 Cases	Subjective	Objective	Possessive
Function (job)	subject predicate pronoun	direct object object of preposition	adjective
	he	him	his
	who	whom	whose

The pronoun *he* has three forms: *he, him, his*. Use *he* when the pronoun functions as a subject, *him* when the pronoun functions as an object, and *his* when the pronoun functions as an adjective in order to show ownership.

The pronoun *who* also has three forms: *who, whom, whose*. Use *who* when the pronoun functions as a subject, *whom* when the pronoun functions as an object, and *whose* when the pronoun functions as an adjective in order to show ownership.

Read each sentence. Should the dependent clause begin with *who, whom,* or *whose*? Write the correct word in the blank.

Dorinda, _____whose_____ situation was distressing, valued the library's distractions.

Frederick, _____whom_____ Dorinda accompanied, had a particular book in mind.

Frederick, _____who_____ wanted to teach Dorinda, found the right book.

The main character, _____whose_____ name was Scarlett, fancied extravagant parties.

Dorinda admired Scarlett, _____whose_____ sunny personality won her many friends.

Scarlett, _____whom_____ Dorinda related to, planned a lavish party for her friends.

The friends _____who_____ accepted the invitation admired the swan centerpiece.

Scarlett's puppy, _____whom_____ she spoiled, ate a cupcake.

Help students locate the subject and verb of each dependent clause. Consider the function of the missing word. Test by substituting *he, him,* and *his*.

A thorough explanation for the first three are below.

1. The first word of the *who* clause shows ownership. It functions as an adjective (her situation). Whose situation? *whose* (Dorinda's)

2. The subject of the *who* clause is *Dorinda*. Dorinda accompanied *him* (objective case) Use *whom* (objective case).

3. The subject of the *who* clause is *who*, referring to Frederick. *He* (subjective case) wanted. Use *who* (subjective case).

Read It!	Mark It!	Fix It!	Day 1

The frog who she detested had irritated her again she slammed the book down and **ignobly** fled to the palace grounds along the way she approached the well.

ignobly
not honorably

1 coordinating conjunction (cc)
2 prepositional phrases
3 [main clauses]
1 *who/which* clause (w/w)
4 subject-verb pairs (s v)
3 openers

? indents   **0**
? capitals   **2**
? commas   **2**
? end marks   **2**
1 usage

      (1) subject
      s   w/w whom   s   v   v   v

[The frog, (~~who~~ she detested), had irritated her

      (1) subject
     s   v   cc

again]. [she slammed the book down and **ignobly**

                 (2) prepositional
  v

fled to the palace grounds]. along the way

  s   v

[she approached the well].

Conjunction	*and* connects two verbs: *slammed* and *fled* MC cc 2nd verb
S V Pairs MC	*frog had irritated*
w/w	*whom* **she detested** Change *who* (subjective) to *whom* (objective). The subject is *She*. Rule: Use *whom* when the subject of the clause is not *who*. The *whom* clause describes *frog*, the noun it follows. (adjective clause) It is nonessential because it does not change the meaning of the sentence. Without the *who* clause, the frog had still irritated her.
MC	*She slammed, fled*
MC	*she approached*
Commas	Place commas around a nonessential *who/which* clause.
Usage	Change *who* (subjective) to *whom* (objective). She detected *whom* (direct object). Use *who* when the pronoun functions as a subject and *whom* when the pronoun functions as an object.

Rewrite It!   The frog, whom she detested, had irritated her again. She slammed the book down and ignobly fled to the palace grounds. Along the way she approached the well.

Read It!	Mark It!	Fix It!	Day 2

Suddenly she notices an old woman who's feeble hands were struggling to draw water from the deep well the woman **futilely** tried to turn the crank which would not budge.

futilely
without success; uselessly

1 prepositional phrase	? indents	**1**
2 [main clauses]	? capitals	**1**
2 *who/which* clauses (w/w)	? commas	**2**
4 subject-verb pairs (s v)	? end marks	**1**
2 openers	2 usage	

(3) -ly adverb

         S   V
         noticed   w/w whose

¶ Suddenly [she ~~notices~~ an old woman], (~~who's~~ feeble

  S   V   V

hands were struggling to draw water from the deep

      (1) subject
               S   V

well). [the woman **futilely** tried to turn the crank],

w/w S   V   V

(which would not budge).

Indentation	new topic	
S V Pairs	MC	*she noticed*
	w/w	*whose* **hands were struggling** The subject of the clause is *hands*. The word *whose* functions as an adjective. (Whose (woman's) feeble hands were struggling.) The *whose* clause describes *woman*, the noun it follows. (adjective clause)
		It is nonessential because it does not change the meaning of the sentence. Without the *whose* clause, Dorinda still noticed an old woman.
	MC	*woman tried*
	w/w	**which would budge** The *which* clause describes *crank*, the noun it follows.
Commas	Place commas around a nonessential *who/which* clause.	
Usage	Change *notices* (present tense) to *noticed* (past tense).	
	Change *who's* (contraction for who is) to *whose* (possessive case pronoun). Use *who* when the pronoun functions as a subject and *whose* when the pronoun functions as an adjective.	

Rewrite It!   Suddenly she noticed an old woman, whose feeble hands were struggling to draw water from the deep well. The woman futilely tried to turn the crank, which would not budge.

Read It!	Mark It!	Fix It!	Day 3

Clearly her finger's ached **hampering** her task grasping the wooden bucket proved useless hearing steps the woman turned toward the girl who rude stared but didnt offer any assistance.

hampering
hindering or impeding the movement or progress

Mark It!	
1 coordinating conjunction (cc)	
1 prepositional phrase	
3 [main clauses]	
1 who/which clause (w/w)	
4 subject-verb pairs (s v)	
3 openers	

Fix It!	Day 3
? indents	**0**
? capitals	**2**
? commas	**4**
? end marks	**2**
2 apostrophes	
1 usage	

③ -ly adverb

Clearly, [her finger's ached], **hampering** her task.

① subject

[grasping the wooden bucket proved useless].

④ -ing

hearing steps, [the woman turned toward the girl],

(who ~~rude~~ stared but didn't offer any assistance).

Conjunction	*but* connects two verbs: *stared* but *did offer*
S V Pairs	MC *fingers ached*
	MC *Grasping proved* What proved? *Grasping* (subject noun)
	MC *woman turned*
	w/w *who stared*, *did offer* The contraction *didn't* includes both a helping verb (did) and an adverb (not). The subject is *who*. Rule: Use *who* when the subject of the clause is *who*. The *who* clause describes *girl*, the noun it follows. (adjective clause) It is nonessential because it does not change the meaning of the sentence. Without the *who* clause, the woman still turned toward the girl.
Commas	Use a comma if an -ly adverb opener modifies the sentence. It was clear that her fingers ached.
	Use a comma when a -ing phrase at the end of a sentence describes a noun other than the word it follows.
	Use a comma after an -ing opener. **PATTERN -ing word/phrase, main clause** The thing after the comma must be the thing doing the inging. *Woman* is doing the *hearing*.
	Place commas around a nonessential *who/which* clause.
Usage	Change the adjective *rude* to the adverb *rudely*. *Rudely* modifies the verb *stared*.

Rewrite It! Clearly, her fingers ached, hampering her task. Grasping the wooden bucket proved useless. Hearing steps, the woman turned toward the girl, who rudely stared but didn't offer any assistance.

Read It!	Mark It!	Fix It!	Day 4

Lovely princess the woman began I have
arthritis in my hands and me cannot lift the
brimming bucket would you kindly fetch me a
cup of water

brimming
filled to the top

1 coordinating conjunction (cc)
2 prepositional phrases
4 [main clauses]
4 subject-verb pairs (s v)

? indents   **1**
? capitals   **2**
? commas   **3**
? end marks   **2**
4 quotation marks
1 usage

¶ "Lovely princess," [the woman began], "[I have
arthritis in my hands], and [me cannot lift the
brimming bucket]. [would you kindly fetch me a
cup of water]?"

Indentation	new speaker
Conjunction	**and** connects two main clauses. A subject and verb pair (I have) comes before the cc, and a subject and verb pair (I can lift) comes after the cc. A comma is required. MC, cc MC
S V Pairs MC	**woman began**
MC	**I have**
MC	**I can lift** The compound word *cannot* includes both a helping verb (can) and an adverb (not).
MC	**you Would fetch**
Ask Students	Titles used without a name are usually lowercase. Why is *Princess* capitalized? Titles used alone in speech as a noun of direct address are capitalized because they substitute for the character's name.
Commas	Place commas around a noun of direct address (NDA). **Lovely Princess,**
	Use a comma to separate an attribution from a direct quote. **PATTERN** "Quote," attribution, "rest of quoted sentence."
	Use a comma to separate two main clauses connected with a cc. **PATTERN MC, cc MC**
Usage	Change the pronoun *me* (objective) to *I* (subjective). Who cannot lift? *I* (subject)

Rewrite It!   "Lovely Princess," the woman began, "I have arthritis in my hands, and I cannot lift the brimming bucket. Would you kindly fetch me a cup of water?"

Learn It!

Overusing Coordinating Conjunctions

Week 2 you learned that a coordinating conjunction (cc) connects the same type of words, phrases, or clauses. The items must be grammatically the same: two or more adjectives, two or more prepositional phrases, two or more main clauses, and so forth.

[Frederick ate fresh crickets], ~~and~~ burping loudly.

> *And* incorrectly connects the noun *crickets* and the participial (-ing) phrase *burping loudly*. These items are not grammatically the same.

~~And~~ Dorinda laughed.

> In formal writing a sentence should not start with a cc; in dialogue it may.

Fix It!   When a *cc* is used incorrectly, remove it or rewrite the sentence.

Week 10 you learned that one way to fix a run-on is to connect two main clauses with a comma + cc. **PATTERN MC, cc MC.**

Of the seven coordinating conjunctions, *and* is the most common and most overused. The pattern *MC, and MC* is effective when *and* is the most logical way to relate the two main clauses.

Same Idea
The two clauses happen at the same time and express similar ideas.

The chef made Frederick fly soup, and the maids fluffed his pillow.

> Both sentences refer to the special treatment that Frederick enjoyed.

Sequential
The second clause happens after the first.

The orderly brought Frederick fly soup, and he gratefully drank it.

> Frederick drank the soup after the orderly brought it to him.

Writers can overuse the coordinating conjunction *and*. Check that *and* is the best way to connect the main clauses. If the main clauses express different ideas, they belong in separate sentences.

Fix It!   When the main clauses express different ideas, replace the *comma + and* with a period. Capitalize the first word of the new sentence.

Because of its vast collection, [Frederick spent time in the
library]. ~~and~~ [he developed a guessing game with book titles].

The same types of words, phrases, or clauses must be specific. For example, a cc cannot connect two clauses where one is a main clause and the other is dependent. It cannot connect two nouns where one is a subject noun and the other is the object of a preposition.

FANBOYS
for, and, nor, but, or, yet, so

Read It!	Mark It!	Fix It!	Day 1

Tossing her golden locks Dorinda impulsively turned away why do people think I am his servant she grumbled. Treating other's attentively, and respectfully **evaded** her.

evaded
was avoided or not understood

Mark It!
1 coordinating conjunction (cc)
4 [main clauses]
1 *that* clause (that)
5 subject-verb pairs (s v)
2 openers

Fix It!
? indents   **1**
? capitals   **1**
? commas   **2**
? end marks   **2**
2 quotation marks
1 apostrophe
1 usage

④ -ing

                                         s

¶ Tossing her golden locks, [Dorinda impulsively

v   *v*   *s*   *v*   *that*   *s*   *v*   *their*

turned away]. "[why do people think] ((that) I am ~~his~~

                                    ① subject

        s   *v*   *s*

servant)?" [she grumbled]. [Treating other's attentively,

cc   *v*

and respectfully **evaded** her].

Indentation	new speaker	
Conjunction	**and** connects two adverbs: *attentively* and *respectfully* a and b	
S V Pairs	MC	**Dorinda turned**
	MC	**people do think**
	that	*(that)* **I am** This is an invisible *that* clause. It does not express a complete thought.
	MC	**she grumbled**
	MC	**Treating evaded** What evaded? *Treating* (subject noun)
Ask Students	Why is the first sentence a #4 -ing opener and the last sentence a #1 subject opener? *Tossing her golden locks* is a participial (-ing) phrase. If removed, a sentence remains. The thing after the comma is doing the inging. *Treating others attentively and respectfully* cannot be removed from the sentence. *Treating* is the subject of the sentence.	
Commas	Use a comma after an -ing opener. **PATTERN -ing word/phrase, main clause** The thing after the comma must be the thing doing the inging. *Dorinda* is doing the *tossing*. Do not use a comma to separate two items connected with a cc. **PATTERN a and b**	
Usage	Change the pronoun *his* (singular) to *their* (plural). The plural noun *people* is the antecedent of *their*.	

Rewrite It!   Tossing her golden locks, Dorinda impulsively turned away. "Why do people think I am their servant?" she grumbled. Treating others attentively and respectfully evaded her.

Read It!	Mark It!	Fix It!	Day 2

Manners were essential, politeness was expected the old lady a fairy in disguise **brandished** her wand, and zapped princess Dorinda into a toad. And at last, the Princess would receive their punishment.

brandished
waved something in a threatening or excited manner

2 coordinating conjunctions (cc)   ? indents   **1**
3 prepositional phrases   ? capitals   **4**
4 [main clauses]   ? commas   **5**
4 subject-verb pairs (s v)   ? end marks   **1**
1 invisible *who/which* clause (w/w)   1 semicolon
3 openers   1 usage

① subject

¶ [Manners were essential]; [politeness was expected].
   s   v   s   v

① subject

[the old lady, ((who was) a fairy in disguise), **brandished** her
   s   w/w   v

wand, and zapped princess Dorinda into a toad]. ~~And~~
       cc   v   cc

② prepositional

at last, [the Princess would receive ~~their~~ punishment].
         s   v   v   her

Indentation	new topic
Conjunction	**and** connects two verbs: *brandished* and *zapped* MC cc 2nd verb
	and does not connect anything. Remove *and*. Coordinating conjunctions connect items that are grammatically the same. They do not usually begin sentences.
S V Pairs MC	**Manners were**
MC	**politeness was** The adjective *expected* follows the linking verb and describes the subject.
MC	**lady brandished, zapped**
MC	**princess would receive**
Invisible w/w	(who was) a fairy in disguise is an invisible *who* clause. With the words *who was* removed, the noun *fairy* follows the noun *lady* and renames it. *Fairy* functions as an appositive because the subject and the verb (who was) are not in the phrase.
Ask Students	Why can you fix the run-on (comma splice) with a semicolon? Both main clauses, *manners were essential* and *politeness was expected*, express a single idea and are similar in length and construction.
Commas	Do not use a comma to separate two main clauses. MC, MC is always wrong.
	Place commas around a nonessential invisible *who/which* clause (appositive phrase).
	Do not use a comma before a cc when it connects two verbs. **PATTERN MC cc 2nd verb**
	Do not use a comma if a prepositional opener has fewer than five words.
Usage	Change the pronoun *their* (plural) to *her* (singular). The singular noun *princess* is the antecedent of *her*.

Rewrite It!   Manners were essential; politeness was expected. The old lady, a fairy in disguise, brandished her wand and zapped Princess Dorinda into a toad. At last the princess would receive her punishment.

Read It!	Mark It!	Fix It!	Day 3

Instantly Dorinda plummeted to the ground, and all that remains was her crown which was miniaturized to fit her diminished stature and her beauty spot which was **prominent**, among the other toady warts.

prominent
particularly noticeable

Mark It!	
2 coordinating conjunctions (cc)	
2 prepositional phrases	
2 [main clauses]	
2 who/which clauses (w/w)	
1 that clause (that)	
5 subject-verb pairs (s v)	
2 openers	

Fix It!	
? indents	**0**
? capitals	**1**
? commas	**5**
? end marks	**1**
1 usage	

③ -ly adverb

①subject

Instantly [Dorinda plummeted to the ground]. ~~and~~ [all
(that ~~remains~~) was her crown, (which was miniaturized
to fit her diminished stature), and her beauty spot],
(which was **prominent**, among the other toady warts).

Conjunction	**and** connects two main clauses. However, the main clauses express different ideas, so they should be in different sentences. Replace the comma + cc with a period. Capitalize *All*.
	and connects two nouns (predicate nouns): *crown* and *beauty spot* a and b
Ask Students	Why is there a comma before *and* when it is connecting only two nouns?
	A nonessential *which* clause comes between the two nouns.
	When two comma rules contradict, follow the rule that says to use a comma.
S V Pairs	MC **Dorinda plummeted**
	MC **All was**
	that **that remained** The *that* clause describes *All*, the pronoun it follows. (adjective clause)
	w/w **which was** The adjective *miniaturized* follows the linking verb and describes the subject.
	The *which* clause describes *crown*, the noun it follows. (adjective clause)
	w/w **which was** The *which* clause describes *spot*, the noun it follows. (adjective clause)
	Both *which* clauses are nonessential because they do not change the meaning of the sentence.
	Without the *which* clauses, all that remained was her crown and her beauty spot.
Commas	Place commas around a nonessential *who/which* clause.
	Do not put a comma in front of a prepositional phrase.
Usage	Change *remains* (present tense) to *remained* (past tense).
Note	Real toads do not have actual warts, just bumps that appear like warts.

Rewrite It! Instantly Dorinda plummeted to the ground. All that remained was her crown, which was miniaturized to fit her diminished stature, and her beauty spot, which was prominent among the other toady warts.

Read It!	Mark It!	Fix It!	Day 4

That will teach you the fairy snapped, you
must learn humility, as a toad, and if you find a noble
gallant prince, who kiss you in kindheartedness
you will be restored to normal

gallant
brave and chivalrous

Mark It!	
1	coordinating conjunction (cc)
3	prepositional phrases
4	[main clauses]
1	who/which clause (w/w)
1	adverb clause (AC)
6	subject-verb pairs (s v)

Fix It!	
? indents	**1**
? capitals	**2**
? commas	**7**
? end marks	**3**
1 usage	

¶ "[That will teach you]," [the fairy snapped]. "[you
must learn humility, as a toad]. and (if you find a noble,
gallant prince), (who kiss you in kindheartedness),
[you will be restored to normal]."

Indentation		new speaker
Conjunction		**and** connects two main clauses. However, the main clauses *You must learn humilty as a toad* and *you will be restored to normal* express different ideas, so they should be in different sentences. Replace the comma + cc with a period. Capitalize *If*.
S V Pairs	MC	**That will teach** This is a main clause because it expresses a complete thought. The demonstrative pronoun *That* is the subject pronoun.
	MC	**fairy snapped**
	MC	**You must learn**
	AC	**If you find** Restored how? *if you find …* (adverb clause)
	w/w	**who kisses** The *who* clause describes *prince*, the noun it follows. (adjective clause)
Ask Students		Is this *who* clause nonessential (needs commas) or essential? The *who* clause is essential to the sentence. It is not enough to find a prince. The prince must kiss her. Removing it from the sentence changes the meaning.
	MC	**you will be restored**
Commas		Use a comma to separate an attribution from a direct quote. PATTERN "Quote," attribution.
		Do not use a comma to separate two main clauses. Use a period. MC, MC is always wrong.
		Do not put a comma in front of a prepositional phrase.
		Use a comma to separate coordinate adjectives (noble, gallant prince).
		Use a comma after an adverb clause that comes before a main clause. PATTERN AC, MC There is no comma after *prince* because the *who* clause is essential to the AC. Do not place commas around an essential adjective clause.
Usage		Change *kiss* to *kisses*. The *who* clause describes the singular noun *prince*, the noun it follows. Therefore, the subject *who* is singular and requires a singular verb (kisses).

Rewrite It! "That will teach you," the fairy snapped. "You must learn humility as a toad. If you find a noble, gallant prince who kisses you in kindheartedness, you will be restored to normal."

Learn It!

Run-On

Week 10 you learned that a **run-on** occurs when a sentence has main clauses that are not connected properly. A run-on can be either a **fused sentence** or a **comma splice**.

For more information about run-ons, see page G-17.

You also learned three simple ways to fix a run-on:

- Place a period at the end of each main clause.

; Use a semicolon when two main clauses express a single idea and are similar in length or construction.

, cc Use a comma + coordinating conjunction (cc) when a cc logically expresses the relationship between the two main clauses.

A fourth way to fix a run-on is to change one of the clauses into an adverb clause by inserting a www word. Use a comma after, not before, an adverb clause.

Adverb Clause

because

[Dorinda's reduced height was a problem], [attendants were not used to looking down].

This passage contains two main clauses connected with a comma, which is a run-on (comma splice). Fix the run-on by inserting a www word before the second main clause, forming a dependent adverb clause. **PATTERN MC AC**

If

[The princess rested on the floor in the great hall], [someone might step on her].

This passage contains two main clauses connected with no punctuation, which is a run-on (fused sentence). Fix the run-on by inserting a www word before the first main clause, forming a dependent clause. **PATTERN AC, MC**

The www words are conjunctions that turn main clauses into dependent clauses. Because they subordinate—make secondary—the clause, they are called subordinating conjunctions.

To subordinate means to place at a lower order. Another term for a dependent clause is a subordinate clause because it is of less importance than the main clause.

Continue to look for and fix run-ons. Fix It! will indicate if you should fix a run-on with a coordinating conjunction (cc) or with an adverb clause (AC). Follow the comma rules.

Fix It   To *fix a run-on with cc,* insert a cc between two main clauses. Follow comma rule. **PATTERN MC, cc MC**

but

Dorinda deserved her punishment, she did not like it.

To *fix a run-on with AC,* insert a www word before a main clause, making it an adverb clause. Follow comma rules. **PATTERN AC, MC or MC AC**

Although

Dorinda deserved her punishment, she did not like it.

although

Dorinda deserved her punishment, she did not like it.

Contrasting Items

A **contrast** shows a striking difference between things. In writing we often use the words *not, although, while,* or *whereas* to show contrast.

❞ Use a comma to separate contrasting parts of a sentence.

Use a comma before *not* when it begins a contrasting phrase.

Everyone treated Dorinda as a toad**, not** a princess.
> A toad is strikingly different from a princess. Use a comma.

Use a comma before the www words *although, while,* or *whereas* when the adverb clause is strikingly different from the main clause before it.

You have learned you should not place a comma before an adverb clause (MC AC). Contrasting items, however, do take commas. Therefore, when an adverb clause is strikingly different from the main clause before it, use a comma. When two comma rules contradict, follow the rule that says to use a comma.

Palace staff used to cater to her**, whereas** now they mocked her.
> The adverb clause *whereas now they mocked her* is strikingly different from the statement *Palace staff used to cater to her.*

Fix It!   Use a comma before *not* when it begins a contrasting phrase.

Use a comma before *although, while,* or *whereas* when it begins a contrasting clause.

Dorinda was rude, not gracious.

She loathed her transformation, although there was one real benefit.

She could hide in rooms and eavesdrop, while that was impossible before.

While means "at the same time as" when it does not start a contrasting clause.

If you can replace the www word with *but,* it probably starts a contrasting clause.

When two comma rules contradict, follow the rule that says to use a comma.

Read It!	Mark It!	Fix It!	Day 1

Every day, the princess **mourned** her new lot in life. She found it difficult to convince anyone at the palace of her true identity, the crown, and beauty spot proved, she is the princess.

mourned
felt or expressed sorrow; grieved

1 coordinating conjunction (cc)
4 prepositional phrases
3 [main clauses]
1 *that* clause (that)
4 subject-verb pairs (s v)

? indents **1**
? capitals **1**
? commas **3**
? end marks **0**
1 usage
(fix run-on with AC)

¶ *(on)* Every day, [the princess **mourned** her new lot

Although

in life]. [She found it difficult to convince anyone

at the palace of her true identity], [the crown, and

beauty spot proved], *(that)* she ~~is~~ the princess).

Sentence openers are not marked in this passage because they may change once the passage has been fixed.

Indentation	new time
Conjunction	***and*** connects two nouns (subject nouns): *crown* and *beauty spot* a and b
S V Pairs	MC ***princess mourned***
	MC ***She found***
	MC ***crown, beauty spot proved***
	that *(that)* **she was** This is an invisible *that* clause. It does not express a complete thought.
Run-On	This passage contains three main clauses. A comma connects the second and third, which forms a run-on (comma splice). Fix the run-on by inserting a www word, forming a dependent clause: ***Although*** she found it difficult to convince anyone at the palace of her true identity, the beauty spot and crown proved she was the princess. **PATTERN AC, MC**
	The passage could also be fixed like this: She found it difficult to convince anyone at the palace of her true identity ***although*** the beauty spot and crown proved she was the princess. **PATTERN MC AC**
Invisible #2	*Every day* is a reference to time. Insert *on*. *(on) Every day* follows the prepositional **PATTERN preposition + noun (no verb).**
Commas	Do not use a comma if a prepositional opener has fewer than five words.
	Do not use a comma to separate two items connected with a cc. **PATTERN a and b**
	Do not put a comma in front of a *that* clause.
Usage	Change *is* (present tense) to *was* (past tense).

Rewrite It!   Every day the princess mourned her new lot in life. Although she found it difficult to convince anyone at the palace of her true identity, the crown and beauty spot proved she was the princess.

Read It!	Mark It!	Fix It!	Day 2

Lady Constance puzzled over the crown which looked familiar she tested Dorinda. If you truly are the princess she began Tell me about your **bona fide** wart not about that silly, beauty spot

bona fide
genuine; real

3 prepositional phrases	? indents **1**
4 [main clauses]	? capitals **1**
1 *who/which* clause (w/w)	? commas **6**
1 adverb clause (AC)	? end marks **1**
6 subject-verb pairs (s v)	4 quotation marks
1 opener	(fix run-on with cc)

① subject

¶ [Lady Constance puzzled over the crown], (which looked familiar), [she tested Dorinda]. "(If you truly are the princess)," [she began], "[(you) Tell me about your bona fide wart, not about that silly, beauty spot]."

Indentation	new speaker
S V Pairs MC	**Lady Constance puzzled**
w/w	**which looked** The *which* clause describes *crown*, the noun it follows. (adjective clause) It is nonessential because it does not change the meaning of the sentence. Without the *which* clause, Lady Constance still puzzled over the crown.
MC	**she tested**
AC	**If you are** Tell why? *If you truly are the princess* (adverb clause)
MC	**she began**
MC	**(you) tell** The subject of an imperative sentence is always *you*.
Run-On	This passage contains four main clauses. The first two are in one sentence, which forms a run-on (fused sentence). Fix the run-on by inserting a comma + cc: Lady Constance puzzled over the crown, which looked familiar, **so** she tested Dorinda. **PATTERN MC, cc MC**
Commas	Place commas around a nonessential *who/which* clause.
	Use a comma after an adverb clause. Although an attribution interrupts the quoted sentence, the pattern does not change: **PATTERN AC, MC**
	Use a comma to separate an attribution from a direct quote. **PATTERN** "Quote," attribution, "rest of quoted sentence."
	Use a comma to separate contrasting parts of a sentence (about your bona fide wart, **not** about that silly beauty spot).
	Do not use a comma to separate cumulative adjectives (silly beauty spot). *Silly* describes *beauty spot*. The word *beauty* forms a compound noun with the noun *spot*, similar to *ice cream* or *hot dog*.

Rewrite It!   Lady Constance puzzled over the crown, which looked familiar, so she tested Dorinda. "If you truly are the princess," she began, "tell me about your bona fide wart, not about that silly beauty spot."

Read It! **Mark It!** **Fix It!**

Luckily, that one was easy its true I have a
wart, hiding behind all my hair Dorinda croaked,
a palace maid **snickered** thats the reason
she never let us style her hair in 2 braids

snickered
uttered a partly stifled laugh

(3) -ly adverb

2 <u>prepositional phrases</u>	? indents **2**
6 [main clauses]	? capitals **3**
1 *that* clause (that)	? commas **3**
7 subject-verb pairs (s v)	? end marks **5**
2 openers	4 quotation marks
	2 apostrophes
	1 number

¶ Luckily, [that one was easy]. "[it's true]. [I have a

wart], hiding <u>behind all my hair</u>," [Dorinda croaked],.

(6) vss

¶ [a palace maid **snickered**]. "[that's the reason]

that
((that) she never let us style her hair <u>in 2 braids</u>)."
two

Indentation		new speaker; new speaker
S V Pairs	MC	**one was** This is a main clause. The word *that* functions as an adjective. Which one? *that*
	MC	**It's** The contraction *It's* includes both a subject (It) and a verb (is).
	MC	**I have**
	MC	**Dorinda croaked**
	MC	**maid snickered** *Snickered* is not a speaking verb. The period communicates that she snickers first and then speaks. If this were an attribution, she must snicker out these words, which is hard to do.
	MC	**That's** The contraction *That's* includes both a subject (That) and a verb (is). This is a main clause because it expresses a complete thought.
	that	**(that) she let** This is an invisible *that* clause. It does not express a complete thought.
Note		*(To) style* is an infinitive. It does not function as a verb. The word *to* is implied, not written. Although students might not recognize that this is an infinitive, they should know that they cannot mark a word as a verb unless it has a subject. Every verb has a subject.
Commas		Do not use a comma when a -ing phrase at the end of a sentence describes the word it follows.
		Use a comma to separate an attribution from a direct quote. **PATTERN "Quote," attribution.**
		Do not use a comma to separate two main clauses. Use a period. MC, MC is always wrong.
Number		Spell out numbers that can be expressed in one or two words.

Rewrite It!   Luckily, that one was easy. "It's true. I have a wart hiding behind all my hair,"
Dorinda croaked.

A palace maid snickered. "That's the reason she never let us style her hair in two
braids."

Read It!	Mark It!	Fix It!	Day 4

Dorinda glared. Lady Constance wasnt convinced, she pressed her again what was your nickname, when you were a toddler. Dorinda sighs **testily**, and tries to roll her eyes.

testily
impatiently; with irritation

Mark It!		Fix It!	
1 coordinating conjunction (cc)		? indents	**3**
5 [main clauses]		? capitals	**1**
1 adverb clause (AC)		? commas	**2**
6 subject-verb pairs (s v)		? end marks	**2**
		2 quotation marks	
		1 apostrophe	
		2 usage	
		(fix run-on with AC)	

¶ [Dorinda glared]. ¶ [Because Lady Constance wasn't convinced], [she pressed her again]. "[what was your nickname], AC (when you were a toddler),?" ¶ [Dorinda ~~sighs~~ **sighed testily**, cc and ~~tries~~ **tried** to roll her eyes].

Sentence openers are not marked in this passage because they may change once the passage has been fixed.

Indentation	new topic; new speaker; new topic
End Marks	The first quoted sentence is a question. Replace the period with a question mark.
Conjunction	**and** connects two verbs: *sighed* and *tried* MC cc 2nd verb
S V Pairs	MC **Dorinda glared**
	MC **Lady Constance was convinced** The contraction *wasn't* includes both a helping verb (was) and an adverb (not).
	MC **she pressed**
	MC **What was** *What* is an interrogative pronoun that begins a question. The noun *nickname* follows the linking verb and renames the subject.
	AC when **you were** Was when? *when you were a toddler* (adverb clause)
	MC **Dorinda sighed, tried**
Run-On	This passage contains five main clauses. A comma connects the second and third, which forms a run-on (comma splice). Fix the run-on by inserting a www word, forming a dependent clause: ***Because** Lady Constance wasn't convinced, she pressed her again.* **PATTERN AC, MC**
Commas	Do not put a comma in front of an adverb clause. **PATTERN MC AC**
	Do not use a comma before a cc when it connects two verbs. **PATTERN MC cc 2nd verb**
Usage	Change *sighs* (present tense) to *sighed* (past tense) and *tries* (present tense) to *tried* (past tense) .

Rewrite It!   Dorinda glared.

Because Lady Constance wasn't convinced, she pressed her again. "What was your nickname when you were a toddler?"

Dorinda sighed testily and tried to roll her eyes.

Learn It!

Words as Words

When referring to a specific word as a word, italicize the word or place it in quotation marks. If handwriting, place the word in quotation marks.

Dorinda used "please" to get her own way.

Dorinda used [the word] "please" to get her own way.
> If you can insert "the word" before the word in question, it is a word used as a word.

This rule also applies to letters. She wrote the [letter] "s" carefully.

Single Quotation Marks

Use **single quotation marks** for a quotation inside another quotation. The inside quotation may be the direct quote of someone's words, a title that needs quotations, or a word used as a word.

Fix It   Use quotations marks around words used as words.

Add single quotation marks for a quotation inside another quotation.

Dorinda's friends called her "Toady" because of the wart on her head.

Frederick said, "My favorite poem is 'The Purple Cow.'"

Adjective Clause and Appositive Phrase

Week 15 you learned that an adjective can be a single word, a phrase, or a clause.
A **clause** is a group of related words that contains both a subject and a verb.
A **phrase** is a group of related words that contains either a noun or a verb, never both.

An **adjective clause** commonly begins with *who, whom, whose,* or *which* and includes a subject and a verb. An adjective clause can also begin with *when, where,* or *that.* The entire clause describes the noun it follows and does the job of an adjective.

The toad (who wore a crown) was Princess Dorinda.
> *Who wore a crown* describes *toad,* the noun it follows. It begins with the word *who* and includes a subject (who) and a verb (wore).

The adjective clause usually comes immediately after the noun it modifies.

Most adjective clauses are essential (no commas) or nonessential (commas). *That* adjective clauses are always essential.

An **appositive** is a noun or noun phrase that renames the noun it follows. It is a phrase because it includes a noun, never a verb.

Princess Dorinda, the toad, felt sorry for herself.
> *The toad* is a noun phrase that renames the noun *Princess Dorinda.* It includes an article (the) and a noun (toad), not a verb.
> Another name for an appositive is the invisible *who/which* clause.
> Princess Dorinda, (who was) a toad, felt sorry for herself. Because the subject and verb (who was) are removed, the appositive is a phrase, not a clause.

Because the comma rules for the adjective clause and the appositive phrase are the same, students can mentally insert *who was* to determine if the appositive phrase requires commas.

Phrase or Clause?

A **phrase** is a group of related words that contains either a noun or a verb, never both.
A **clause** is a group of related words that contains both a subject and a verb.

Read each sentence and decide if the bolded words form a phrase or a clause.
    Circle the correct answer.

Lady Constance, **who raised the girls**, tested the toad's story.

phrase   (clause)

Lady Constance, **their governess**, wondered if a toad could be Dorinda.

(phrase)   clause

The toad's story, **which was an incredible tale**, seemed unbelievable.

phrase   (clause)

Frederick, **a prince in disguise**, believed the toad.

(phrase)   clause

Identify the opener as a #2 prepositional opener or a #5 clausal opener.
    Insert a comma if needed.

② prepositional

Pattern:
preposition + noun
(no verb)

comma if 5+ words

⑤ clausal

Pattern:
www word +
subject + verb

comma after clause
AC, MC

[**5**] Since the fairy had changed Dorinda, only Frederick believed her.

[**2**] Since that horrible event Dorinda felt sad.

[**5**] As she was no longer human, Dorinda viewed the world differently.

[**2**] As a toad Dorinda better appreciated Frederick.

[**2**] Before her transformation Dorinda cared only about herself.

[**5**] After the fairy changed her, Dorinda was more sympathetic.

[**2**] Until the event at the well, Dorinda was thoroughly selfish.

[**5**] Until she was restored, Dorinda would learn to manage as a toad.

[**2**] Because of Dorinda's new condition, palace staff mocked her.

[**5**] Because a toad's life was challenging, Dorinda became grateful for any kindness.

Read It!

as a child I was called toady I had a wart on the back of my head. As I aged my friends dropped it, since they realized that I wasnt a **toady** at all she snapped.

toady
someone who flatters excessively

Mark It!

4 <u>prepositional phrases</u>
4 [main clauses]
1 *that* clause (that)
2 adverb clauses (AC)
7 subject-verb pairs (s v)

Fix It!

? indents	**0**
? capitals	**2**
? commas	**3**
? end marks	**0**

4 quotation marks
1 apostrophe
(fix run-on with AC)

———

s   v   v   *because* s v

"as a child [I was called 'toady'] [∧ I had a wart

                           AC s   v   s

on the back of my head]. (As I aged), [my friends

v   AC   s   v   *that* s   v

dropped it], (since they realized) (that I wasn't a

s   v

toady at all)," [she snapped].

Capitalization	**Toady** uppercase, proper noun *Toady* was Dorinda's nickname.
Note	This is a pun on *toady*. The unkind nickname her friends gave Dorinda was due to the wart. To be a toady is to flatter someone in hopes of gain. Dorinda does not flatter others but expects others to toady to her.
Quotations	Place quotation marks around words used as words. *"As a child I was called [the word] 'Toady'* Since Dorinda is speaking, use single quotes around *Toady* for a quote within a quote.

S V Pairs					
	MC	*I was called*		MC	*I had*
	AC	*As I aged* Dropped when? *As I aged* (adverb clause)		MC	*friends dropped*
	AC	*since they realized* Dropped why? *since they realized*			
	that	*that I was* The contraction *wasn't* includes both a linking verb (was) and an adverb (not).		MC	*she snapped*

Ask Students	Explain the difference between *As a child* and *As I aged*. *As a child* is a prepositional phrase opener. Because it has three words, it does not have a comma. **PATTERN preposition + noun (no verb)** *As I aged* is an adverb clause opener and requires a comma. **PATTERN www word + subject + verb**
Run-On	This passage contains four main clauses. The first two are in one sentence, which forms a run-on (fused sentence). Fix the run-on by inserting a www word, forming a dependent clause: As a child, I was called 'Toady' **because** I had a wart on the back of my head. **PATTERN MC AC**
Commas	Use a comma after an adverb clause. **PATTERN AC, MC** Do not put a comma in front of an adverb clause. **PATTERN MC AC** Use a comma to separate an attribution from a direct quote. **PATTERN "Quote," attribution.**

Rewrite It! "As a child I was called 'Toady' because I had a wart on the back of my head. As I aged, they dropped it since they realized that I wasn't a toady at all," she snapped.

Read It! | **Mark It!** | **Fix It!** Day 2

The palace took her in no one wanted to touch her. Her skin in fact were rough warty and **repulsive** some acknowledged her whereas others ignored her the footmen, who once pampered her, snubbed her.

repulsive
causing deep dislike or aversion

1 coordinating conjunction (cc)	? indents **1**
1 prepositional phrase	? capitals **2**
5 [main clauses]	? commas **6**
1 who/which clause (w/w)	? end marks **2**
1 adverb clause (AC)	1 usage
7 subject-verb pairs (s v)	(fix run-on with cc)
4 openers	

① subject

s   v   **but**   s   v

¶ [The palace took her in], [no one wanted to touch her].

① subject   s   v

was   cc

[Her skin, in fact, ~~were~~ rough, warty, and **repulsive**].

① subject

s   v   AC   s   v

[some acknowledged her], (whereas others ignored her).

① subject   s   w/w   s   v   v

[the footmen, (who once pampered her), snubbed her].

Indentation		new topic
Conjunction		**and** connects three adjectives: *rough*, *warty*, and *repulsive* a, b, and c
S V Pairs	MC	**palace took**
	MC	**no one wanted** No one is a compound word. It is an indefinite pronoun.
	MC	**skin was**
	MC	**Some acknowledged**
	AC	*whereas* **others ignored** Acknowledged when? *whereas others ignored her* (adverb)
	MC	**footmen snubbed**
	w/w	**who pampered** The *who* clause describes *footmen*, the noun it follows. (adjective clause)
Note		This *who* clause could be either essential or nonessential.
		With commas it is saying that all footmen snubbed her, and, incidentally, all once toadied to her.
		Without commas it is saying that only those footmen who used to toady to her snubbed her.
Run-On		This passage contains five main clauses. The first two are in one sentence, which forms a run-on (fused sentence). Fix the run-on by inserting a comma + cc: The palace took her in, **but** no one wanted to touch her. **PATTERN MC, cc MC**
Commas		Place commas around a transitional prepositional phrase. **, in fact,**
		When two comma rules contradict, follow the rule that says to use a comma.
		A comma is needed after *her* because of this rule: Use a comma to separate contrasting parts of a sentence (Some acknowledged her, **whereas** others ignored her).
		A comma is not needed after *her* because of this rule: Do not put a comma in front of an adverb clause. **PATTERN MC AC**
Usage		Change *were* to *was*. The singular subject *skin* requires a singular verb (ends in *s*).

Rewrite It!   The palace took her in, but no one wanted to touch her. Her skin, in fact, was rough, warty, and repulsive. Some acknowledged her, whereas others ignored her. The footmen, who once pampered her, snubbed her.

Read It!	Mark It!	Fix It!	Day 3

Maribella normally a sympathetic sister shuddered, whenever Dorinda **pattered**, into the room and even King Morton had nothing hopeful to offer his daughter.

pattered
walked lightly or quickly

1 coordinating conjunction (cc)	? indents	**0**
1 prepositional phrase	? capitals	**1**
2 [main clauses]	? commas	**4**
1 adverb clause (AC)	? end marks	**1**
3 subject-verb pairs (s v)		
1 invisible who/which clause (w/w)		
2 openers		

(1) subject
S   w/w

[Maribella, ((who was) normally a sympathetic sister),

    v   AC   s   v

shuddered], (whenever Dorinda **pattered**, into the

        cc   (1) subject   s   v

room). ~~and~~ [even King Morton had nothing hopeful

to offer his daughter].

Conjunction	**and** connects two main clauses. However, the main clauses express different ideas and work better as different sentences. Replace the coordinating conjunction with a period. Capitalize *Even*.
S V Pairs	MC *Maribella shuddered*
	AC whenever **Dorinda pattered** Shuddered when? *whenever Dorinda pattered into the room* (adverb clause)
	MC *King Morton had*
Invisible w/w	*(who was) normally a sympathetic sister* is an invisible *who* clause. With the words *who was* removed, the noun *sister* follows the noun *Maribella* and renames it. *Sister* functions as an appositive because the subject and the verb (who was) are not in the phrase.
Commas	Place commas around a nonessential invisible *who/which* clause (appositive phrase).
	Do not put a comma in front of an adverb clause. **PATTERN MC AC**
	Do not put a comma in front of a prepositional phrase.

Rewrite It! Maribella, normally a sympathetic sister, shuddered whenever Dorinda pattered into the room. Even King Morton had nothing hopeful to offer his daughter.

Read It!	Mark It!	Fix It!	Day 4

Dorindas basic needs were met the **luster** had gone out of her life. Moping around the palace Dorinda complained constantly. Living as a toad devastated the princess

luster
brightness

3 <u>prepositional phrases</u>
4 [main clauses]
4 subject-verb pairs (s v)

? indents	0
? capitals	0
? commas	2
? end marks	1
1 apostrophe	
(fix run-on with AC)	

Although

[∧Dorinda's basic needs were met], [the **luster** had gone out of her life]. Moping around the palace,

[Dorinda complained constantly]. [Living as a toad devastated the princess].

Sentence openers are not marked in this passage because they may change once the passage has been fixed.

S V Pairs	MC ***needs were met***
	MC ***luster had gone***
	MC ***Dorinda complained***
	MC ***Living devastated*** What devastated? *Living* (subject noun)
Run-On	This passage contains four main clauses. The first two are in one sentence, which forms a run-on (fused sentence). Fix the run-on by inserting a www word, forming a dependent clause: ***Although*** Dorinda's basic needs were attended to, the luster had gone out of her life. PATTERN AC, MC The passage could also be fixed like this: Dorinda's basic needs were met ***although*** the luster had gone out of her life. PATTERN MC AC
Commas	Use a comma after an -ing opener. PATTERN -ing word/phrase, main clause The thing after the comma must be the thing doing the inging. *Dorinda* is doing the *moping*.

Rewrite It! Although Dorinda's basic needs were met, the luster had gone out of her life. Moping around the palace, Dorinda complained constantly. Living as a toad devastated the princess.

Learn It!

#4 -ing Opener

Week 5 you learned that a **#4 -ing opener** is a sentence that begins with a participial (-ing) phrase. A legal, grammatical #4 sentence opener follows the PATTERN **-ing word/phrase, main clause.**

For more information about illegal #4 openers, see page G-44.

Legal #4 Opener

A #4 -ing opener is a legal, grammatically correct #4 -ing opener when the thing after the comma (subject of main clause) is the thing doing the inging.

④ -ing

Adjusting his crown, King Morton sighed.

> *King Morton* is the thing (subject of main clause) after the comma. *King Morton* is doing the *adjusting*. This is a legal #4 -ing opener.

Illegal #4 Opener

A #4 -ing opener is an illegal, grammatically incorrect #4 -ing opener when the thing after the comma is not the thing doing the inging.

 -ing

Adjusting his crown, it was heavy.

> *It* is the thing (subject of main clause) after the comma. *It* (the crown) is not doing the *adjusting*.

> This is an illegal #4 -ing opener and must be rewritten so that the person adjusting the crown is the thing (subject of main clause) after the comma.

 -ing

Raising his voice, King Morton's impatience was obvious.

> It looks like King Morton is the thing after the comma. However, *King Morton's* is an adjective describing *impatience*. *Impatience* is not doing the *raising*.

> This is an illegal #4 -ing opener and must be rewritten so that King Morton, the person raising his voice, is the thing (subject of main clause) after the comma.

An illegal #4 is either a dangling modifier or a misplaced modifier.

A dangling modifier occurs when the noun that the -ing phrase describes is not in the sentence.

A misplaced modifier occurs when the noun that the -ing phrase describes is in the sentences but is not the subject of the sentence.

Find It!   Check that the thing (subject of main clause) after the comma is the thing doing the inging.

Ask students to check if the thing after the comma is the thing doing the inging.

Fix It!   Rewrite if necessary.

④ -ing   *heavy*   *King Morton sighed.*

Adjusting his crown, ~~it was heavy~~.
                  ∧

④ -ing   *King Morton showed impatience.*

Raising his voice, ~~King Morton's impatience was obvious~~.

There is often more than one way to rewrite an illegal #4 sentence.

Rewrite so *King Morton* is the thing (subject of main clause) after the comma. In this case, a verb must be added to the main clause.

Rewrite so *King Morton* is the thing (subject of main clause) after the comma.

If a main clause does not follow the comma, the sentence is neither a #2 prepositional opener nor a #4 -ing opener. It is a #1 subject opener. Remove the comma.

If the sentence begins with *concerning*, *according to*, *regarding*, or *during*, it is a #2 prepositional opener. Use a comma if 5+ words.

If the sentence is a #4 -ing opener, make sure the thing after the comma is the thing doing the inging.

Dipping (S) improved (V) is a #1 subject opener. Remove the comma.

Dorinda is not dripping; the bread is. The thing after the comma should be *bread*.

During is a preposition. Remove the comma because this prepositional opener has three words.

According to is a preposition. Leave the comma because this prepositional opener has five words.

The thing after the comma (*Frederick*) is doing the hopping. This is a legal #4. The comma is correct.

Back is not the one leaping; *Dorinda* is. *Dorinda's* is an adjective, not a thing. The thing (subject) after the comma should be Dorinda. Remove the comma.

Straining (S) made (V) is a #1 subject opener. Remove the comma.

The thing after the comma (*Frederick*) is doing the opening. This is a legal #4. The comma is correct.

What Is the Sentence Opener?

As you learned Week 18, an impostor #4 begins with a #1 subject opener (the subject of the sentence) or a #2 prepositional opener (concerning, according to, regarding, during).

A legal #4 -ing opener follows the **PATTERN -ing word/phrase, main clause.**
The thing after the comma is the thing doing the inging.

An illegal #4 appears to follow the pattern, but the thing after the comma is not the thing doing the inging. The sentence is grammatically incorrect.

Read each sentence and decide if it begins with a #1 subject opener, #2 prepositional opener, #4 -ing participial opener or if the sentence is illegal (grammatically incorrect). Remove the comma if it is incorrect.

Dipping her bread in the fly soup, improved its taste.

(#1) #2 #4 illegal

Dripping in cream, Dorinda gobbled her bread.

#1 #2 #4 (illegal)

During the afternoon, Frederick and Dorinda escaped to the library.

#1 (#2) #4 illegal

According to the head librarian, Frederick's book sat on the lowest shelf.

#1 (#2) #4 illegal

Hopping into the room, Frederick reached the bookshelf before Dorinda.

#1 #2 (#4) illegal

Leaping onto the footstool, Dorinda's back was sore.

#1 #2 #4 (illegal)

Straining her back, made Dorinda irritable.

(#1) #2 #4 illegal

Opening the cover, Frederick sighed with contentment.

#1 #2 (#4) illegal

Read It!	Mark It!	Fix It!	Day 1

Miserably, Dorinda wandered into the infirmary to **commiserate**, with her fellow amphibian. Mending rapidly Dorinda shared her gloomy thoughts, while Frederick listened sympathetically.

commiserate
share in feelings of sadness or sympathy

Mark It!	
2 prepositional phrases	
2 [main clauses]	
1 adverb clause (AC)	
3 subject-verb pairs (s v)	
2 openers	

Fix It!	
? indents	1
? capitals	0
? commas	4
? end marks	0
1 illegal #4 opener	

③ -ly adverb

¶ Miserably, [Dorinda wandered into the infirmary to
  s   v

④ -ing

commiserate, with her fellow amphibian]. Mending

  s   v   AC
rapidly, [Dorinda shared her gloomy thoughts], (while

  s   v   *while Dorinda shared her gloomy thoughts*
Frederick listened sympathetically) ∧ .

Indentation	new topic	
S V Pairs	MC ***Dorinda wandered***	
	MC ***Dorinda shared***	
	AC *while **Frederick listened*** Shared when? *while Frederick listened sympathetically* (adverb clause)	
Ask Students	Is the thing after the comma the thing doing the inging?	
	No, it is not Dorinda who is mending but Frederick. This is an illegal #4 opener (a dangling modifier).	
Illegal #4	Rewrite the second sentence so that Frederick is the thing (subject of main clause) after the comma: *Mending rapidly, Frederick listened sympathetically while Dorinda shared her gloomy thoughts.*	
Commas	Do not use a comma if an -ly adverb opener modifies the verb. Dorinda wandered in a miserable manner.	
	Do not put a comma in front of a prepositional phrase.	
	Use a comma after an -ing opener. **PATTERN -ing word/phrase, main clause** The thing after the comma must be the thing doing the inging. *Frederick* is doing the *mending*.	
	Do not put a comma in front of an adverb clause. **PATTERN MC AC**	

Rewrite It!   Miserably Dorinda wandered into the infirmary to commiserate with her fellow amphibian. Mending rapidly, Frederick listened sympathetically while Dorinda shared her gloomy thoughts.

Read It!	Mark It!	Fix It!	Day 2

According to Frederick "being a frog wasnt that dreadful," while people werent always **humane** he was free to live as he pleased. Dorinda whom remained discouraged listened yet doubted.

humane
showing compassion for people and animals

Mark It!		Fix It!	
1 coordinating conjunction (cc)		? indents	**0**
1 <u>prepositional phrase</u>		? capitals	**1**
3 [main clauses]		? commas	**4**
1 *who/which* clause (w/w)		? end marks	**1**
2 adverb clauses (AC)		2 quotation marks	
6 subject-verb pairs (s v)		2 apostrophes	
3 openers		1 usage	

② prepositional

<u>According to Frederick</u> ["being a frog wasn't that dreadful],". (while people weren't always **humane**),

[he was free to live] (as he pleased). [Dorinda,

(w̶h̶o̶m̶ remained discouraged), listened yet doubted].

Quotations	Do not use quotation marks around an indirect quote. The same sentence using a direct quote: "Being a frog isn't that dreadful. While people aren't always humane, I am free to live as I please."
Conjunction	**yet** connects two verbs: *listened* yet *doubted* MC cc 2nd verb
Ask Students	What four prepositions end with the letters *ing*? concerning, according to, regarding, during
Preposition	*According to Frederick* is a prepositional phrase, not a participial (-ing) phrase. Mark it as a #2 prepositional opener. It contains three words, so it does not need a comma.
S V Pairs	MC **being was** What wasn't? *being* (subject noun) The contraction *wasn't* includes both a linking verb (was) and an adverb (not).
	AC *while* **people were** The contraction *weren't* includes both a linking verb (were) and an adverb (not). Was free to live how? *while people weren't always humane* (adverb clause)
	MC **he was**
	AC *as* **he pleased** Was free to live how? *as he pleased* (adverb clause)
	MC **Dorinda listened, doubted**
	w/w **who remained** Change *whom* (objective) to *who* (subjective). The subject is *who*. Rule: Use *who* when the subject of the clause is *who*. The *who* clause describes *Dorinda*, the noun it follows. (adjective clause) It is nonessential because it does not change the meaning of the sentence.
Commas	Do not use a comma to separate two main clauses. Use a period. MC, MC is always wrong. Use a comma after an adverb clause that comes before a main clause. **PATTERN AC, MC** Place commas around a nonessential *who/which* clause.
Usage	Change the pronoun *whom* (objective) to *who* (subjective).

Rewrite It! According to Frederick being a frog wasn't that dreadful. While people weren't always humane, he was free to live as he pleased. Dorinda, who remained discouraged, listened yet doubted.

Read It!	Mark It!	Fix It!	Day 3

Trying to cheer her Dorinda agreed when Frederick offered to read a few stories he **regaled** her with humorous, fairy tales and wild stirring adventures, from the novel "the arabian nights."

regaled
entertained agreeably

Mark It!	Fix It!
1 coordinating conjunction (cc)	? indents **1**
2 prepositional phrases	? capitals **4**
2 [main clauses]	? commas **4**
1 adverb clause (AC)	? end marks **1**
3 subject-verb pairs (s v)	2 quotation marks
1 invisible who/which clause (w/w)	1 illegal #4 opener
2 openers	

④ -ing

¶ Trying to cheer her, [Dorinda agreed] (when Frederick offered to read a few stories)]. [he regaled her with humorous, fairy tales and wild, stirring adventures, from the novel] (which was) "the arabian nights)."

①subject

Indentation	new topic
Capitalization	*The Arabian Nights* is the title of a book. Capitalize the first letter of every word in this title.
Quotations	Do not use quotation marks around the title of a novel (book). The title should be italicized if typed and underlined if handwritten.
Conjunction	**and** connects two nouns (objects of the preposition): *tales* and *adventures* a and b
S V Pairs	MC **Dorinda agreed**
	AC *when Frederick offered* Agreed when? *when Frederick offered* (adverb clause)
Illegal #4	Dorinda was not trying; Frederick was. Rewrite so *Frederick* is the thing (subject of main clause) after the comma: *Trying to cheer her, Frederick offered to read a few stories.* It is also correct to write *Trying to cheer her, Frederick offered to read a few stories. Dorinda agreed.*
	MC **He regaled**
Invisible w/w	*(which was) The Arabian Nights* is an invisible *which* clause. With the words *which was* removed, the book title *The Arabian Nights* follows the noun *novel* and renames it. *The Arabian Nights* functions as an essential appositive because it defines which novel Frederick regaled her with. Do not use commas.
Commas	Use a comma after an -ing opener. **PATTERN -ing word/phrase, main clause** The thing after the comma must be the thing doing the inging. *Frederick* is doing the *trying*.
	Do not use a comma to separate cumulative adjectives (humorous fairy tales). *Humorous* describes *fairy tales*. The word *fairy* forms a compound noun with the noun *tales*, similar to *ice cream* or *hot dog*.
	Use a comma to separate coordinate adjectives (wild, stirring adventures).
	Do not put a comma in front of a prepositional phrase.

Rewrite It!   Trying to cheer her, Frederick offered to read a few stories. He regaled her with humorous fairy tales and wild, stirring adventures from the novel *The Arabian Nights*.
Note: Students underline book titles when handwriting.

Read It!	Mark It!	Fix It!	Day 4

Day after day Frederick entertained Dorinda. Gradually, she grew to appreciate his companionship, and to respect his positive **demeanor**, and living daily, without complaint characterized Fredericks life.

demeanor
conduct; behavior

Mark It!	Fix It!	
2 coordinating conjunctions (cc)	? indents	0
3 prepositional phrases	? capitals	1
3 [main clauses]	? commas	5
3 subject-verb pairs (s v)	? end marks	1
3 openers	1 apostrophe	

② prepositional

(during) Day after day, [Frederick entertained Dorinda].
                        s   v

③ -ly adverb
                    s   v
Gradually, [she grew to appreciate his companionship,

                                          ① subject
        cc   cc   s
and to respect his positive **demeanor**. ~~and~~ [living daily,

                        v
without complaint characterized Frederick's life].

Conjunction	**and** connects two infinitive phrases: *to appreciate* ... and *to respect* ... a and b
	and connects two main clauses. However, the main clauses express different ideas and work better as different sentences. Replace the comma + cc with a period. Capitalize *Living*.
S V Pairs	MC ***Frederick entertained***
	MC ***she grew***
	MC ***Living characterized*** What characterized? *Living* (subject noun)
Invisible #2	*Day* is a reference to time. Insert *during*. *(during) Day* follows the prepositional **PATTERN preposition + noun (no verb)**.
Commas	If two or more prepositional phrases open a sentence, follow the last phrase with a comma.
	Do not use a comma if an -ly adverb opener modifies the verb. Dorinda grew to appreciate in a gradual manner.
	Do not use a comma to separate two items connected with a cc. **PATTERN a and b**
	Do not put a comma in front of a prepositional phrase.

Rewrite It! Day after day, Frederick entertained Dorinda. Gradually she grew to appreciate his companionship and to respect his positive demeanor. Living daily without complaint characterized Frederick's life.

Learn It!

Usage with Affect and Effect
Usage errors occur when a word is used incorrectly.

For more information about usage, see page G-35.

v
Dorinda was deeply affected by her transformation.
  Affect is a verb that means to have an influence or to cause.

The definitions given for *affect* and *effect* are the most commonly used.

n
One effect of becoming a toad was surprisingly positive.
  Effect is a noun that means the result of some action.

Fix It!   Cross out the incorrect use of *affect* or *effect*.

Trials did not negatively affect/~~effect~~ Frederick.

Dorinda noticed the ~~affect~~/effect of his positive attitude.

Verb Review
Every verb has a subject. A verb acts alone or in phrases to perform different actions.
  An **action verb** (av) shows action or ownership.
  A **linking verb** (lv) links the subject to a noun or to an adjective.
  A **helping verb** (hv) helps an action verb or a linking verb. The helping verb and the verb it helps (action or linking) form a verb phrase.

Mark every subject. Mark every verb as an action verb (*av*), linking verb (*lv*), or helping verb (*hv*) in the following sentences.

Remind students that adjectives follow linking verbs and describe the subject.

  s   *av*   *s* *hv* *av*
Frederick thought that he would gag at the strange food.

 s *lv*   *s* *hv*   *av*   *av*
He was surprised that he did not choke but swallowed it easily.

In the second sentence *Surprised* is an adjective, not a verb. He did not surprise anyone. *Was* is a linking verb that links the subject *He* to the adjective *surprised*.

  s   *lv*   *s*   *av*
The food tasted bitter, but it satisfied his hunger.

  s   *av*   *av*
The chef kindly prepared and served him insect delicacies.

In the third sentence *tasted* is a linking verb that links the subject *food* to the adjective *bitter*.

  s   *hv* *av*   *s*   *av*
Frederick had encouraged Dorinda to eat, but she refused.

 s *hv* *hv* *lv*
She should have been grateful.

When *to* comes before a word, the word does not function as a verb. *To eat* is an infinitive. It does not have a subject and does not function as a verb.

Review It!   Weeks 24–25 mark every verb as an action verb (*av*), linking verb (*lv*), or helping verb (*hv*).

In the final sentence *should have been* is a linking verb with its helping verbs that links the subject *She* to the adjective *grateful*.

Semicolon Review

A **semicolon** connects two main clauses that are closely related. The two main clauses express a single idea and are similar in length or construction.

Put a √ in the blanks of the following sentences that use a semicolon correctly. Put an X in the blank of those that misuse the semicolon. Replace misused semicolons with periods.

X Frederick counted ten flies in his soup;. around the bowl and above the table hovered twenty more flies watching for the next dish.

√ The frog side of his personality enjoyed the flies; the human side was disgusted by them.

X The orderly was kind to bring him fly soup on a tray;. that way, spills were better contained.

√ Frederick sometimes savored a snail; he even relished an occasional slug.

√ Dorinda could not eat a spider; she would not touch the worm.

X Frederick explained that mealworms and crickets were healthy food for toads;. Dorinda shuddered at the mere thought of them.

The main clauses express two different ideas and differ in length. The first main clause tells that Frederick counted the flies in his soup. The second main clause talks about other flies in the area. These should be separate sentences.

The main clauses are similar in length and meaning. They express the two sides of Frederick's personality. The semicolon is correct.

The main clauses are similar in length, but they express two different ideas. The first main clause tells that the orderly was kind to use a tray. The second main clause tells the benefit of the tray. These should be separate sentences.

The main clauses are similar in length and meaning. They express two things he would enjoy eating. The semicolon is correct.

The main clauses are similar in length and meaning. They talk about different foods that Dorinda would not eat. The semicolon is correct.

The main clauses express two different ideas. The first main clause tells what Frederick said about toads' diets. The second main clause gives Dorinda's reaction to his words. These should be separate sentences.

Read It!	Mark It!	Fix It!	Day 1

Frederick always cheerfully greeted the orderly delivering his **odious** fly soup he didnt grumble, although the chef served him chocolate-covered beetles for dessert.

odious
highly offensive; repugnant; disgusting

Mark It!
1 prepositional phrase
2 [main clauses]
1 adverb clause (AC)
3 subject-verb pairs (s v)
2 openers

Fix It!
? indents   **0**
? capitals   **1**
? commas   **1**
? end marks   **1**
1 apostrophe

(1) subject
S
             V
             av

[Frederick always cheerfully greeted the orderly

(1) subject
     S   V   V
       hv   av

delivering his **odious** fly soup]. [he didn't grumble],

AC   S   V
              av

(although the chef served him chocolate-covered

beetles for dessert).

S V Pairs	MC	**Frederick greeted**
	MC	**He did grumble** The contraction *didn't* includes both a helping verb (did) and an adverb (not).
	AC	*although* **chef served** Did not grumble why? *although chef served him … beetles for dessert* (adverb clause)
Commas		Do not put a comma in front of an adverb clause. **PATTERN MC AC**
Note		Compound words can be spelled as one word, one hyphenated word, or two words. *chocolate-covered*

Rewrite It!   Frederick always cheerfully greeted the orderly delivering his odious fly soup. He didn't grumble although the chef served him chocolate-covered beetles for dessert.

Read It!	Mark It!	Fix It!	Day 2

Stumbling over his hurt leg Frederick didnt **chastise** Dorinda for her clumsiness, but readily forgave her, and she was grateful. His joyful attitude had a positive affect/effect on her.

chastise
criticize severely

- 2 coordinating conjunctions (cc)
- 3 prepositional phrases
- 3 [main clauses]
- 3 subject-verb pairs (s v)
- 2 openers

? indents	0
? capitals	0
? commas	3
? end marks	1
1 apostrophe	
2 usage	
1 illegal #4	

④ -ing

Dorinda was grateful that
s   v
hv

Stumbling <u>over his hurt leg</u>, [Frederick didn't

v
av   her   cc

chastise ~~Dorinda~~ <u>for her clumsiness</u>, but readily

v   s   v   ① subject
av   cc   lv

forgave her]. ~~and~~ [~~she was grateful~~]. [His joyful

s   v
av

attitude had a positive ~~affect~~/effect <u>on her</u>].

Conjunction		***but*** connects two verbs: *did chastise* but *forgave* MC cc 2nd verb ***and*** connects two main clauses. However, the main clauses express different ideas and work better as different sentences. Replace the comma + cc with a period.
S V Pairs	MC	***Frederick did chastise, forgave***
Illegal #4		Frederick was not stumbling; Dorinda was. Rewrite so *Dorinda* is the thing (subject of main clause) after the comma. As a subject, *Dorinda* requires a verb. One way to fix this passage is to move the main clause *she [Dorinda] was grateful*. There are other ways this could be rewritten.
	MC	***she was***
	MC	***attitude had***
Commas		Use a comma after an -ing opener. **PATTERN** -ing word/phrase, main clause The thing after the comma must be the thing doing the inging. *Dorinda* is doing the *stumbling*. Do not use a comma before a cc when it connects two verbs. **PATTERN** MC cc 2nd verb
Usage		Change *Dorinda* to *her* to avoid repetition. Use *effect*, a noun that refers to the result of some action.

Rewrite It!   Stumbling over his hurt leg, Dorinda was grateful that Frederick didn't chastise her for her clumsiness but readily forgave her. His joyful attitude had a positive effect on her.

Mark It! Fix It! Day 3

How do you always remain so cheerful,
Dorinda inquired 1 day. Unpleasant things
happen you show **empathy** for others. Clearly
trials do not affect/effect you

empathy
the ability to identify with someone else's feelings

Mark It!	
2 <u>prepositional phrases</u>	
5 [main clauses]	
5 subject-verb pairs (s v)	

Fix It!	
? indents	**1**
? capitals	**1**
? commas	**3**
? end marks	**2**
4 quotation marks	
1 number	
1 usage	
(fix run-on with AC)	

¶ "[How do you always remain so cheerful],?"
[Dorinda inquired (on) 1 day]. "[Although Unpleasant things
happen], [you show **empathy** <u>for others</u>]. Clearly,
[trials do not affect/effect you]."

Indentation	new speaker
End Marks	The first quoted sentence is a question. Replace the comma between the quote and the attribution with a question mark. **PATTERN** "Quote?" attribution.
S V Pairs	MC *you do remain*
	MC *Dorinda inquired*
	MC *things happen*
	MC *you show*
	MC *trials do affect*
Run-On	This passage contains five main clauses. Nothing connects the third and fourth, which forms a run-on (fused sentence). Fix the run-on by inserting a www word, forming a dependent clause: ***Although*** unpleasant things happen, you show empathy for others. **PATTERN AC, MC**
Commas	Use a comma if an -ly adverb opener modifies the sentence. It was clear that trials do not affect you.
Number	Spell out numbers that can be expressed in one or two words.
Usage	Use *affect*, a verb that means to have an influence or to cause.

Rewrite It!   "How do you always remain so cheerful?" Dorinda inquired one day. "Although unpleasant things happen, you show empathy for others. Clearly, trials do not affect you."

Read It!	Mark It!	Fix It!	Day 4

Oh thats simple. When I am angry folks avoid me, when I am kind they spend time with me. After all why should I be **discontent** I am comfortable fed and watered

discontent
dissatisfied or unhappy

Mark It!
1 coordinating conjunction (cc)
2 prepositional phrases
5 [main clauses]
2 adverb clauses (AC)
7 subject-verb pairs (s v)

Fix It!
? indents — **1**
? capitals — **0**
? commas — **7**
? end marks — **2**
2 quotation marks
1 semicolon
1 apostrophe

¶ "Oh, [that's simple]. (When I am angry), [folks avoid me]; (when I am kind), [they spend time with me]. After all, [why should I be **discontent**]? [I am comfortable, fed, and watered]."

Indentation	new speaker		
Interjection	*Oh,* is an interjection that expresses a mild emotion.		
Conjunction	*and* connects three adjectives: *comfortable, fed,* and *watered* a, b, and c		
S V Pairs	MC	*that's* The contraction *That's* includes both a subject (That) and a verb (is).	
	AC	*when **I am*** Avoid when? *when I am angry* (adverb clause)	
	MC	*folks avoid*	
	AC	*when **I am*** Spend time when? *when I am kind* (adverb clause)	
	MC	*they spend*	
	MC	*I should be*	
	MC	*I am*	
Ask Students	What is the best way to fix the run-on (comma splice)? Use a semicolon. Both main clauses begin with an adverb clause and express a single idea.		
Comma	Use a comma after an interjection that does not expresses strong emotion. *Oh,*		
	Use a comma after an adverb clause. **PATTERN AC, MC**		
	Do not use a comma to separate two main clauses. Use a period or semicolon. MC, MC is always wrong.		
	Use a comma if a prepositional opener functions as a transition. *After all,*		
	Use commas to separate three or more items in a series connected with a cc. **PATTERN a, b, and c**		

Rewrite It!   "Oh, that's simple. When I am angry, folks avoid me; when I am kind, they spend time with me. After all, why should I be discontent? I am comfortable, fed, and watered."

Learn It!

Usage with Between and Among

Usage errors occur when a word is used incorrectly.

Surely <u>between the two</u> of them, they could get along.

> *Between* is a preposition that refers to two items.

<u>Among their various activities</u> Dorinda enjoyed reading best.

> *Among* is a preposition that refers to three or more items.

Fix It!   Cross out the incorrect use of *among* or *between.*

Dorinda searched for berries among/~~between~~ the worms on her plate.

Frederick waited for Dorinda ~~among~~/between the twin pillars.

Comparative and Superlative Adjectives

Comparative and superlative adjectives describe a noun by making a comparison.

A **comparative adjective** compares two items. Form it by adding the adverbs *more* or *less* or the suffix *-er* to an adjective.

Dorinda was the younger daughter; Maribella was the older daughter.

> This sentence compares two girls: Dorinda and Maribella. The comparative adjectives *younger* and *older* are used.

Dorinda was younger than all of her cousins.

> One or both of the items may form a group. Although this sentence mentions all of her cousins, it compares two items: Dorinda and cousins. The comparative adjective *younger* is used.

A **superlative adjective** compares three or more items. Form it by adding the adverbs *most* or *least* or the suffix *-est* to an adjective.

The great hall was the largest and most majestic room in the castle.

> This sentence compares the great hall with all the rooms in the castle. Since there are more than two rooms, the superlative adjectives *largest* and *most majestic* are used.

Than signals a comparison of two items.

Follow these rules to form comparative and superlative adjectives.

one syllable add suffix	three or more syllables use the adverbs	two syllables add suffix or use the adverbs	Some words form irregular comparatives and superlatives.	
-er -est	more or less most or least	In some cases, either way is acceptable although one form may be more common than the other.		
young younger youngest	**dangerous** more or less dangerous most or least dangerous	**clever** cleverer or more clever cleverest or most clever	**good** better best	**bad** worse worst

Do not make a double comparison.

> Incorrect: She was *more younger* than her sister.

If a two-syllable adjective ends in -y (tiny), -le (little), or -ow (narrow), use the suffix, not the adverb (tinier, not more tiny). Use a dictionary if in doubt.

Fix It!   Cross out the incorrect comparative or superlative adjective.

Frederick was kinder/~~kindest~~ than Dorinda.

Students continue to number every sentence opener in the story that Frederick reads except questions and quoted dialogue.

More on Quotation Marks

On Day 3 Frederick begins reading a story to Dorinda. Since he is speaking the words of the story, each paragraph must open with quotation marks to remind the reader that someone is still speaking. Closing quotation marks are used only when the speaker has finished.

Noun and Pronoun Function Review

A **noun** names a person, place, thing, or idea. A **pronoun** replaces a noun in order to avoid repetition. Week 11 you learned that both nouns and pronouns perform many functions (jobs) in a sentence; however, they can do only one function (job) at a time.

A **subject** is a noun or pronoun that performs a verb action. It tells who or what the clause is about.

An **object of the preposition** is a noun or pronoun at the end of a prepositional phrase. PATTERN preposition + noun (no verb)

A **noun of direct address** is a noun used to directly address someone. It only appears in a quoted sentence.

A **direct object** is a noun or pronoun that follows an action verb and answers the question *what* or *whom*. A direct object receives the verb's action. That means it completes the verb's meaning.

A **predicate noun** is a noun or pronoun that follows a linking verb and answers the question *what* or *whom*. A predicate noun renames the subject. The subject and predicate noun are different names for the same person, place, thing, or idea.

An **appositive** is a noun or noun phrase that renames the noun that comes immediately before it. It is a phrase because it includes a noun, never a verb.

In the following sentences mark every verb as an action verb (*av*), linking verb (*lv*), or helping verb (*hv*). Mark the function of every noun and pronoun.

> sn   av   nda   hv sp av   do
> Frederick asked, "Dorinda, can we play a game?"

> sn   sn   av   do
> Frederick and Dorinda played a game.

> sp   av   do   app   op
> They played checkers, a game on the table.

> sn   lv   pn   op
> Cribbage was another game on the table.

Review It!   Continue to mark every verb as *av*, *lv*, or *hv*.

This week mark every subject noun (*sn*), subject pronoun (*sp*), object of the preposition (*op*), noun of direct address (*nda*), direct object (*do*), predicate noun (*pn*), and appositive (*app*).

Read It!	Mark It!	Fix It!	Day 1

The next day, Frederick **rummaged** through the bookshelves in the library, he remembered a tale that his mother had read to him, when he was a boy; he searched for the story among/between the books.

rummaged
searched through actively

13 noun/pronoun jobs
6 prepositional phrases
3 [main clauses]
1 *that* clause (that)
1 adverb clause (AC)
5 subject-verb pairs (s v)
3 openers

? indents   **1**
? capitals   **2**
? commas   **3**
? end marks   **2**
1 semicolon
1 usage

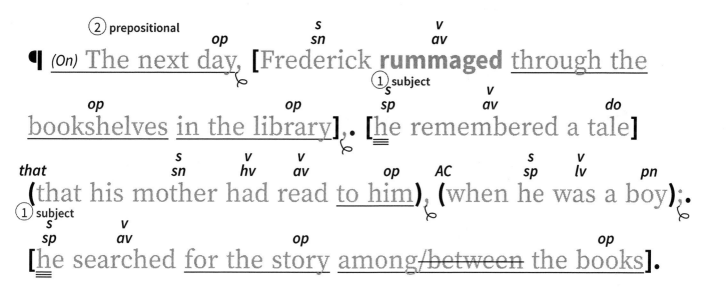

Indentation	new time
S V Pairs	MC ***Frederick rummaged***
	MC ***He remembered*** He remember what? The noun *tale* follows the AV and functions as the direct object.
	that *that **mother had read***
	AC *when **he was*** The noun *boy* follows the linking verb and renames the subject. *Boy* functions as a predicate noun. Read when? *when he was a boy* (adverb clause)
	MC ***he searched***
Invisible #2	*The next day* is a reference to time. *(On) The next day* follows the prepositional **PATTERN preposition + noun (no verb).** Mark as a #2 prepositional opener.
Semicolon	The second and third main clauses express two different ideas and are different in length and construction. The main clauses should be separate sentences.
Commas	Do not use a comma if a prepositional opener has fewer than five words.
	Do not use a comma to separate two main clauses. Use a period. MC, MC is always wrong.
	Do not put a comma in front of an adverb clause. **PATTERN MC AC**
Usage	Use *among*, a preposition that refers to three or more items.

Rewrite It!   The next day Frederick rummaged through the bookshelves in the library. He remembered a tale that his mother had read to him when he was a boy. He searched for the story among the books.

| Read It! | Mark It! | Fix It! | Day 2 |

At last he saw a thin book among/between 2 large volumes. He desired this **precise** book, because it included the hound and the king's nephew. She would hear the story, she would learn a lesson.

precise
exact; specific

13 noun/pronoun jobs	? indent **0**
1 conjunction (cc)	? capitals **4**
2 prepositional phrases	? commas **2**
4 [main clauses]	? end marks **0**
1 adverb clause (AC)	1 semicolon
5 subject-verb pairs (s v)	2 quotation marks
3 openers	1 number
	1 usage

② prepositional

At last [he saw a thin book ~~among~~/between 2̶ large volumes]. [He desired this **precise** book], (because it included "the hound and the king's nephew)."
[She would hear the story]; [she would learn a lesson].

Capitalization	"The Hound and the King's Nephew" is the title of a short story found within a book. Do not capitalize conjunctions (and) or articles (the) unless they are the first or last word in the title.
Quotations	Place titles found within a larger source in quotation marks.
Conjunction	**and** connects two nouns: *Hound* and *Nephew* a and b
S V Pairs MC	**he saw** He saw what? The noun *book* follows the AV and functions as the direct object.
MC	**He desired** He desired what? The noun *book* follows the AV and functions as the direct object.
AC	*because **it included*** It included what? The noun phrase "The Hound and the King's Nephew" follows the AV and functions as the direct object. The words *Hound* and *Nephew* are both nouns in the story's title. Desired why? *because it included* ... (adverb clause)
MC	**She would hear** She would hear what? The noun *story* follows the AV and functions as the direct object.
MC	**she would learn** She would learn what? The noun *lesson* follows the AV and functions as the direct object.
Semicolon	A comma connects the third and fourth main clauses, which forms a run-on (comma splice). MC, MC is always wrong. Fix the run-on by inserting a semicolon. Both main clauses, *She would hear the story* and *she would learn a lesson*, express a single idea and are similar in length and construction.
Commas	Do not put a comma in front of an adverb clause. **PATTERN MC AC**
Number	Spell out numbers that can be expressed in one or two words.
Usage	Use *between*, a preposition that refers to two items.

Rewrite It!   At last he saw a thin book between two large volumes. He desired this precise book because it included "The Hound and the King's Nephew." She would hear the story; she would learn a lesson.

Read It!

Students should mark the openers in the story that Frederick reads. They do not mark openers for dialogue or conversational quotations between characters.

"Dorinda listen as I read. "King Arthur" he began "was riding with his nephew. Robert the elder/eldest son of his sisters 3 boys enjoyed the kings special favor regrettably he was a **mute** child.

mute
incapable of speech

Mark It!

11 noun/pronoun jobs
2 prepositional phrases
5 [main clauses]
1 adverb clause (AC)
6 subject-verb pairs (s v)
1 invisible who/which clause (w/w)
3 openers

Fix It!   Day 3

? indents	**2**
? capitals	**1**
? commas	**6**
? end marks	**1**
2 apostrophes	
1 number	
1 usage	

¶ "Dorinda, [(you) listen] (as I read). ¶ "[King Arthur," [he began], "was riding with his nephew]. [Robert, ((who was) the elder/eldest son of his sister's 3 boys), enjoyed the king's special favor]. regrettably, [he was a **mute** child].

Since Frederick has not finished reading the story, do not end the passage with quotation marks.

Indentation	new speaker; new topic
Quotations	The quotation marks in this passage are correct. In continued speech with a new topic, end the first paragraph with no quotation marks to indicate a speaker is not finished. Start the new paragraph with quotation marks to remind the reader that someone is still speaking.
S V Pairs	MC **(you) listen** The subject of an imperative sentence is always *you*.
	AC *as I read* Listen when? *as I read* (adverb clause)
	MC **King Arthur was riding**
	MC **he began**
	MC **Robert enjoyed** Enjoyed what? The noun *favor* follows the action verb and functions as a direct object.
	MC **he was** He was what? The noun *child* follows the linking verb and renames the subject. *Child* functions as a predicate noun.
Invisible w/w	*(who was) the eldest son of his sister's three boys* is an invisible *who* clause. With the words *who was* removed, the noun *son* follows the noun *Robert* and renames it. *Son* functions as an appositive because the subject and the verb (who was) are not in the phrase.
Commas	Place commas around a noun of direct address (NDA). **Dorinda,**
	Use a comma to separate an attribution from a direct quote.
	PATTERN "Quote," attribution, "rest of quoted sentence."
	Place commas around a nonessential invisible *who/which* clause (appositive phrase).
	Use a comma if an -ly adverb opener modifies the sentence. It was regrettable that he was a mute child.
Number	Spell out numbers that can be expressed in one or two words.
Usage	Use the superlative adjective *eldest* because there are three boys.

Rewrite It!

"Dorinda, listen as I read.

"King Arthur," he began, "was riding with his nephew. Robert, the eldest son of his sister's three boys, enjoyed the king's special favor. Regrettably, he was a mute child.

Read It!	Mark It!	Fix It!	Day 4

They rode through the royal forest where they often hunted. Roberts beloved hound Balin remained, among/between them. They passed through a Cedar Grove Balin ran ahead barking **emphatically**.

emphatically
with force or insistence

Mark It!	
9 noun/pronoun jobs	
3 <u>prepositional phrases</u>	
4 [main clauses]	
5 subject-verb pairs (s v)	
3 openers	

Fix It!	
? indents	0
? capitals	2
? commas	6
? end marks	0
1 apostrophe	
1 usage	
(fix run-on with cc)	

(1) subject

s   v

sp   av   op   s / sp

[They rode <u>through the royal forest</u>], (*(which was)* where they

v / av   (1) subject   s / sn   app   v / av

often hunted). [Robert's beloved hound, Balin, remained,

(1) subject   s / sp   v / av

op

~~among~~/between them]. [They passed <u>through a C̸edar</u>

op   and   s / sn   v / av

<u>C̸rove</u>], [Balin ran ahead], barking **emphatically**.

Capitalization	Do not capitalize the common name of animals and plants. Just as you do not capitalize *oak tree* or *pine forest*, do not capitalize *cedar grove*.
S V Pairs	MC ***They rode***
	DC *where **they hunted*** The *where* clause describes *forest*, the noun it follows. (adjective clause)
	MC ***hound remained*** The noun *Balin* follows the noun *hound* and renames it. *Balin* functions as an appositive. Encourage students to mentally insert *who was. (who was) Balin* is an invisible *who* clause.
	MC ***They passed***
	MC ***Balin ran***
Run-On	This passage contains four main clauses. The last two are in one sentence, which forms a run-on (fused sentence). Fix the run-on by inserting a comma + cc: They passed through a cedar grove, ***and*** Balin ran ahead, barking emphatically. **PATTERN MC, cc MC**
Commas	Place commas around a nonessential adjective clause.
	Place commas around a nonessential appositive.
	Do not use a comma in front of a prepositional phrase.
	Use a comma when a -ing phrase at the end of a sentence describes a noun other than the word it follows.
Usage	Use *between*, a preposition that refers to two items.

Rewrite It!   They rode through the royal forest, where they often hunted. Robert's beloved hound, Balin, remained between them. They passed through a cedar grove, and Balin ran ahead, barking emphatically.

Learn It!

Usage with Than and Then
Usage errors occur when a word is used incorrectly.

The hound was brighter than its litter mates.
> *Than* is a word used to show a comparison.
> *Than* is often used with comparative adjectives.

What happened then was unexpected.
> *Then* is an adverb meaning next or immediately after.

Fix It!   Cross out the incorrect use of *than* or *then*.

Robert ~~than~~/then knew something was wrong.

More than/~~then~~ anything, he longed to alert his uncle.

Comparative Adjectives and Superlative Adjectives
Last week you learned the difference between comparative and superlative adjectives. In order to use the correct form of the adjective, determine how many items are being compared.

Balin was the largest hound in the litter.
> This sentence compares Balin with each individual hound in the litter, which would include three or more puppies.
> The superlative adjective *largest* is used.

Balin was larger than the other hounds in the litter.
> Although this sentence mentions many hounds, the word *than* forms a comparison of two items. This sentence compares Balin with the litter (a group).
> The comparative adjective *larger* is used.

Comparative and Superlative Adjective Review
Read each sentence and determine if it needs a comparative adjective or a superlative adjective.
> Fill in the blank with the comparative (add *more* or *-er*) or superlative (add *most* or *-est*) form of the adjective in parentheses.

Balin was the **cleverest or most clever** hound in the litter of five pups. (clever)

He was trained to be the **fastest** runner of them all. (fast)

His eyesight was **sharper** than the eyesight of the other pups. (sharp)

He was **more alert** to danger than his master. (alert)

Balin is compared to five pups. Use the superlative: *cleverest* or *most clever*.

Balin is compared to them all (five pups). Use the superlative: *fastest*.

Than signals the need for a comparative adjective. His eyesight is compared to the eyesight of the other pups (a group). Use the comparative: *sharper*.

Balin is compared to his master. Use the comparative: *more alert*.

Read It!	Mark It!	Fix It!	Day 1

Balin barked louder/loudest than/then ever before; Robert was surprised, since his hound never barked, without a **credible** reason. He recognized the sound as a warning, concern gripped his heart.

credible
believable; trustworthy

Mark It!		Fix It!	
2 prepositional phrases		? indents	**0**
4 [main clauses]		? capitals	**0**
1 adverb clause (AC)		? commas	**2**
5 subject-verb pairs (s v)		? end marks	**1**
3 openers		1 semicolon	
		2 usage	
		(fix run-on with cc)	

①subject
s   v

[Balin barked louder/~~loudest~~ than/~~then~~ ever before];.

①subject
s   v   AC   s   v

[Robert was surprised], (since his hound never barked,

①subject
s   v

without a **credible** reason). [He recognized the sound

and   s   v

as a warning], [concern gripped his heart].

Ask Students	How do you know *as a warning* is a prepositional phrase?	
	It begins with a preposition (as) and ends with a noun (warning). It has an article (a) in between but no verb.	
S V Pairs	MC ***Balin barked***	
	MC ***Robert was*** Remind students that an adjective often follows the linking verb and describes the subject. *Surprised* is an adjective because it describes Robert's emotional state. It does not indicate an action.	
	AC since ***hound barked*** Surprised why? *since his hound never barked without a credible reason* (adverb clause)	
	MC ***He recognized***	
	MC ***concern gripped***	
Semicolon	The main clauses express two different ideas and are different in length and construction. The main clauses should be separate sentences.	
Run-On	This passage contains four main clauses. The last two are in one sentence, which forms a run-on (comma splice). Fix the run-on by inserting a cc: He recognized the sound as a warning**, *and*** concern gripped his heart. **PATTERN MC, cc MC**	
Commas	Do not put a comma in front of an adverb clause. **PATTERN MC AC**	
	Do not use a comma in front of a prepositional phrase.	
Usage	Use the comparative adjective *louder* because two things are compared: now and before.	
	Use *than*, a word used to show a comparison.	

Rewrite It! Balin barked louder than ever before. Robert was surprised since his hound never barked without a credible reason. He recognized the sound as a warning, and concern gripped his heart.

Read It!	Mark It!	Fix It!	Day 2

By contrast his uncle seemed **undaunted**, or perhaps oblivious to the noise, which the dog was making riding for hours the king had developed a potent thirst.

undaunted
not discouraged

1 coordinating conjunction (cc)
3 prepositional phrases
2 [main clauses]
1 *who/which* clause (w/w)
3 subject-verb pairs (s v)
2 openers

? indents **0**
? capitals **1**
? commas **4**
? end marks **1**

② prepositional

By contrast, [his uncle seemed **undaunted**, or perhaps oblivious to the noise], (which the dog was making).

④ -ing

riding for hours, [the king had developed a potent thirst].

Conjunction	*or* connects two adjectives: *undaunted* or *oblivious*. Both adjectives follow the linking verb *seemed* and describe the subject, the word *uncle*. a and b
S V Pairs MC	**uncle seemed** The adjectives *undaunted* and *oblivious* follow the linking verb and describe the subject.
w/w	*which* **dog was making** The *which* clause describes *noise*, the noun it follows. (adjective clause) It is essential because it defines which noise his uncle seemed oblivious to. The uncle did not seem obvious to all noise, only the noise the dog was making. Removing it from the sentence changes the meaning.
MC	**king had developed**
Commas	Use a comma if a prepositional opener functions as a transition. ***By contrast,***
	Do not use a comma to separate two items connected with a cc. **PATTERN a and b**
	Do not place commas around an essential *who/which* clause.
	Use a comma after an -ing opener. **PATTERN -ing word/phrase, main clause** The thing after the comma must be the thing doing the inging. *King* is doing the *riding*.

Rewrite It!   By contrast, his uncle seemed undaunted or perhaps oblivious to the noise which the dog was making. Riding for hours, the king had developed a potent thirst.

Read It!   **Mark It!**   **Fix It!**

"At a mountain stream where cool water trickled over some rocks King Arthur knelt, and than/then cupped his hands it was a **mere** dribble. Longing for a drink the king's hands waited to fill with water.

mere
small; nothing more than

Mark It!		Fix It!	
1 coordinating conjunction (cc)		? indents	0
4 prepositional phrases		? capitals	1
3 [main clauses]		? commas	4
4 subject-verb pairs (s v)		? end marks	1
3 openers		1 illegal #4	
		1 usage	

This paragraph correctly opens with quotation marks to remind the reader that someone is still speaking.

② prepositional

s   v
"At a mountain stream, ((which was) where cool water trickled

s   v   cc
over some rocks), [King Arthur knelt, and than/then

v   ⑥ vss   ④ -ing
cupped his hands]. [it was a **mere** dribble]. Longing

                    waited for his hands to fill with water.
                    king   s   v
for a drink, [the king's hands waited to fill with water].

Indentation	new location
Quotations	This paragraph correctly opens with quotation marks to remind the reader that someone is still speaking. Since Frederick has not finished reading the story, do not end the passage with quotation marks.
Conjunction	**and** connects two verbs: *knelt* and *cupped* MC cc 2nd verb
S V Pairs	DC *where* **water trickled** The *where* clause describes *stream*, the noun it follows. (adjective clause)
	MC **King Arthur knelt**, *cupped*
	MC **It was**
	MC **hands waited**
Illegal #4	The king's hands were not longing; the king was. Rewrite the last sentence so that the king, not the king's hands, is the thing (subject of main clause) after the comma: *Longing for a drink, the king waited for his hands to fill with water.*
Commas	Place commas around a nonessential adjective clause.
	Do not use a comma before a cc when it connects two verbs. **PATTERN MC cc 2nd verb**
	Use a comma after an -ing opener. **PATTERN -ing word/phrase, main clause** The thing after the comma must be the thing doing the inging. *King* is doing the *longing*.
Usage	Use *then*, an adverb meaning next or immediately after.

Rewrite It!   "At a mountain stream, where cool water trickled over some rocks, King Arthur knelt and then cupped his hands. It was a mere dribble. Longing for a drink, the king waited for his hands to fill with water.

Read It!		Mark It!		Fix It!	Day 4

"Anxiously Robert watched, and listened, while Balin barked madly although he feared that something in the water might be **noxious** Robert couldnt warn his Uncle.

noxious
poisonous

1 coordinating conjunction (cc)
1 prepositional phrase
2 [main clauses]
1 *that* clause (that)
2 adverb clauses (AC)
5 subject-verb pairs (s v)
2 openers

? indents **1**
? capitals **2**
? commas **3**
? end marks **1**
1 apostrophe

③ -ly adverb

¶ "Anxiously [Robert watched, and listened], (while Balin barked madly). (although he feared) (that something in the water might be **noxious**), [Robert couldn't warn his U̶ncle].

⑤ clausal

(s v over Robert watched, cc, v listened, AC while; s v Balin barked, AC madly although; s v he feared, that; s v something ... might be; s Robert; v v couldn't warn his Uncle)

Indentation	new topic
Quotations	Quotation marks remind the reader that someone is still speaking.
Conjunction	**and** connects two verbs: *watched* and *listened* MC cc 2nd verb
Ask **Students**	When are words like *uncle* capitalized? *Uncle* is capitalized when it is used as a proper noun in place of a person's name or when it is used as a title directly before the name.
S V Pairs	MC **Robert watched, listened** AC *while* **Balin barked** Watched and listened when? *while Balin barked madly* (adverb clause) AC *although* **he feared** Couldn't warn why? *Although he feared* (adverb clause) that *that* **something might be** The adjective *noxious* follows the linking verb and describes the subject. MC **Robert could warn** The contraction *couldn't* includes both a helping verb (could) and an adverb (not).
Commas	Do not use a comma before a cc when it connects two verbs. **PATTERN MC cc 2nd verb** Do not put a comma in front of an adverb clause. **PATTERN MC AC** Use a comma after an adverb clause that comes before a main clause. **PATTERN AC, MC** There is no comma after *feared* because the *that* clause is essential to the AC. Do not put a comma in front of a *that* clause.

Rewrite It!   "Anxiously Robert watched and listened while Balin barked madly. Although he feared that something in the water might be noxious, Robert couldn't warn his uncle.

Review It!

Commas with Cordinating Conjunctions

Review the FANBOYS and the comma rules.

ACRONYM FANBOYS

Coordinating conjunctions connect the same type of words, phrases, or clauses.

FANBOYS

for, and, nor, but, or, yet, so

$\mathbf{9}$| a, b, and c
  | MC, cc MC

✗| a and b
  | MC cc 2nd verb

Use a comma before a cc that joins three items in a series or two main clauses.

Do not use a comma before a cc that joins two items in a series, including two verbs with the same subject.

Read the following sentences and underline the words, phrases, or clauses that each cc connects. Insert commas where needed.

The king was <u>thirsty</u> and <u>eager</u> to drink the water.

and connects two adjectives

   a and b

Balin <u>grew</u> anxious**,** <u>barked</u> loudly, and <u>tried</u> to warn the king.

and connects three verbs

   a, b, and c

<u>Balin sensed something was wrong</u>**,** but <u>Robert could not call out a</u>

<u>warning</u>.

but connects two main clauses

   MC, cc MC

Robert <u>realized</u> that something was wrong but <u>could</u> not <u>call</u> out a

warning.

but connects two verbs

   MC cc 2nd verb

Robert knew <u>that Balin was warning them</u> and $\wedge$ *(that)* <u>the water could be tainted</u>.

and connects two dependent (that) clauses. The second *that* is an invisible *that* clause. The sentence does not make sense with two MCs.

   a and b

<u>Robert wiggled the king's hands</u>**,** and <u>the water spilled</u>.

and connects two main clauses

   MC, cc MC

Dialogue Review

Dialogue includes quoted sentences and attributions.

What is an attribution? _____

___*An attribution is the person speaking and the speaking verb.*___

What is the difference between a direct quote and an indirect quote?

___*A direct quote is the exact words a person spoke. An indirect quote is a*___

___*paraphrase of what someone spoke. It often begins with* **that.**___

Capitalization and punctuation mistakes in quotations are common. Read the following passage and fix the errors.

The king cried. "Stay where you are".

Robert longed to explain that, "he did not trust the water". If he could

speak, he would say "the hound is warning you".

"Be quiet. The king commanded Balin we will leave only after I drink

some water".

Here is the corrected passage with correct punctuation bolded.

The king cried**,** "Stay where you are**."**

Robert longed to explain that he did not trust the water. If he could

speak, he would say**,** "**T**he hound is warning you**."**

"Be quiet**,"** **t**he king commanded Balin. **"W**e will leave only after I drink

some water**."**

He did not trust the water is an indirect quote introduced with the word *that*. It should not be in quotation marks. Here is the sentence rewritten with a direct quote: Robert longed to explain, "I do not trust the water."

Read It!	Mark It!	Fix It!	Day 1

Robert knew that he should not interrupt the king, he had to find a way to alert him; thinking quickly Robert rushed to his uncles side, and knocked the water, from his hands. This **agitated** the king.

agitated
disturbed; angered

Mark It!	
1 coordinating conjunction (cc)	
2 prepositional phrases	
4 [main clauses]	
1 *that* clause (that)	
5 subject-verb pairs (s v)	
3 openers	

Fix It!	
? indents	**0**
? capitals	**1**
? commas	**3**
? end marks	**1**
1 semicolon	
1 apostrophe	
(fix run-on with cc)	

①　subject
s　　　　　v　　that　　　s　　　v　　　　　　　　v
[Robert knew] (that he should not interrupt the king),

　　　　　　　　　　　　　　　　　　　　④ -ing
but　s　　v
∧ [he had to find a way to alert him];. thinking quickly,

s　　　　v
[Robert rushed to his uncle's side, and knocked the
　　　　　　　　　　　　　　cc　　　v

⑥ vss
　　s　　　　　v
water, from his hands]. [This **agitated** the king].

Conjunction	*and* connects two verbs: *rushed* and *knocked* MC cc 2nd verb
S V Pairs	MC *Robert knew*
	that *that he should interrupt*
	MC *he had*
	MC *Robert rushed, knocked*
	MC *This agitated*
Run-On	This passage contains four main clauses. The first two are in one sentence and form a run-on (comma splice). Fix the run-on by inserting a cc: Robert knew that he should not interrupt the king, *but* he had to find a way to alert him. **PATTERN MC, cc MC**
Semicolon	The sentence that begins *Thinking quickly, Robert rushed ...* differs in length and construction from the sentence before it. Additionally, the clauses express different ideas. Replace the semicolon with a period.
Commas	Use a comma after an -ing opener. **PATTERN -ing word/phrase, main clause.** The thing after the comma must be the thing doing the inging. *Robert* is doing the *thinking*. Do not use a comma before a *cc* when it connects two verbs. **PATTERN MC cc 2nd verb** Do not put a comma in front of a prepositional phrase.

Rewrite It!　　Robert knew that he should not interrupt the king, but he had to find a way to alert him. Thinking quickly, Robert rushed to his uncle's side and knocked the water from his hands. This agitated the king.

Read It!	Mark It!	Fix It!	Day 2

"King Arthur shouted, I am **parched**, and need water." "He just wanted a drink Dorinda interrupted Robert should have trusted his uncle not his dog. Of course his uncle was wiser/wisest"

parched
very thirsty

	Fix It!	
1 coordinating conjunction (cc)	? indents	**2**
1 <u>prepositional phrase</u>	? capitals	**0**
6 [main clauses]	? commas	**4**
6 subject-verb pairs (s v)	? end marks	**2**
1 opener	4 quotation marks	
	1 usage	

(1) subject

¶ "[King Arthur shouted], '[I am **parched**, and need water].'" ¶ "[He just wanted a drink]," [Dorinda interrupted]. "[Robert should have trusted his uncle, not his dog]. Of course, [his uncle was wiser/~~wisest~~]."

Indentation	new speaker; new speaker
Quotations	The double quotes are correct because Frederick is reading the story aloud. Place single quotes around the words King Arthur shouted because it is a quote within a quote. *Dorinda interrupted* is an attribution and should not be inside quotation marks.
Conjunction	***and*** connects two verbs: *am* and *need* MC cc 2nd verb
S V Pairs	MC ***King Arthur shouted*** MC ***I am*, *need*** The adjective *parched* follows the linking verb and describes the subject. MC ***He wanted*** MC ***Dorinda interrupted*** MC ***Robert should have trusted*** MC ***uncle was*** The adjective *wiser* follows the linking verb and describes the subject.
Commas	Do not use a comma before a cc when it connects two verbs. **PATTERN MC cc 2nd verb**
	Use a comma to separate an attribution from a direct quote. **PATTERN "Quote," attribution.**
	Use a comma to separate contrasting parts of a sentence (his uncle, ***not*** his dog).
	Use a comma if a prepositional opener functions as a transition. ***Of course,***
Usage	Use the comparative adjective *wiser* because there are two beings: *uncle* and *dog*.

Rewrite It!   "King Arthur shouted, 'I am parched and need water.'"

"He just wanted a drink," Dorinda interrupted. "Robert should have trusted his uncle, not his dog. Of course, his uncle was wiser."

Read It!	Mark It!	Fix It!	Day 3

Humans can be foolish stubborn creatures whereas animal's instinctively sense danger, which humans cannot **detect** Frederick commented listen to the rest of the story

detect
discover; notice the presence of

Mark It!
2 <u>prepositional phrases</u>
3 [main clauses]
1 *who/which* clause (w/w)
1 adverb clause (AC)
5 subject-verb pairs (s v)

Fix It!
? indents **1**
? capitals **1**
? commas **4**
? end marks **2**
3 quotation marks
1 apostrophe

¶ "[Humans can be foolish, stubborn creatures],
(whereas animal's instinctively sense danger),
(which humans cannot **detect**)," [Frederick commented]. "[(you) listen to the rest of the story].

No closing quotation mark because Frederick continues to talk.

Indentation	new speaker
S V Pairs	MC ***Humans can be***
	AC *whereas **animals sense*** Can be why? *whereas animals instinctively sense danger* (adverb clause)
	w/w *which **humans can detect*** The compound word *cannot* includes both a helping verb (can) and an adverb (not). The *which* clause describes *danger*, the noun it follows. (adjective clause) It is essential because it defines the type of danger animals instinctively sense. Removing it from the sentence changes the meaning.
	MC ***Frederick commented***
	MC ***(you) Listen*** The subject of an imperative sentence is always *you*.
Commas	Use a comma to separate coordinate adjectives (foolish, stubborn creatures).
	When two comma rules contradict, follow the rule that says to use a comma.
	A comma is needed after *creatures* because of this rule: Use a comma to separate contrasting parts of a sentence (Humans can be foolish, stubborn creatures**,** *whereas* animals instinctively sense danger). A comma is not needed after *creatures* because of this rule: Do not put a comma in front of an adverb clause. **PATTERN MC AC**
	Do not place commas around an essential *who/which* clause.
	Use a comma to separate an attribution from a direct quote. **PATTERN** "**Quote," attribution.**

Rewrite It!   "Humans can be foolish, stubborn creatures, whereas animals instinctively sense danger which humans cannot detect," Frederick commented. "Listen to the rest of the story.

"Cupping his hands again King Arthur collected more of the precious liquid flowing over the rocks persistently Robert than/then **jiggled** his uncles' hands signaling that they should check the source, before they drank.

jiggled
moved with short, quick jerks

Mark It!	Fix It!	
2 prepositional phrases	? indents	0
2 [main clauses]	? capitals	1
1 *that* clause (that)	? commas	3
1 adverb clause (AC)	? end marks	1
4 subject-verb pairs (s v)	1 apostrophe	
2 openers	1 usage	

This paragraph correctly opens with quotation marks to remind the reader that someone is still speaking.

④ -ing

"Cupping his hands again, [King Arthur collected
                     s   v

more of the precious liquid] flowing over the rocks.

③ -ly adverb

         s   v
[persistently Robert ~~than~~/then **jiggled** his uncle's

                that   s   v   v
hands], signaling (that they should check the source),

AC   s   v
(before they drank).

Indentation	new topic
Quotations	The paragraph correctly opens with quotation marks to remind the reader that Frederick is reading the book. Since Frederick is not finished reading the story, do not end the passage with quotation marks.
S V Pairs	MC *King Arthur collected* MC *Robert jiggled* that *that they should check* AC *before they drank* Check when? *before they drank* (adverb clause)
Commas	Use a comma after an -ing opener. **PATTERN -ing word/phrase, main clause** The thing after the comma must be the thing doing the inging. *King Arthur* is doing the *cupping*. Use a comma when a -ing phrase at the end of a sentence describes a noun other than the word it follows. Do not put a comma in front of an adverb clause. **PATTERN MC AC**
Usage	Use *then*, an adverb meaning next or immediately after.

Rewrite It!   "Cupping his hands again, King Arthur collected more of the precious liquid flowing over the rocks. Persistently Robert then jiggled his uncle's hands, signaling that they should check the source before they drank.

Review It!

Unnecessary Commas

Using the list below, explain why the comma is wrong.

A	subject + verb	**I**	#3 opener modifies verb
B	a and b	**J**	MC AC
C	MC cc 2nd verb	**K**	end-sentence participial (-ing)
D	comma splice	**L**	essential appositive
E	before prep phrase	**M**	essential adj clause begins with *who* or *which*
F	*that* clause		
G	cumulative adjectives	**N**	essential adj clause begins with *when* or *where*
H	#2 opener < 5 words		

If students struggle, encourage them to look at Unnecessary Comma Rules on page 50.

__J__ Dorinda softened, as she listened to the story about King Arthur.

__B__ She wondered if she would be impatient, or if she would listen to the warning.

__F__ She realized, that like the king she had been unkind.

__K__ She was ashamed because she had mistreated the girls, seeking her friendship.

__L__ Dorinda once pushed her friend, Clarissa, off a swing.

__H__ In the same week, Dorinda made fun of Jane's haircut.

__D__ Clarissa forgave her, Jane did not.

__G__ Even Maribella suffered from Dorinda's early, childish behavior.

__I__ Knowingly, Dorinda faked tears when Maribella was praised.

__A__ Each birthday in Dorinda's youth, was more extravagant than the one before.

__C__ Dorinda pouted, and even cried if Maribella received a nicer gift.

__M__ She felt she was the one, who deserved the best!

__N__ She then thought of the garden, where she had met Frederick.

__E__ She realized much had changed, since that time.

Read It!	Mark It!	Fix It!	Day 1

The king who's frustration had escalated **callously** pushed Robert away, suddenly Balin appeared jumping on the king knocking him over and spilling the water.

callously
insensitively; unsympathetically

Mark It!		
1 coordinating conjunction (cc)	? indents	**0**
1 prepositional phrase	? capitals	**1**
2 [main clauses]	? commas	**6**
1 *who/which* clause (w/w)	? end marks	**1**
3 subject-verb pairs (s v)	1 usage	
2 openers		

①subject
    s   w/w *whose*   s   v   v
[The king, (~~who's~~ frustration had escalated), **callously**

    v   ③ -ly adverb   s   v
pushed Robert away]. suddenly [Balin appeared],

                        cc
jumping on the king, knocking him over, and spilling

the water.

Conjunction		***and*** connects three participial (-ing) phrases: *jumping on the king, knocking him over,* and *spilling the water.* a, b, and c
S V Pairs	MC	***king pushed***
	w/w	*whose **frustration had escalated** The subject of the clause is *frustration*. The word *whose* functions as an adjective. (Whose (king's) frustration had escalated.) The *whose* clause describes *king*, the noun it follows. (adjective clause) It is nonessential because it does not change the meaning of the sentence. Without the *whose* clause, the king still pushed Robert away.*
	MC	***Balin appeared***
Commas		Place commas around a nonessential *who/which* clause.
		Do not use a comma to separate two main clauses. Use a period. MC, MC is always wrong.
		Use a comma when a -ing phrase at the end of a sentence describes a noun other than the word it follows.
		Use commas to separate three or more items in a series connected with a cc. **PATTERN a, b, and c**
Usage		Change *who's* (contraction for who is) to *whose* (possessive case pronoun). Use *who* when the pronoun functions as a subject and *whose* when the pronoun functions as an adjective.

Rewrite It! The king, whose frustration had escalated, callously pushed Robert away. Suddenly Balin appeared, jumping on the king, knocking him over, and spilling the water.

Read It!	Mark It!	Fix It!	Day 2

"King Arthur lost all patience because of your relentless **insubordination** you, and your miserable hound dog are forever banished from my Kingdom he snapped at his nephew cowering, at his uncle's rage.

insubordination
defiance of authority

Mark It!	Fix It!
1 coordinating conjunction (cc)	? indents **1**
4 prepositional phrases	? capitals **2**
3 [main clauses]	? commas **3**
3 subject-verb pairs (s v)	? end marks **2**
1 opener	2 quotation marks

⑥ vss

¶ ["King Arthur lost all patience]. 'because of your relentless **insubordination**, [you, and your miserable hound dog are forever banished from my Kingdom]!' [he snapped at his nephew] cowering, at his uncle's rage.

Indentation	new topic (or speaker)
Quotations	The paragraph begins with double quotes to remind the reader that Frederick is reading the story.
	Place single quotes around the words that King Arthur said because it is a quote within a quote.
End Marks	The first main clause is a complete thought, not an attribution.
	The direct quote is an exclamation, so an exclamation mark, not a comma, separates the quote from the attribution. The word *he* is not capitalized. **PATTERN** "Quote!" attribution.
Conjunction	**and** connects two subjects: *you* and *dog* a and b
S V Pairs	MC **King Arthur lost**
	MC **you, dog are banished**
	MC **he snapped**
Commas	Use a comma if a prepositional opener has five words or more.
	Do not use a comma to separate two items connected with a cc. **PATTERN a and b**
	Do not use a comma in front of a prepositional phrase.

Rewrite It!   "King Arthur lost all patience. 'Because of your relentless insubordination, you and your miserable hound dog are forever banished from my kingdom!' he snapped at his nephew cowering at his uncle's rage.

Read It!	Mark It!	Fix It!	Day 3

"**Grievingly** Robert turned away realizing, that he could insist on his way, or obey his uncle since he feared the king he decided that obedience was a better/best option.

grievingly
with distress or great sorrow

Mark It!	Fix It!	
1 coordinating conjunction (cc)	? indents	1
1 <u>prepositional phrase</u>	? capitals	1
2 [main clauses]	? commas	4
2 *that* clauses (that)	? end marks	1
1 adverb clause (AC)	1 usage	
5 subject-verb pairs (s v)		
2 openers		

③ -ly adverb

¶"**Grievingly** [Robert turned away], realizing, (that he could insist on his way, or obey his uncle). (since he feared the king), [he decided] (that obedience was a better/best option).

Indentation	new topic
Conjunction	*or* connects two verbs: *insist* or *obey* MC cc 2nd verb
S V Pairs	MC **Robert turned**
	that *that* **he could insist, obey**
	AC *Since* **he feared** Decided why? *Since he feared the king* (adverb clause)
	MC **he decided**
	that *that* **obedience was**
Commas	Use a comma when a -ing phrase at the end of a sentence describes a noun other than the word it follows.
	Do not put a comma in front of a *that* clause.
	Do not use a comma before a cc when it connects two verbs. **PATTERN MC cc 2nd verb**
	Use a comma after an adverb clause that comes before a main clause. **PATTERN AC, MC**
Usage	Use the comparative adjective *better* because there are two options: *insist* or *obey*.

Rewrite It!   "Grievingly Robert turned away, realizing that he could insist on his way or obey his uncle. Since he feared the king, he decided that obedience was a better option.

Read It!	Mark It!	Fix It!	Day 4

"King Arthur decided to follow the path among/between the rocks to the top of the cliff where the water originated, wanting to drink without interference he made the **laborious** climb.

laborious
requiring much work and effort

4 <u>prepositional phrases</u>
2 [main clauses]
3 subject-verb pairs (s v)
2 openers

? indents   **1**
? capitals   **1**
? commas   **3**
? end marks   **1**
1 usage

①subject

¶ "[King Arthur decided to follow the path among/~~between~~ the rocks to the top of the cliff],

((which was) where the water originated), ④-ing wanting to drink without interference, [he made the **laborious** climb].

Indentation	new place		
S V Pairs	MC	***King Arthur decided***	
	DC	*where **water originated*** The *where* clause describes *cliff*, the noun it follows. (adjective clause)	
Ask Students		Why does *where Frederick now stayed* require a comma? It is a nonessential adjective clause. It describes the noun *cliff*. If you remove it, King Arthur still followed the path to the top of the cliff.	
	MC	***he made***	
Commas		Place commas around a nonessential adjective clause.	
		Do not use a comma to separate two main clauses. Use a period. MC, MC is always wrong.	
		Use a comma after an -ing opener. **PATTERN** -ing word/phrase, main clause The thing after the comma must be the thing doing the inging. *He* is doing the *wanting*.	
Usage		Use *among*, a preposition that refers to three or more items. There were more than two rocks.	

Rewrite It!   "King Arthur decided to follow the path among the rocks to the top of the cliff, where the water originated. Wanting to drink without interference, he made the laborious climb.

Learn It!

Usage with Accept and Except

Usage errors occur when a word is used incorrectly.

> Dorinda decided she would accept his offer of friendship.
> *Accept* is a verb meaning to take something offered or to agree to a suggestion.

> Dorinda liked every dish the chef prepared except for caviar.
> *Except* is a preposition or conjunction that introduces the one person or thing that is not included in the main statement.

Fix It!   Cross out the incorrect use of *accept* or *except*.

> The chef worked everyday of the week ~~accept~~/except Sunday.

> Frederick would gratefully accept/~~except~~ any dish they brought.

Sentence Opener Review

You have learned six types of sentence openers—six ways to open or begin a sentence. Using different sentence openers makes writing more interesting.

A #1 subject opener is written below. Use the idea of that sentence to write sentences that begin with each type of opener. Add commas where required. There are multiple right answers.

#1 Subject _____ *Dorinda no longer minded being a toad.* _____

#2 Prepositional ___ In fact, Dorinda no longer minded being a toad. ___

#3 -ly Adverb ___ Surprisingly, Dorinda no longer minded being a toad. ___

#4 -ing ___ Demanding less than she used to, Dorinda no longer minded being a toad. ___

#5 Clausal ___ As she discovered, Dorinda no longer minded being a toad. ___

#6 Vss ___ Dorinda was content. ___

Encourage students to practice forming sentences with different openers orally. Students who can easily create oral sentences struggle less when writing.

The written samples are only suggestions.

comma if 5+ words or transition

comma if -ly adverb modifies sentence

comma after phrase

comma after clause

2–5 words

Read It!	Mark It!	Fix It!	Day 1

"At the top, he discovered a dead snake. The enormous snakes poison had contaminated the water. Balin, and Robert had been trying too save the king's life, he had been two **arrogant** to listen.

arrogant
disdainfully proud

1 coordinating conjunction (cc)
1 prepositional phrase
4 [main clauses]
4 subject-verb pairs (s v)
3 openers

? indents   **1**
? capitals   **0**
? commas   **2**
? end marks   **0**
1 apostrophe
2 usage
(fix run-on with cc)

②prepositional   ①subject

             s   *v*

¶ "At the top, [he discovered a dead snake]. [The

             s   *v*   *v*

enormous snake's poison had contaminated the water].

①subject

s   *cc*   *s*   *v*   *v*   *v*   *to*

[Balin, and Robert had been trying ~~too~~ save the king's

   but   *s*   *v*   *v*   *too*

life], [he had been ~~two~~ **arrogant** to listen].

Indentation	new place
Conjunction	*and* connects two nouns (subject nouns): *Balin* and *Robert* a and b
S V Pairs	MC ***he discovered***
	MC ***poison had contaminated***
	MC ***Balin, Robert had been trying***
	MC ***he had been***
Note	In the verb phrase *had been trying*, *been* functions as a helping verb because it it is followed by another verb (trying). Remember, a word that ends in -ing functions as a verb if it follows a helping verb. In the verb phrase *had been*, *been* is an linking verb because it does not have a verb after it. See *Think About It!* on page 26.
Run-On	This passage contains four main clauses. The last two are in one sentence, which forms a run-on (comma splice). Fix the run-on by inserting a cc: Balin and Robert had been trying to save his life, ***but*** he had been too arrogant to listen. **PATTERN MC, cc MC**
Commas	Do not use a comma if a prepositional opener has fewer than five words.
	Do not use a comma to separate two items connected with a cc. **PATTERN a and b**
Usage	Use *to*, the infinitive marker.
	Use *too*, an adverb meaning to an excessive degree.

Rewrite It!   "At the top he discovered a dead snake. The enormous snake's poison had contaminated the water. Balin and Robert had been trying to save the king's life, but he had been too arrogant to listen.

Read It!	Mark It!	Fix It!	Day 2

"When the king returned to the castle he called,
for his nephew finding Robert in his room, with his
servant Arthur humbled himself **contritely**. Can you
accept/except my apology, and forgive me, He began.

contritely
with genuine sorrow or regret

Mark It!	
1 coordinating conjunction (cc)	
4 prepositional phrases	
4 [main clauses]	
1 adverb clause (AC)	
5 subject-verb pairs (s v)	
2 openers	

Fix It!	
? indents	1
? capitals	2
? commas	6
? end marks	2
2 quotation marks	
1 usage	

⑤ clausal

¶ ("When the king returned to the castle), [he called,
AC   s   v   s   v

④ -ing

for his nephew]. finding Robert in his room, with his

s   v
servant, [Arthur humbled himself **contritely**]. '[Can you
                                                              v   s

v   cc   v   s   v
accept/except my apology, and forgive me],?' [He began].

Indentation	new place (or speaker)
Capitalization	*he* lowercase The attribution does not begin the sentence, so it should be lowercase.
End Marks	The direct quote is a question, so a question mark, not a comma, separates the quote from the attribution. **PATTERN** "Quote?" attribution.
Conjunction	*and* connects two verbs: *accept* and *forgive* MC cc 2nd verb
S V Pairs	AC *When **king returned** Called when? When the king returned* (adverb clause)
	MC ***he called***
	MC ***Arthur humbled***
	MC ***you Can accept, forgive***
	MC ***he began***
Commas	Use a comma after an adverb clause. **PATTERN AC, MC**
	Do not put a comma in front of a prepositional phrase.
	Use a comma after an -ing opener. **PATTERN** -ing word/phrase, main clause
	The thing after the comma must be the thing doing the inging. *Arthur* is doing the *finding*.
	Do not use a comma before a cc when it connects two verbs. **PATTERN MC cc 2nd verb**
Usage	Use *accept*, the verb that means to take or receive.

Rewrite It!   "When the king returned to the castle, he called for his nephew. Finding Robert in his
                       room with his servant, Arthur humbled himself contritely. 'Can you accept my apology and
                       forgive me?' he began.

Read It!	Mark It!	Fix It!	Day 3

While you trusted Balin myself depended on no one, accept/except myself. Robert for your loyalty I shall elevate you to the **coveted** position of arm bearer to the king and Balin shall dine on steak every day.

coveted
greatly desired

Mark It!		Fix It!	
1 coordinating conjunction (cc)		? indents	**0**
7 prepositional phrases		? capitals	**0**
3 [main clauses]		? commas	**4**
1 adverb clause (AC)		? end marks	**0**
4 subject-verb pairs (s v)		2 quotation marks	
		2 usage	

AC
s   v   s   v
‘(While you trusted Balin), [~~myself~~ depended on no one,

~~accept~~/except myself]. Robert, for your loyalty [I shall
                                                    s   v

v
elevate you to the **coveted** position of arm bearer

cc   s   v   v
to the king], and [Balin shall dine on steak every day].’

Quotations	Place single quotes around the words that King Arthur said because it is a quote within a quote.
Conjunction	**and** connects two main clauses. A subject and verb pair (I shall elevate) comes before the cc, and a subject and verb pair (Balin shall dine) comes after the cc. A comma is required. MC, cc MC
S V Pairs	AC *While **you trusted*** Depended when? *While you trusted Balin* (adverb clause) MC **I depended** MC **I shall elevate** MC **Balin shall dine**

Commas	Use a comma after an adverb clause. **PATTERN AC, MC**
	Do not put a comma in front of a prepositional phrase.
	When two comma rules contradict, follow the rule that says to use a comma.
	   A comma is needed after *Robert* because of this rule: Place commas around a noun of direct address (NDA). **Robert,**
	   A comma is not needed after *Robert* because of this rule: Do not put a comma in front of an prepositional phrase.
	Use a comma to separate two main clauses connected with a cc. **PATTERN MC, cc MC**

Usage	In the first line change the pronoun *myself* (reflexive) to *I* (subjective). The pronoun *myself* in the phrase *except myself* is correct. Use a reflexive pronoun when the pronoun following the verb refers to the subject. Use *except*, which means excluding, save, or but.

Rewrite It!   ‘While you trusted Balin, I depended on no one except myself. Robert, for your loyalty I shall elevate you to the coveted position of arm bearer to the king, and Balin shall dine on steak every day.’

Read It!	Mark It!	Fix It!	Day 4

"Robert signed to his servant who translated for him. Your safety matters I am pleased to serve you and I shall diligently work in the position which you are **entrusting** to me."

entrusting
charging with a responsibility

1 coordinating conjunction (cc)
4 prepositional phrases
4 [main clauses]
2 *who/which* clauses (w/w)
6 subject-verb pairs (s v)
1 opener

? indents   **1**
? capitals   **0**
? commas   **2**
? end marks   **1**
2 quotation marks

(1) subject
     s   v   w/w   s   v

¶ "[Robert signed to his servant], (who translated

for him). '[Your safety matters]. [I am pleased

to serve you], and [I shall diligently work in the

position] (which you are **entrusting** to me).'"

Indentation	new topic (or speaker)
Quotations	Place single quotes around the words that Robert's servant spoke. This is a quote within a quote. The double quotation marks at the end of the passage indicate that Frederick is done reading. The period belongs inside both the single quotation mark indicating the end of Robert's words and the double quotation mark indicating the end of Frederick's words.
Conjunction	*and* connects two main clauses. A subject and verb pair (I am) comes before the cc, and a subject and verb pair (I shall work) comes after the cc. A comma is required. MC, cc MC
S V Pairs MC	*Robert signed*
w/w	*who translated* The *who* clause describes *servant*, the noun it follows. (adjective clause) It is nonessential because it does not change the meaning of the sentence. There is only one servant. Without the *who* clause, Robert still signed to his servant.
MC	*safety matters*
MC	*I am* The adjective *pleased* follows the linking verb and describes the subject.
MC	*I shall work*
w/w	*which you are entrusting* The *which* clause describes *position*, the noun it follows. (adjective clause) It is essential because it defines the type of position Robert will diligently work in. Removing it from the sentence changes the meaning.
Commas	Place commas around a nonessential *who/which* clause.
	Use a comma to separate two main clauses connected with a cc. **PATTERN MC, cc MC**
	Do not place commas around an essential *who/which* clause.

Rewrite It!   "Robert signed to his servant, who translated for him. 'Your safety matters. I am pleased to serve you, and I shall diligently work in the position which you are entrusting to me.'"

Review It!

Fill in the blanks below with different parts of speech in order to create a silly story about Dorinda and Frederick.

After you have completed the list on this page, transfer your words to the blanks in the story on page 181.

1 noun _____

1 interjection _____

1 speaking verb _____

2 adjectives _____ _____

1 speaking verb _____

1 adjective _____

1 verb (past tense) _____

1 adjective _____

1 noun (clothing) _____

1 verb (past tense) _____

1 noun (body part) _____

1 -ly adverb _____

2 verbs (past tense) _____ _____

1 adjective _____

1 noun (food) _____

1 verb (past tense) _____

1 noun (body part) _____

2 -ing words _____ _____

1 verb (past tense) _____

1 interjection _____

1 adjective _____

1 speaking verb _____

1 -ly adverb _____

Read It!	Mark It!	Fix It!	Day 1

At that moment, Dorinda realized the message of the story, she understood the offense, which was committed yet **poignantly** forgiven considering the boys kindness she examined her own heart.

poignantly
in a profoundly moving way

Mark It!
1 coordinating conjunction (cc)
2 prepositional phrases
3 [main clauses]
1 who/which clause (w/w)
4 subject-verb pairs (s v)
3 openers

Fix It!
? indents   **1**
? capitals   **2**
? commas   **4**
? end marks   **2**
1 apostrophe

② prepositional

¶ At that moment, [Dorinda realized the message of
① subject

the story]. [she understood the offense], (which was
committed yet **poignantly** forgiven). considering the
④ -ing

boy's kindness, [she examined her own heart].

Indentation	new topic
Conjunction	*yet* connects two verbs: *committed* yet *forgiven* MC cc 2nd verb
S V Pairs	MC *Dorinda realized*
	MC *She understood*
	w/w *which was committed, forgiven* The *which* clause describes offense. (adjective clause) It is essential because it defines the type of offense she understood. She does not claim to understand all offenses. Removing it from the sentence changes the meaning.
	MC *she examined*
Commas	Do not use a comma if a prepositional opener has fewer than five words.
	Do not use a comma to separate two main clauses. Use a period. MC, MC is always wrong.
	Do not place commas around an essential *who/which* clause.
	Use a comma after an -ing opener. PATTERN -ing word/phrase, main clause The thing after the comma must be the thing doing the inging. *She* is doing the *considering*.

Rewrite It!   At that moment Dorinda realized the message of the story. She understood the offense which was committed yet poignantly forgiven. Considering the boy's kindness, she examined her own heart.

Read It!	Mark It!	Fix It!	Day 2

Why had she not recognized that her behavior had been **abhorrent**. Frederick had only desired that she keep her promise, truthfully she had treated him as dreadfully, as the king had treated Robert his nephew.

abhorrent
hateful; loathsome; detestable

3 [main clauses]	? indents 0
2 *that* clauses (that)	? capitals 1
1 adverb clause (AC)	? commas 4
6 subject-verb pairs (s v)	? end marks 2
2 openers	

      v   s   v   *that*   s   v

[Why had she not recognized] (that her behavior had

① subject

  v   s   v   v   *that*   s

been **abhorrent**)**?** [Frederick had only desired] (that she

③ -ly adverb

  v   s   v   v

keep her promise)**.** truthfully**,** [she had treated him as

    AC   s   v   v

dreadfully]**,** (as the king had treated Robert**,** his nephew)**.**

S V Pairs	MC	*she had recognized*
	that	*that behavior had been*
	MC	*Frederick had desired*
	that	*that she keep* She did not keep her promise, so the subjunctive mood *she keep* is correct. For more information about the subjunctive case, see page G-11.
	MC	*she had treated* The first *as* is followed by a single word: dreadfully. It does not begin an adverb clause. Rather, it is an adverb which tells to what extent.
	AC	*as king had treated* Had treated to what extent? *as the king had treated Robert* (adverb clause) The noun *nephew* follows the noun *Robert* and renames it. *Nephew* functions as an appositive. Encourage students to mentally insert *who was. (who was) his nephew* is an invisible *who* clause.
Commas		Do not use a comma to separate two main clauses. Use a period. MC, MC is always wrong.
		Use a comma if an -ly adverb opener modifies the sentence. It was truthful that she had treated him as dreadfully as the king had treated Robert.
		Do not put a comma in front of an adverb clause. **PATTERN MC AC**
		Place commas around a nonessential appositive.

Rewrite It!   Why had she not recognized that her behavior had been abhorrent? Frederick had only desired that she keep her promise. Truthfully, she had treated him as dreadfully as the king had treated Robert, his nephew.

Read It!	Mark It!	Fix It!	Day 3

Dorinda now knew, that kindness to others was more/most beneficial than/then nurturing ones selfish interests, with heartfelt **remorse**, she kissed Frederick, on his cheek.

remorse
deep regret for wrongdoing

Mark It!		
3 prepositional phrases	? indents	0
2 [main clauses]	? capitals	1
1 *that* clause (that)	? commas	4
3 subject-verb pairs (s v)	? end marks	1
2 openers	1 apostrophe	
	2 usage	

(1) subject
 s   v   *that*   s   v
[Dorinda now knew], (that kindness to others was

more/~~most~~ beneficial than/~~then~~ nurturing one's selfish

(2) prepositional
 s   v
interests),. with heartfelt **remorse**, [she kissed Frederick,

on his cheek].

S V Pairs	MC ***Dorinda knew***
	that *that **kindness was*** The adjective *beneficial* follows the linking verb and describes the subject.
	MC ***she kissed***
Commas	Do not put a comma in front of a *that* clause.
	Do not use a comma to separate two main clauses. Use a period. MC, MC is always wrong.
	Do not use a comma if a prepositional opener has fewer than five words.
	Do not use a comma in front of a prepositional phrase.
Usage	Use the comparative adjective *more beneficial* because two things are compared: kindness to others and nurturing one's selfish interests.
	Use *than*, a word used to show a comparison.

Rewrite It!   Dorinda now knew that kindness to others was more beneficial than nurturing one's selfish interests. With heartfelt remorse she kissed Frederick on his cheek.

Read It!	Mark It!	Fix It!	Day 4

What do you think Frederick did after that kiss.
He kissed her back of course poof the curses' were
reversed, instantly, a noble gallant prince appeared
beside a humble kindhearted princess.

reversed
changed to an opposite state or condition

3 <u>prepositional phrases</u>
4 [main clauses]
1 *that* clause (that)
5 subject-verb pairs (s v)
4 openers

? indents   **2**
? capitals   **3**
? commas   **5**
? end marks   **4**
1 apostrophe

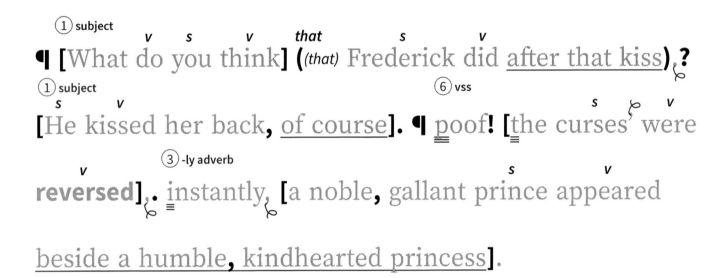

Indentation	new topic; new topic
Note	The passage begins with the narrator addressing the reader. The second indentation is needed when the story continues after the narrator's interruption.
Interjection	***Poof!*** is an interjection that expresses a strong emotion. Use an exclamation mark and capitalize *The*.
S V Pairs	MC ***you do think***
	that *(that)* ***Frederick did*** This is an invisible *that* clause. It does not express a complete thought.
	MC ***He kissed***
	MC ***curses were reversed***
	MC ***prince appeared***
Commas	Place commas around a transitional prepositional phrase. **, *of course***
	Do not use a comma to separate two main clauses. Use a period. MC, MC is always wrong.
	Do not use a comma if an -ly adverb opener modifies the verb. Prince appeared in an instant manner.
	Use a comma to separate coordinate adjectives (noble, gallant prince; humble, kindhearted princess).

Rewrite It!   What do you think Frederick did after that kiss? He kissed her back, of course.

         Poof! The curses were reversed. Instantly a noble, gallant prince appeared beside a

humble, kindhearted princess.

Learn It!

Use the words you chose on page 175 to complete the story.

Birthday Surprise

by _____

One _____ Princess Dorinda and Prince Frederick found a kitten.
     noun

" _____ ! Where did you come from?" Dorinda _____ .
   interjection   speaking verb

"Are you _____ ?"
         adjective

"He will be the _____ gift for Maribella's birthday!" Frederick
                adjective

_____ .
speaking verb

Dorinda hid the kitten in her _____ bedroom. Later, Maribella
                              adjective

_____ into the room, looking for a _____ _____ .
verb (past tense)   adjective   noun (clothing)

Out _____ the kitten, landing on Maribella's _____ . Maribella
    verb (past tense)   noun (body part)

_____ _____ from the room. She _____ right
-ly adverb   verb (past tense)   verb (past tense)

into Frederick, who was carrying a _____ birthday _____ . It
                                   adjective   noun (food)

flew up in the air and _____ on Maribella's _____ . She sat on
                        verb (past tense)   noun (body part)

the floor _____ . The kitten perched _____ on the stairs while
          -ing word   -ing word

Dorinda _____ Maribella.
        verb (past tense)

" _____ ! What a _____ birthday surprise!" Frederick
  interjection   adjective

_____ _____ .
speaking verb   -ly adverb

Appendices

Appendix I: Complete Story

Appendix IV: Grammar Glossary

Frog Prince

In the recent past in an obscure kingdom among the Alps, a decorous king reigned faithfully. His family line of monarchs stretched back to the Middle Ages. King Morton had inherited the throne from his father nearly three decades before. Like his father King Morton ruled fairly and showed compassion to all. As a kindhearted ruler, King Morton loved his subjects. The people of the land esteemed him. Maribella and Dorinda, the king's daughters, lived with him. Everyone in the land admired his devotion to his girls. His younger daughter, however, frustrated him greatly.

Princess Dorinda had been an obstinate child from toddlerhood. As a child she often escaped from the nursery and found mischief. She once stole into the throne room, swung on the chandeliers, and landed at the feet of the scandalized courtiers. On another occasion she upset the prestigious new chef and her staff. They were experimenting with sturgeon roe ice cream. Dorinda sneaked a taste and expected a sweet treat, but instead of bits of chocolate, the taste of salty fish eggs first surprised and then repulsed her.

The princess, who had earned a reputation for beauty, considered herself quite chic because she wore her hair in a French twist and had a beauty spot on her cheek. Her beauty was flawed by her reputation for fastidiousness and self-centeredness.

King Morton hoped that she would consider several young suitors. Dorinda refused them time after time, yet they continued to court her. None were wealthy, handsome, or titled enough for her highness. King Morton, whose patience was dwindling, shook his head in despair and sighed deeply when his daughter voiced her desires.

Clearly, Dorinda annoyed many in the palace. Lady Constance, who had cared for her since childhood, had virtually stopped training her young charge. Although Dorinda had seemed a lovable, tractable, and contented child in her youth, many years of indulgence had spoiled her. She complained constantly. Unfortunately, no expense had been spared to gratify the two girls when the girls' mother was alive. They enjoyed custom dolls with complete wardrobes and assorted furniture, but they always asked for more. When they were young girls, they were disappointed that their fairy-tale playground did not resemble Cinderella's castle. As a teenager Dorinda stomped her foot and pouted when a new television was delivered. Declaring it minuscule, she demanded a theater room with sound, lighting, and comfort. Although Lady Constance did not approve, she met Dorinda's demands because she did not want to argue with her.

On a crisp spring morning, Princess Dorinda played with her latest plaything, which was a golden ball. Tossing it up, she wandered among the plants in the conservatory.

From a distance the king observed his daughter and her golden ball. Eyeing the glass windows, he suggested, "Dorinda, why don't you toss that ball in the garden?"

Dorinda rolled her eyes. Crossly she grabbed her stylish boots and jacket and went outside. With her ball in hand, the princess roamed through the expansive castle gardens. Meandering aimlessly through the stately imperial gardens, Princess Dorinda repeatedly tossed her ball up and down and caught it with slick confidence. At the corner of the well, a most regrettable event occurred. Carelessly she tossed her precious golden ball too high, and down it fell with a splash. Dorinda gasped. The heavy ball sank to the bottom of the deep, dark well. Angry salty tears flowed, and Dorinda, who was inconsolable, stomped her foot in frustration.

"I've lost my golden baaall!" Dorinda wailed. "I would reward my benefactor handsomely if only I could have my ball back."

"I would be honored to assist you," a throaty voice offered.

Instantly Dorinda's tears dried as she looked around for the person who was speaking. In fact, she could turn her tears on and off on a whim. Seeing no one, Dorinda asked, "Oh! Who has proposed such a generous, thoughtful offer?"

Hopping toward her on the rim of the well, an amphibian croaked, "It was I."

As she let loose a spine-tingling shriek, Dorinda started to run. Of course, her inquisitiveness got the better of her, and she turned back to the frog. "How can you talk, Mr. Frog?"

"It's a long, dull story, but I might tell it to you in the future. Would you like me to find your ball?"

"Yes, I would appreciate that."

"I'll gladly do it with one unique stipulation," the frog responded.

"I'll do anything that you want! My dad will kill me if I lose that ball, which cost him a royal fortune," she replied. "You must jump in and retrieve my ball sitting at the bottom of the well."

"I'll salvage your ball if you'll allow me to stay for one night in the palace, feasting at your fancy table and eating from your own plate."

"Well, of course," Dorinda responded hastily.

The frog hopped into the water, disappeared for a few moments, and returned, holding Dorinda's treasure. Gleefully Dorinda snatched the wet, slippery ball.

"It's solid gold," he finally wheezed. Skipping back to the palace, Princess Dorinda didn't hear him pattering behind her. The exhausted amphibian hoped that Princess Dorinda's word was trustworthy.

While the royal family dined sumptuously, they heard a faint tap at the castle door. Within moments a footman appeared and delivered a message to Princess Dorinda.

"Princess," he began, "you have a visitor at the door."

Excusing herself from the table, Dorinda hastened away. She hoped that the visitor was her new friend, for she was eager to eat dessert with her.

When she opened the door, blood drained from her face. There sat the frog squatting and looking at Dorinda with sad huge eyes.

"You forgot your pledge to treat me hospitably," he croaked.

Dorinda slammed the door. Truthfully, she hoped that the audacious, annoying amphibian would leave, forget her promise, and never return.

"Dorinda, who knocked?" King Morton inquired when she returned.

Despite her deficiencies Dorinda truthfully answered her father. "It was a frog."

King Morton's eyes widened, and he inquired, "What did he want?"

Crying yet again, Dorinda sobbed the story of the frog's considerate rescue and of her foolish promise. She miserably wailed, "I will not touch that ugly, despicable thing!"

Dorinda's theatrics frustrated her father; her tears annoyed him. "Daughter," he urged, "you are a royal princess. Your word must be trustworthy."

Reluctantly Princess Dorinda slunk to the door. She opened it just wide enough for the frog to squeeze through. "You may enter," she sighed audibly.

Hopping behind her, the frog followed Dorinda to the elaborate dining hall. "I appreciate your hospitality, Sire. I'm Frederick," the frog volunteered.

"Dorinda, pick up Frederick," her father commanded, "and feed him from your golden plate."

"Yuck! Then I won't touch another bite," she whined.

Patiently King Morton, who valued integrity, explained that a promise was a promise. Additionally, he reminded Dorinda about her royal duties and the expectations of the people, the nation's citizens.

Dorinda complied. Because she would not touch the frog with her own precious fingers, she held her napkin between her thumb and first finger. Unceremoniously she grabbed one of Frederick's hind legs and deposited him on the table beside her plate. He was a revolting green amphibian. Promptly she receded into her chair.

After supper King Morton invited Frederick to the guest room, which was a splendid suite. Velvet carpeted the floor; silk blanketed the bed. Frederick knew that he would relish his palace stay.

Evidently, Dorinda, Maribella, and King Morton had not deduced the frog's true identity. Frederick was not a lowly frog but a royal prince. When he had lived at his father's castle, Frederick had been a swollen-headed, pretentious teenager.

On a humid afternoon in July, young Frederick had been riding his horse, a strong thoroughbred, through a forest in his father's vast kingdom. After he had ridden for several miles, his horse reared up because a thin young boy stood in the path.

"Please, sir, I've lost my way," the boy explained. "Can I have a ride out of this daunting forest?"

"Get out of my way, peasant," the rude, thoughtless prince retorted. He was oblivious that the boy was a wizard in disguise.

Instantly the boy's voice thundered, "For your lack of compassion and decency, you must spend your days as a frog, a worthless creature." Staring reproachfully, the boy zapped the air, and the prince found himself hopping off the saddle and plummeting to the ground. The wizard continued, "As a frog you might learn humility and gratitude for simple kindnesses which people offer you. You will be restored to normal if a princess kisses you in true kindheartedness. If you ever confess that you are a prince, you will be fated to froghood forever."

The frog had kept his secret for six long years, hoping he would eventually return to normal. Frederick had resided as a frog in King Morton's sequestered expansive garden, and he had wished one of the princesses, who frequently spent time in the garden, would be his friend. Unfortunately for him, he had met Dorinda before he had met Maribella.

That evening he assessed the situation and conjectured how to charm Dorinda, the younger princess.

The next morning during a substantial breakfast of omelets, pastries, and fruit, King Morton, who always treated his guests with generosity, graciously insisted that Frederick stay for a week.

Dorinda groaned. Glancing down, she noticed that Frederick's hind leg was inadvertently touching her omelet. "Ew!" she cried as she swept him from her plate and spitefully hurled him against the wall.

"Ow!" he grunted. "I believe my leg is broken!"

Dorinda feigned remorse for her unkind actions, mumbling an apology. "I wish I had broken all of your legs," she muttered pitilessly.

Dorinda's behavior mortified her father. King Morton gently lifted the frog, placed him on a silver tray, and carried him to the doctor caring for the animals. He ordered Dorinda to follow.

In the infirmary the palace vet positioned the frog on the adjustable exam table, where he treated his smallest patients. After he examined Frederick, he set the broken frog leg, which dangled oddly.

"Frogs are animals which heal slowly, so it will be a lengthy convalescence," the vet informed King Morton and Dorinda. "He will stay in the infirmary for a month."

Hearing the doctor's announcement, Dorinda became sullen. After her father insisted that she deliver Frederick's meals, she regretted the day when the accident happened. Dorinda resolved to avoid the infirmary, where Frederick now stayed. When the king ordered her to assist Frederick while he recuperated, she knew it would be difficult. She knew that she would have to treat him royally, but she could be a royal pain.

"Dorinda, read to Frederick your favorite stories in the imperial library," the king announced and walked away.

Every day Dorinda took Frederick to the library. Whenever they entered, the frog marveled at the hundreds of colorful books that covered the walls from floor to ceiling.

At last Frederick had an idea. "Let's play a game!" he eagerly proffered as he searched the row in front of him. "I'll read the first line of a story, and you tell me the name of the book." Agreeing hesitantly, Dorinda sat beside Frederick, whose scrawny skeletal fingers opened a book. "In the light of the moon a little egg lay on a leaf," read Frederick.

Dorinda thought for a moment. "That has to be *The Very Hungry Caterpillar*," she responded. She had enjoyed that book, a favorite of hers, since she was a young child.

Playing the game improved her mood. "Let me do one," she said. "There was a boy called Eustace Clarence Scrubb, and he almost deserved it." Hoping to stump Frederick, she smirked.

Guessing confidently, Frederick answered, "Oh! That's easy! It's *The Voyage of the Dawn Treader*!" Playing the game amused him. He chose another. "Jenna's reputation was only as good as her word."

Dorinda, who didn't know, walked over to look. The words on the cover were *One Good Turn Deserves Another*. Reading the title made Dorinda suspicious. At that moment she decided the game was over. The frog, whom she detested, had irritated her again. She slammed the book down and ignobly fled to the palace grounds. Along the way she approached the well.

Suddenly she noticed an old woman, whose feeble hands were struggling to draw water from the deep well. The woman futilely tried to turn the crank, which would not budge. Clearly, her fingers ached, hampering her task. Grasping the wooden bucket proved useless. Hearing steps, the woman turned toward the girl, who rudely stared but didn't offer any assistance.

"Lovely Princess," the woman began, "I have arthritis in my hands, and I cannot lift the brimming bucket. Would you kindly fetch me a cup of water?"

Tossing her golden locks, Dorinda impulsively turned away. "Why do people think I am their servant?" she grumbled. Treating others attentively and respectfully evaded her.

Manners were essential; politeness was expected. The old lady, a fairy in disguise, brandished her wand and zapped Princess Dorinda into a toad. At last the princess would receive her punishment. Instantly Dorinda plummeted to the ground. All that remained was her crown, which was miniaturized to fit her diminished stature, and her beauty spot, which was prominent among the other toady warts.

"That will teach you," the fairy snapped. "You must learn humility as a toad. If you find a noble, gallant prince who kisses you in kindheartedness, you will be restored to normal."

Every day the princess mourned her new lot in life. Although she found it difficult to convince anyone at the palace of her true identity, the crown and beauty spot proved she was the princess.

Lady Constance puzzled over the crown, which looked familiar, so she tested Dorinda. "If you truly are the princess," she began, "tell me about your bona fide wart, not about that silly beauty spot."

Luckily, that one was easy. "It's true. I have wart hiding behind all my hair," Dorinda croaked.

A palace maid snickered. "That's the reason she never let us style her hair in two braids." Dorinda glared.

Because Lady Constance wasn't convinced, she pressed her again. "What was your nickname when you were a toddler?"

Dorinda sighed testily and tried to roll her eyes. "As a child I was called 'Toady' because I had a wart on the back of my head. As I aged, they dropped it since they realized that I wasn't a toady at all," she snapped.

The palace took her in, but no one wanted to touch her. Her skin, in fact, was rough, warty, and repulsive. Some acknowledged her, whereas others ignored her. The footmen, who once pampered her, snubbed her. Maribella, normally a sympathetic sister, shuddered whenever Dorinda pattered into the room. Even King Morton had nothing hopeful to offer his daughter. Although Dorinda's basic needs were met, the luster had gone out of her life. Moping around the palace, Dorinda complained constantly. Living as a toad devastated the princess.

Miserably Dorinda wandered into the infirmary to commiserate with her fellow amphibian. Mending rapidly, Frederick listened sympathetically while Dorinda shared her gloomy thoughts. According to Frederick being a frog wasn't that dreadful. While people weren't always humane, he was free to live as he pleased. Dorinda, who remained discouraged, listened yet doubted.

Trying to cheer her, Frederick offered to read a few stories. He regaled her with humorous fairy tales and wild, stirring adventures from the novel *The Arabian Nights*. Day after day, Frederick entertained Dorinda. Gradually she grew to appreciate his companionship and to respect his positive demeanor. Living daily without complaint characterized Frederick's life. Frederick always cheerfully greeted the orderly delivering his odious fly soup. He didn't grumble although the chef served him chocolate-covered beetles for dessert. Stumbling over his hurt leg, Dorinda was grateful that Frederick didn't chastise her for her clumsiness but readily forgave her. His joyful attitude had a positive effect on her.

"How do you always remain so cheerful?" Dorinda inquired one day. "Although unpleasant things happen, you show empathy for others. Clearly, trials do not affect you."

"Oh, that's simple. When I am angry, folks avoid me; when I am kind, they spend time with me. After all, why should I be discontent? I am comfortable, fed, and watered."

The next day Frederick rummaged through the bookshelves in the library. He remembered a tale that his mother had read to him when he was a boy. He searched for the story among the books. At last he saw a thin book between two large volumes. He desired this precise book because it included "The Hound and the King's Nephew." She would hear the story; she would learn a lesson.

"Dorinda, listen as I read.

"King Arthur," he began, "was riding with his nephew. Robert, the eldest son of his sister's three boys, enjoyed the king's special favor. Regrettably, he was a mute child. They rode through the royal forest, where they often hunted. Robert's beloved hound, Balin, remained between them. They passed through a cedar grove, and Balin ran ahead, barking emphatically. Balin barked louder than ever before. Robert was surprised since his hound never barked without a credible reason. He recognized the sound as a warning, and concern gripped his heart. By contrast, his uncle seemed undaunted or perhaps oblivious to the noise which the dog was making. Riding for hours, the king had developed a potent thirst.

"At a mountain stream, where cool water trickled over some rocks, King Arthur knelt and then cupped his hands. It was a mere dribble. Longing for a drink, the king waited for his hands to fill with water.

"Anxiously Robert watched and listened while Balin barked madly. Although he feared that something in the water might be noxious, Robert couldn't warn his uncle. Robert knew that he should not interrupt the king, but he had to find a way to alert him. Thinking quickly, Robert rushed to his uncle's side and knocked the water from his hands. This agitated the king.

"King Arthur shouted, 'I am parched and need water.'"

"He just wanted a drink," Dorinda interrupted. "Robert should have trusted his uncle, not his dog. Of course, his uncle was wiser."

"Humans can be foolish, stubborn creatures, whereas animals instinctively sense danger which humans cannot detect," Frederick commented. "Listen to the rest of the story.

"Cupping his hands again, King Arthur collected more of the precious liquid flowing over the rocks. Persistently Robert then jiggled his uncle's hands, signaling that they should check the source before they drank. The king, whose frustration had escalated, callously pushed Robert away. Suddenly Balin appeared, jumping on the king, knocking him over, and spilling the water.

"King Arthur lost all patience. 'Because of your relentless insubordination, you and your miserable hound dog are forever banished from my kingdom!' he snapped at his nephew cowering at his uncle's rage.

"Grievingly Robert turned away, realizing that he could insist on his way or obey his uncle. Since he feared the king, he decided that obedience was a better option.

"King Arthur decided to follow the path among the rocks to the top of the cliff, where the water originated. Wanting to drink without interference, he made the laborious climb.

"At the top he discovered a dead snake. The enormous snake's poison had contaminated the water. Balin and Robert had been trying to save the king's life, but he had been too arrogant to listen.

"When the king returned to the castle, he called for his nephew. Finding Robert in his room with his servant, Arthur humbled himself contritely. 'Can you accept my apology and forgive me?' he began. 'While you trusted Balin, I depended on no one except myself. Robert, for your loyalty I shall elevate you to the coveted position of arm bearer to the king, and Balin shall dine on steak every day.'

"Robert signed to his servant, who translated for him. 'Your safety matters. I am pleased to serve you, and I shall diligently work in the position which you are entrusting to me.'"

At that moment Dorinda realized the message of the story. She understood the offense which was committed yet poignantly forgiven. Considering the boy's kindness, she examined her own heart. Why had she not recognized that her behavior had been abhorrent? Frederick had only desired that she keep her promise. Truthfully, she had treated him as dreadfully as the king had treated Robert, his nephew. Dorinda now knew that kindness to others was more beneficial than nurturing one's selfish interests. With heartfelt remorse she kissed Frederick on his cheek.

What do you think Frederick did after that kiss? He kissed her back, of course.

Poof! The curses were reversed. Instantly a noble, gallant prince appeared beside a humble, kindhearted princess.

-ly Adverb

An **-ly adverb** dresses up writing because it creates a strong image or feeling.

Strong Verb

A **strong verb** dresses up writing because it creates a strong image or feeling. A strong verb is an action verb, never a linking or helping verb.

Quality Adjective

A **quality adjective** dresses up writing because it creates a strong image or feeling. A quality adjective is more specific than a weak adjective, which is overused, boring, or vague.

Pronoun

A **pronoun** replaces a noun in order to avoid repetition.

A **personal pronoun** takes the place of common and proper nouns. It should agree with its antecedent in number, person, and case.

A **reflexive pronoun** ends in -self or -selves and refers to the subject of the same sentence.

An **intensive pronoun** ends in *-self* or *-selves,* functions as an appositive, and intensifies the noun or pronoun it refers to. Intensive pronouns can be removed from the sentence.

	Case	Subjective	Objective	Possessive		Reflexive/Intensive
2 numbers	Function (job) 3 persons	subject predicate pronoun	object of preposition direct object indirect object	adjective	pronoun	
singular	1st	I	me	my	mine	myself
singular	2nd	you	you	your	yours	yourself
singular	3rd	he, she, it	him, her, it	his, her, its	his, hers, its	himself, herself, itself
plural	1st	we	us	our	ours	ourselves
plural	2nd	you	you	your	yours	yourselves
plural	3rd	they	them	their	theirs	themselves

A **relative pronoun** begins a dependent *who/which* clause. The pronoun *who* has three forms: *who* (subjective), *whom* (objective), *whose* (possessive).

who, whom, whose, which, that

An **interrogative pronoun** is used to ask a question.

what, whatever, which, whichever, who, whoever, whom, whose

A **demonstrative pronoun** points to a particular person or thing. When a word on the demonstrative list is placed before a noun, it functions as an adjective, not a pronoun.

this, that, these, those

An **indefinite pronoun** is not definite. It does not refer to any particular person or thing. When a word on the indefinite list is placed before a noun, it functions as an adjective, not a pronoun.

Singular and Plural	Plural	Singular			
all	both		each	much	one
any	few	another	either	neither	other
more	many	anybody	everybody	nobody	somebody
most	others	anyone	everyone	no one	someone
none	own	anything	everything	nothing	something
some	several	anywhere	everywhere	nowhere	somewhere

Preposition

A **preposition** starts a phrase that shows the relationship between a noun or pronoun and another word in the sentence. **PATTERN preposition + noun (no verb)**

This is not an exhaustive list. When in doubt, consult a dictionary.

aboard	amid	beneath	down	into	opposite	throughout	up	
about	among	beside	during	like	out	to	upon	
above	around	besides	except	minus	outside	toward	with	
according to	as	between	for	near	over	under	within	
across	at	beyond	from	of	past	underneath	without	
after	because of	by	in	off	regarding	unlike		
against	before	concerning	inside	on	since	until		
along	behind	despite	instead of	onto	through	unto		

Verb

A **verb** shows action, links the subject to another word, or helps another verb.

An **action verb** shows action or ownership.

A **linking verb** links the subject to a noun or adjective.

am, is, are, was, were, be, being, been (be verbs)

seem, become, appear, grow, remain, taste, sound, smell, feel, look (verbs dealing with the senses)

A **helping verb** helps an action verb or a linking verb.

am, is, are, was, were, be, being, been (be verbs)

have, has, had, do, does, did, may, might, must, can, will, shall, could, would, should

Conjunction

A **conjunction** connects words, phrases, or clauses.

An **coordinating conjunction** (cc) connects the same type of words, phrases, or clauses.

FANBOYS   for, and, nor, but, or, yet, so

A **subordinating conjunction** (www word) connects an adverb clause to a main clause.

www.asia.b   when, while, where, as, since, if although, because

before, after, until, unless, whenever, whereas, than

Clause

A **clause** is a group of related words that contains both a subject and a verb.

Label the subject-verb pairs to determine how many clauses are in each sentence. Focus on the word that begins the clause and on its placement in the sentence to determine if it is a main clause or a dependent clause. After you have identified each clause, follow the comma rules.

Main Clause

A **main clause** expresses a complete thought, so it can stand alone as a sentence.

[Dorinda's dress was expensive].
> Every sentence must have a main clause.

[Dorinda's dress was expensive]**, and** [this frustrated her father].
> When a coordinating conjunction best expresses the relationship between the two main clauses, connect the main clauses with a comma and a coordinating conjunction. **MC, cc MC.**

[The dress had tiny pearls]; [it had gold embroidery].
> When the main clauses express a single idea and are similar in length or construction, connect the main clauses with a semicolon. Use a semicolon sparingly. **MC; MC.**

Dependent Clause

A **dependent clause** does not express a complete thought, so it cannot stand alone as a sentence.

Adjective Clause

An **adjective clause** describes the noun it follows.

A *who/which* clause is an adjective clause.

[Dorinda's dress**, (**which she purchased online**),** was expensive].
> begins with *who, whom, whose, which, when, where, that* (a relative pronoun)
> ❯ use commas unless essential

Noun Clause

All the words in a **noun clause** work together to do a noun job.

A *that* clause is usually a noun clause.

[It frustrated the king] (that Dorinda purchased the dress).
> commonly begins with *that* (a relative pronoun)
> ✗ do not use commas

Adverb Clause

An **adverb clause** modifies a verb in the sentence.

(Although Dorinda did not need another dress)**,** [she purchased this one] (because it had real gold).
> begins with a www word (a subordinating conjunction)
> ❯ use a comma after but not before **AC, MC   MC AC**

Phrase

A **phrase** is a group of related words that contains either a noun or a verb, never both.

④ -ing

Watching his daughter, [King Morton was relaxing <u>in the conservatory</u>, his favorite place]. [Dorinda had grown restless], wandering <u>among the flowers</u>.

Prepositional Phrase

in the conservatory   among the flowers

A **prepositional phrase** begins with a preposition and ends with a noun.

It adds imagery or information to a sentence because the entire phrase functions as an adjective describing a noun or as an adverb modifying a verb or adjective.

 if a prepositional phrase opener has 5 + words
around a transition

Verb Phrase

was relaxing   had grown

A **verb phrase** includes a main verb (action or linking) and its helping verbs.

It tells what a subject does in a sentence. The helping verbs often indicate the tense.

Participial (-ing) Phrase

watching his daughter   wandering among the flowers

A **participial (-ing) phrase** begins with a verb form that ends in -ing and usually includes additional words like adverbs, nouns, infinitives, prepositional phrases, or dependent clauses.

It describes a noun because the entire phrase functions as an adjective. This is why the thing (subject of main clause) after the comma must be the thing doing the inging.

 mid-sentence use commas unless essential

end-sentence use a comma when it describes a noun other than the word directly before it

Appositive Phrase

his favorite place

An **appositive phrase** is an appositive and the words that describe it. An appositive is a noun that renames the noun it follows. The appositive and the noun it follows are different names for the same person, place, thing, or idea.

Because the comma rules for the *who/which* clause and the appositive phrase are the same, mentally insert *who* or *which* and the *be* verb to determine if the appositive phrase requires commas. This is why the appositive phrase is referred to as an invisible *who/which* clause.

use commas unless essential

Sentence Opener

A **sentence opener** is a descriptive word, phrase, or clause that is added to the beginning of a sentence.

(1) subject

The tired governess wondered how to teach Dorinda.

begins with the subject of the sentence (may include article or adjective)

(2) prepositional

Before the queen's unfortunate death, Constance served the queen.

begins with a prepositional phrase

PATTERN preposition + noun (no verb)

, | if 5 + words or transition

(3) -ly adverb

Clearly, Dorinda embarrassed Lady Constance.

begins with an -ly adverb

, | if adverb modifies sentence (It was ____ that ____.)

(4) -ing

Talking out of turn, Dorinda ignored regal protocol.

begins with a participial phrase

PATTERN -ing word/phrase, main clause

, | after phrase

(5) clausal

When Dorinda disregarded regal protocol, Constance chided the girl.

begins with a www word (subordinating conjunction)

PATTERN www word + subject + verb

, | after clause (AC, MC)

(6) vss

Dorinda exhausted her.

2–5 words

Sometimes it appears that more than one sentence opener begins a sentence. When this happens, place the comma after the last opener. Number the sentence opener based on the first word of the sentence.

Fix It!™
Grammar

Glossary

Listen. Speak. Read. Write. Think!

Fix It!
Grammar

Glossary

FOURTH EDITION

Contents

Parts of Speech

Every word belongs to a word group—a **part of speech**. There are eight parts of speech. Many words can be used as different parts of speech. However, a word will only perform one part of speech at a time. (*Light* is a verb in The fireworks *light* the sky. *Light* is a noun in We need more *light*. *Light* is an adjective in It is a *light* load.)

One must look at how words are used in a sentence to determine their parts of speech. To see how these parts of speech are used as IEW dress-ups and sentence openers, see the Stylistic Techniques section beginning on page G-37.

Noun

A **noun** names a person, place, thing, or idea.

To determine if a word is a noun, ask if an article adjective (a, an, the) comes before it or if it is countable.

> Noun Tests:
> the _____
> two _____

A **common noun** names a general person, place, or thing. It is not capitalized.

A **proper noun** names a specific person, place, or thing. It is capitalized.

> The *king* is a common noun, but *King James* is a proper noun.

> A *beagle* is a common noun, but the name of my pet beagle *Benji* is a proper noun.

A **compound noun** is two or more words combined to form a single noun. They can be written three different ways. To spell compound words correctly, consult a dictionary.

separate words	*fairy tale; Robin Hood; ice cream*
hyphenated words	*merry-go-round; son-in-law; seventy-two*
one word	*grandmother; railroad; moonlight*

Pronoun

A **pronoun** replaces a noun in order to avoid repetition. The noun the pronoun replaces is called an antecedent.

A **personal pronoun** refers back to an antecedent recently mentioned and takes the place of that noun. The pronoun should agree with its antecedent in number, person, and case.

3 cases		*Subjective* function as	*Objective* function as	*Possessive* function as	
		subject subject complement	object of a preposition direct object indirect object	adjective	pronoun
2 numbers	3 persons				
singular	1st	I	me	my	mine
	2nd	you	you	your	yours
	3rd	he, she, it	him, her, it	his, her, its	his, hers, its
plural	1st	we	us	our	ours
	2nd	you	you	your	yours
	3rd	they	them	their	theirs

Number means one (singular) or more than one (plural).

Person means who is speaking (1st), spoken to (2nd), or spoken about (3rd).

Case refers to the way a pronoun functions in a sentence.

Both a **reflexive pronoun** (used in the objective case) and an **intensive pronoun** (used as an appositive) end in *-self* or *-selves* and refer back to a noun or pronoun in the same sentence.

Dorinda fancied *herself* quite stylish.   Dorinda *herself* played as others worked.

A **relative pronoun** (*who, which, that*) begins a dependent clause. Use *who* for people and *which* or *that* for things. See page G-21.

Robin lived in Sherwood Forest, *which* belonged to the king.

Robin knew the other men *who* lived in the forest.

Robin battled with Little John, *whom* he had met on the log.

Robin knew the families *whose* lands had been stolen.

Forms of *who* include *whom* and *whose*.
> *who* subjective case
> *whom* objective case
> *whose* possessive case

An **interrogative pronoun** is used to ask a question. The most common include *what, whatever, which, whichever, who, whoever, whom, whose.*

Who owns that house? *Whatever* do you mean? *Whose* coat is this?

Not all question words are pronouns. Words like *why* and *how* are adverbs.

A **demonstrative pronoun** (*this, that, these, those*) points to a particular person or thing.

This is my mother and *that* is our house.   *These* are mine.   *Those* are yours.

An **indefinite pronoun** is not definite. It does not refer to any particular person or thing.

Everyone will attend.   *All* of the cookies are gone.   *Most* of the cake is gone.

When a word on the demonstrative or indefinite list is placed before a noun, it functions as an adjective, not a pronoun.
> *Both* cookies are gone.
> I live in *that* house.

Singular and Plural	Plural	Singular			
all	both		each	much	one
any	few	another	either	neither	other
more	many	anybody	everybody	nobody	somebody
most	others	anyone	everyone	no one	someone
none	own	anything	everything	nothing	something
some	several	anywhere	everywhere	nowhere	somewhere

Noun and Pronoun Functions

Both nouns and pronouns perform many jobs or functions in a sentence.

A **subject** performs a verb action. It tells who or what the clause is about.

> The soldier marched in formation.
> Who marched? *soldier* (subject)

A **subject complement** follows a linking verb and renames the subject (also called a predicate noun) or describes the subject (also called a predicate adjective).

> The soldier is a *woman*. The king is *he*. The castle is *theirs*.

The **object of a preposition** is the last word in a prepositional phrase. See page G-18.

A **direct object** follows an action verb and answers the question *what* or *whom*.

> The soldier built a fire.
> Built what? *a fire* (direct object)

> The soldier treated him kindly.
> Treated whom? *him* (direct object)

An **indirect object** appears only when there is a direct object. Indirect objects come between the verb and direct object and tell who or what received the direct object.

> The dwarf gave the soldier a purse.
> Gave what? *purse* (direct object). Who received it? *soldier* (indirect object)

> The woman knitted him a scarf.
> Knitted what? *scarf* (direct object). Who received it? *him* (indirect object)

To tell the difference between an indirect object and a direct object, revise the sentence and insert *to* or *for* in front of the indirect object.

> The dwarf gave a purse *to* the soldier.

> The woman knitted a scarf *for* him.

A **possessive case pronoun** that functions as an adjective comes before a noun, whereas a possessive case pronoun that functions as a pronoun is used alone.

> That is *my* house.

> That is *mine*.

A **noun of direct address** (NDA) is a noun used to refer to someone directly. It appears in dialogue and names the person spoken to.

> "Timmy, after dinner we can read books," Johnny said.

An **appositive** is a noun that renames the noun that comes before it.

Place commas around an appositive if it is nonessential to the meaning of the sentence.

> Robin Hood**,** *the archer***,** led his men through the forest.
> (nonessential, commas)

Do not place commas around an appositive if it is essential to the meaning of the sentence. See page G-26.

> The archer *Robin Hood* led his men through the forest.
> (essential, no commas) The appositive is essential because it defines which archer led his men.

Function is different from part of speech.

A noun or pronoun can perform only one function in a sentence.

When the sentence is a command, the subject, *you*, is implied. See imperative mood, page G-11.

The appositive is an invisible *who/which* clause. See page G-39.

Preposition

A **preposition** starts a phrase that shows the relationship between a noun or pronoun and another word in the sentence.

A preposition usually shows a relationship dealing with space or time.

> The squirrel sat *on the branch* (space) *in the morning* (time).

A word functions as a preposition when it is part of a prepositional phrase. See page G-18.

> A prepositional phrase always begins with a preposition and ends with a noun or pronoun. The phrase may have adjectives in between, but never a verb.

> The noun or pronoun that ends the prepositional phrase is called the object of the preposition. When the object of the preposition is a pronoun, it will be one of the objective case pronouns: *me, you, him, her, it, us, you, them.*

Some words on the preposition list may function as another part of speech.

> When a word that looks like a preposition follows a verb but does not have a noun afterward, it is not functioning as a preposition but as an adverb.

> > The mouse fell down. (fell where? *down*)
> > *Down* is not followed by a noun.
> > This is an adverb, not a prepositional phrase.

> > Timmy wore his vest inside (wore vest where? *inside*)
> > *Inside* is not followed by a noun.
> > This is an adverb, not a prepositional phrase.

> When a word that looks like a preposition is followed by a subject and a verb, it is a not functioning as a preposition but as a subordinating conjunction (www word).

> > *As Johnny gave orders*, the mice listened
> > *As Johnny gave orders* contains a subject (Johnny) and a verb (gave).
> > This is a clause, not a prepositional phrase.

> > The mice hid *after the cat arrived.*
> > *After the cat arrived* contains a subject (cat) and a verb (arrived).
> > This is a clause, not a prepositional phrase.

This is not an exhaustive list. When in doubt, consult a dictionary.

PATTERN

preposition + noun
(no verb)

If it is something a squirrel can do with a tree, it is probably a prepositional phrase.

A squirrel climbs *up the tree*, sits *in the tree*, runs *around the tree.*

Prepositions List

aboard	around	between	in	opposite	toward
about	as	beyond	inside	out	under
above	at	by	instead of	outside	underneath
according to	because of	concerning	into	over	unlike
across	before	despite	like	past	until
after	behind	down	minus	regarding	unto
against	below	during	near	since	up, upon
along	beneath	except	of	through	with
amid	beside	for	off	throughout	within
among	besides	from	on, onto	to	without

Verb

A **verb** shows action, links the subject to another word, or helps another verb.

To determine if a word is a verb, use the verb test.

An **action verb** shows action or ownership.

She *chopped* vegetables.

The chef *prepared* lunch.

Dorinda *has* a beauty mark.

They *own* a lovely palace.

A **linking verb** links the subject to a noun or an adjective. When the subject complement is a noun, the noun after the linking verb renames the subject. When the subject complement is an adjective, the adjective after the linking verb describes the subject.

Robin Hood *was* (linking verb) an outlaw (subject complement, noun).
Outlaw is another name for Robin Hood.

The soup *smelled* (linking verb) delicious (subject complement, adjective).
Delicious describes soup.

The soup *is* (linking verb) salty (subject complement, adjective).
Salty describes soup.

A **helping verb** helps an action verb or a linking verb. It is paired with the main verb (action or linking) to indicate tense, voice, and mood.

The chef *would* prepare supper.
Would helps prepare.

The soup *had* tasted strange.
Had helps tasted.

Verb Test:

I _____.

It _____.

Some verbs function as either action or linking verbs.

He *smells* (action) gas.

The gas *smells* (linking) bad.

If you can substitute *is* for the verb, it is probably functioning as a linking verb.

Linking Verbs List

am, is, are, was, were, be, being, been (be verbs)

seem, become, appear, grow, remain

taste, sound, smell, feel, look (verbs dealing with the senses)

Helping Verbs List

am, is, are, was, were, be, being, been (be verbs)

have, has, had, do, does, did, may, might, must

can, will, shall, could, would, should

Be verbs dominate our language and perform important functions as both linking and helping verbs.

Students should memorize the *be* verbs: am, is, are, was, were, be, being, been.

Verbal

A **verbal** is a word formed from a verb that is usually not functioning as a verb.
A verbal often functions as a noun, adjective, or adverb.

An **infinitive** is formed by placing *to* in front of the simple present form of a verb.

An infinitive functions as an adjective, adverb, or noun, but never as a verb.

Dorinda has some things *to learn.*

Frederick is eager *to hear* a story.

A **participle** is formed by adding the suffix *-ing* or *-ed* to the simple present form of a verb.

splash + ing = splashing; splash + ed = splashed

A participle functions as a verb if it has a helping verb.

He *was splashing*, which frightened the fish.

For years, she *had longed* to visit the city.

If a participle does not have a helping verb, it functions as an adjective. A participle-adjective may appear directly before a noun or after a linking verb.

Robin Hood was known for his *hunting* skills.

It was a *botched* case. The case was *botched.*

A participle may also form a participial phrase that describes a noun in the sentence.

Springing to his feet, Robin Hood confronted the challenger.
Springing to his feet describes Robin Hood, the subject after the comma.

Robin Hood whistled merrily, *thinking of Maid Marian.*
Thinking of Maid Marian describes Robin Hood, the subject of the sentence.

A **gerund** is formed by adding the suffix *-ing* to the simple present form of a verb.

splash + ing = splashing

A gerund functions as a noun, never as a verb.

His *splashing* frightened the fish.
Splashing is the subject of the sentence and therefore a noun.

The fish were frightened by his *splashing.*
Splashing is the object of the preposition *by* and therefore a noun.

Tense

Verb tense indicates when an action occurs. There are six tenses in English: simple past, simple present, simple future, past perfect, present perfect, and future perfect.

The **simple tense** is simply formed by using different forms of the verb.

I *biked.* I *bike.* I *will bike.*

He *ran.* He *runs.* He *will run.*

The **perfect tense** is formed by adding a form of *have* to the past participle verb form.

I *had biked.* I *have biked.* I *will have biked.*

He *had run.* He *has run.* He *will have run.*

Most writing occurs in the **past tense**, either simple or perfect. When telling about two events that occurred in the past, the more recent event is written in the simple past tense, and the earlier event is written in the past perfect tense.

The soldiers *cried* (past tense) because they *had lost* (past perfect) their gifts.

To + verb and verbs ending in -ing should not be marked as strong verbs.

For clarity in meaning, avoid splitting infinitives when possible.

To split an infinitive is to insert one or more adverbs between *to* and the verb, as in *to foolishly insert.*

Some words do not form the past participle by adding -ed. There are many irregular verb forms.

eat/eaten
not eated

creep/crept
not creeped

draw/drew
not drawed

If in doubt, consult a dictionary.

Simple past is commonly called *past*; simple present, *present*; and simple future, *future.*

Forms of *have* include *have, has,* and *had.*

Use *had* + the past participle of a verb to form the past perfect.

Voice

Verb voice indicates if the subject is doing or receiving the action. There are two voices in English: active and passive.

In **active voice**, the subject of the sentence is doing the verb action. The active voice creates a strong image and feeling because it highlights the doer of the action. Most sentences should be written in active voice.

> *Will climbed* the tree.
> The subject (Will) is doing the verb (climbed).

In **passive voice**, the subject receives the action of the verb. The subject is not doing any action. The verb is always in the form of a verb phrase (two or more words) that contains a *be* verb and a past participle. Because the passive voice is often wordy and dull, avoid overusing the passive voice.

> The *tree was climbed* by Will. The *tree was climbed*.
> In both sentences the subject (the tree) is not doing the verb action (was climbed). Someone or something else is doing the verb action. In the first sentence who is doing the verb is specified (Will). In the second sentence it is implied.

Action verbs, not linking verbs, can be passive or active.

To create a strong image and feeling, write sentences where the subject actively does the verb action.

Sam kicked the ball is better than *The ball was kicked by Sam.*

 Advanced

PATTERN **subject** (person/thing being acted on) **+ be verb + past participle + by someone or something** (either in the sentence or implied). The passive sentence must have all four elements.

> The tree (thing being acted on) was (be verb) climbed (past participle) by Will (by someone).
> The castle (the thing being acted on) would be (be verb) demolished (past participle) by the soldiers (by someone).

Understanding passive voice helps distinguish if an -ed word is operating as a verb or an adjective.

> The sandwich (the thing being acted on) was (be verb) devoured (past participle).
> Someone must have devoured the sandwich, so the "by someone" is implied.
> Since this sentence follows the passive voice pattern, *devoured* is a verb.

> Molly (subject) was (be verb) famished (-ed word).
> Since *famished* is a state of being, not something being done to Molly, there is no implied "by someone" phrase. Thus, *famished* is an adjective that follows a linking verb (was), describing Molly.

Mood

Verb mood indicates how an action is expressed, telling if it is a fact, opinion, command, or suggestion. There are three moods in English: indicative, imperative, and subjunctive.

The **indicative mood** makes statements or asks questions.

> I will swim. Will you swim with me?

The **imperative mood** gives a command or makes a request. The subject of an imperative sentence is always *you*.

> Swim. Swim to the other side of the pond.

The **subjunctive mood** expresses contrary-to-fact conditions with *wish* or *if* statements in the third person. It is used infrequently.

> If Sam were concerned, he would take swimming lessons.
> Sam is not concerned, so the subjunctive *Sam were* is correct.

> Sam's mother wishes that he were a stronger swimmer.
> Sam is not a stronger swimmer, so the subjunctive *he were* is correct.

Conjunction
A conjunction connects words, phrases, or clauses.

A **coordinating conjunction** connects the same type of words, phrases, or clauses. The items the coordinating conjunction connects must be grammatically the same: two or more nouns, two or more present participles, two or more dependent clauses, two or more main clauses, and so forth.

Memorize the cc's using the acronym FANBOYS:
for, and, nor, but, or, yet, so.

There are seven coordinating conjunctions: *for, and, nor, but, or, yet, so.*

Use a comma before a coordinating conjunction when it connects three or more items in a series.
PATTERN a, b, and c

He *ran* to the window, *opened* it, and *jumped* out.

Use a comma before a coordinating conjunction when it connects two main clauses (a compound sentence).
PATTERN MC, cc MC

The *cook yelled,* and the *mouse ran.*

Do not use a comma before a coordinating conjunction when it connects two items in a series unless they are main clauses.
PATTERN a and b

The cook saw the *vegetables* (no comma) but not the *mouse.*

Do not use a comma before a coordinating conjunction when it connects two verbs (a compound verb) with the same subject.
PATTERN MC cc 2nd verb

The cook *yelled* (no comma) and *ran.*

Starting sentences with a coordinating conjunction is discouraged in formal writing on the basis that a coordinating conjunction connects things of equal grammatical construction within a sentence.

Faulty parallelism occurs when a coordinating conjunction does not connect things of equal grammatical construction. This means that the items in a series are not parallel.

He *ran* to the window, *opened* it, and *jumping* out.
Ran, opened, and jumping are not the same verb form. To correct, change jumping to jumped: He *ran, opened,* and *jumped.*

In academic papers students should avoid beginning a sentence with a cc.

In fictional papers dialogue can mimic real speech patterns. Thoughts often begin with *and* or *but.*

A **subordinating conjunction** (also called a www word) usually connects an adverb clause to a main clause. The adverb clause is a dependent clause, which cannot stand alone as a sentence. It begins with a www word and contains a subject and a verb.

There are many subordinating conjunctions. The most common are taught using the acronym *www.asia.b*: when, while, where, as, since, if, although, because. Other words function as subordinating conjunctions: after, before, until, unless, whenever, whereas, than.

 Use a comma after an adverb clause that comes before a main clause.
PATTERN **AC, MC**

> *When it rained,* Timmy stayed indoors.

 Do not use a comma before an adverb clause.
PATTERN **MC AC**

> Timmy stayed indoors (no comma) *when it rained.*

A word functions as a subordinating conjunction only when it is followed by a subject and verb. This is why recognizing the pattern www word + subject + verb is important. If a verb is not present, the group of words is likely a prepositional phrase and not a clause. See pages G-18 and G-21.

A **conjunctive adverb** connects ideas or provides a transition.

Common conjunctive adverbs are *however, therefore, then, moreover, consequently, otherwise, nevertheless, thus, furthermore, instead, otherwise.*

 Place commas around a conjunctive adverb if it interrupts the flow of the sentence. The exception is one-syllable conjunctive adverbs like *then.*

> *Moreover,* Robin Hood had many followers.
> Robin Hood was a talented archer and, *moreover,* a good leader.
> *Then* (no comma) he took an arrow from his quiver.

If a conjunctive adverb is used to connect two main clauses that express similar ideas, place a semicolon before the conjunctive adverb and a comma after.
PATTERN **MC; ca, MC.**

> The outlaws lived in the forest; *however,* the forest belonged to the king.

PATTERN

www word + subject + verb

Memorize the most common www words using the acronym *www.asia.b*: when, while, where, as, since, if, although, because.

When you add a conjunctive adverb to a main clause, it is still a main clause, which is not the case with subordinating conjunctions or relative pronouns.

Adjective

An **adjective** describes a noun or pronoun. An adjective tells which one, what kind, how many, or whose.

An adjective comes before the noun it describes or follows a linking verb and describes the subject. See page G-9.

> The scared mice jumped from the first basket and ran under the cook's feet.
> What kind of mice? *scared* Which basket? *first* Whose feet? *cook's*

> The mice appeared *scared*.
> *Scared* follows *appeared* (linking verb) and describes *mice* (subject).

An **article adjective** signals a noun is coming. The article adjectives are *a, an, the*. Sometimes adjectives come between the article and its noun.

> *The* tall stranger entered *the* room.

> *The* boy appeared to be *a* reluctant, timid soldier.

A **comparative adjective** is formed by adding the adverb *more* or the ending *-er* to an adjective. A comparative adjective compares two nouns.

> The rose was *more* beautiful than the daisy.

> The boy stood *taller* than his mother.

A **superlative adjective** is formed by adding the adverb *most* or the ending *-est* to an adjective. A superlative adjective compares three or more nouns.

> This is the *most* interesting book I have read.

> The Little Mermaid was the *youngest* in her family.

Most one-syllable adjectives form the comparative and superlative by adding the suffix *-er* or *-est*. Three or more syllable adjectives form the comparative with *more* and the superlative with *most*. Two-syllable adjectives are formed both ways. If in doubt, consult a dictionary.

 Use a comma to separate **coordinate adjectives**. Adjectives are coordinate if each adjective independently describes the noun that follows. The order is not important.

> The woman had a thin face with a pointed**,** protruding nose.
> It sounds right to say both *protruding, pointed nose* and
> *pointed and protruding nose*. The adjectives are coordinate
> and the comma is necessary.

 Do not use a comma to separate **cumulative adjectives**. Adjectives are cumulative if the first adjective describes the second adjective and the noun that follows. Cumulative adjectives follow this specific order: quantity, opinion, size, age, shape, color, origin, material, purpose.

> Robin saw fifteen foresters seated beneath a huge oak tree.
> It does not sound right to say *oak huge tree* or *huge and oak tree*.
> The adjectives are cumulative and should not have a comma.

A **possessive adjective** is a noun functioning as an adjective in order to show ownership. See page G-28.

> The vest belonged to Timmy (noun).

> Timmy's (possessive adjective) vest had several pockets.

Adjective Test:
the _____ pen

> Which pen?
> the *first* pen
> *that* pen

> What kind of pen?
> a *shiny* pen
> the *green* pen

> How many pens?
> *twenty* pens
> *few* pens

> Whose pen?
> the *teacher's* pen
> *my* pen

Some words form irregular comparatives and superlatives. The most common of these are *good, better, best* and *bad, worse, worst*.

Only coordinate adjectives need to be separated with a comma.

Adjectives are coordinate if you can reverse their order or add *and* between them.

Adjectives are cumulative if they must be arranged in a specific order.

Adverb

An **adverb** modifies a verb, an adjective, or another adverb. An adverb tells how, when, where, why, or to what extent.

> I dropped the pen there beside the book.
> Dropped where? *there*

> He seemed genuinely happy when he indicated that he would visit us later.
> How happy? *genuinely* Visit when? *later*

An **-ly adverb** is an adverb that ends in -ly. Not all words that end in -ly are adverbs. Impostor -ly adverbs are adjectives like *chilly, ghastly, ugly,* and *friendly*. If the word ending in -ly describes a noun, it is an adjective and not an adverb.

> Inadvertently Frederick touched Dorinda's omelet with his hind leg.
> Touched how? *inadvertently* Inadvertently is an adverb.

> Dorinda accidentally hurled him across the room.
> Hurled how? *accidentally* Accidentally is an adverb.

> Frederick uttered a ghastly sound when his leg broke.
> What kind of sound? *ghastly* Ghastly is not an -ly adverb. It is an adjective because it describes the noun *sound*.

An **interrogative adverb** is an adverb used to begin a question. The interrogative adverbs are *how, when, where,* and *why*.

> *Why* do bees sting, Baloo?

> *How* will you collect the honey?

A **comparative** or **superlative** adverb is usually formed by adding the adverbs *more* or *most* in front of the adverb. If the adverb is short, the suffix -er or -est is used, as in faster or fastest. If in doubt, consult a dictionary.

Do not place *more* or *most* before the word with -er or -est after. Not *more faster* but *faster*.

Interjection

An **interjection** expresses an emotion.

When an interjection expresses a strong emotion, use an exclamation mark. The next word begins with a capital letter.

> *Help!* My golden ball has vanished.

When an interjection does not express a strong emotion, use a comma.

> *Oh,* I see it now.

The Sentence

Sentences are essential to writing. As the building blocks of sentences, clauses and phrases are the most important structural units of language. For the reader, the ability to recognize clauses and phrases results in greater comprehension. For the writer, the ability to organize clauses and phrases results in clearer communication. The writer must know enough about each to punctuate properly. This section defines these terms and explains the related commas rules.

Sentence

A sentence contains a subject and a verb and expresses one complete thought.

> Every sentence must have a main clause.

A sentence begins with a capital letter and ends with an end mark. It contains at least one subject-verb pair, which is called a main clause. A **subject** is the noun or pronoun that tells who or what the clause is about. A **verb** tells what the subject is doing. Additional words, phrases, and clauses may be added.

A **run-on** occurs when a sentence has two main clauses that are not connected properly. There are two types of run-ons, which are always wrong.

A **fused sentence** is two main clauses placed in one sentence without any punctuation between them. **MC MC.**

Quinn glanced up the door slammed shut.

A **comma splice** is two main clauses placed in one sentence with only a comma between them. **MC, MC.**

Quinn glanced up, the door slammed shut.

There are four main ways to fix a run-on.

> A period is usually the easiest solution for run-ons.

1. Period: Quinn glanced up. The door slammed shut. PATTERN **MC. MC.**

2. Comma + cc: Quinn glanced up, *and* the door slammed shut. PATTERN **MC, cc MC.**

3. Adverb clause: Start one of the clauses with one of the www words.

As Quinn glanced up, the door slammed shut. PATTERN **AC, MC.**

Quinn glanced up *as* the door slammed shut. PATTERN **MC AC.**

> A semicolon is only used when both main clauses are closely related and usually parallel in construction.

4. Semicolon: Quinn glanced up; the door slammed shut. PATTERN **MC; MC.**

Of these options for this example, the adverb clause is the best solution because *as* explains how the two clauses are related.

A **fragment** occurs when a sentence does not contain a main clause. The group of words may contain a phrase and/or a dependent clause, but it is only part of a sentence.

Fragments that do not leave the reader hanging and that fit the flow of the paragraph are dramatic and effective. *Fix It!* stories permit such fragments, especially in dialogue.

Timmy saw his dear friend. (sentence)
Greeting him kindly. (unacceptable fragment)
"Hello, Johnny!" (acceptable fragment)

Phrase

A phrase is a group of related words that contains either a noun or a verb, never both.

A **prepositional phrase** begins with a preposition and ends with a noun. There might be other words between the preposition and the noun, but there is never a verb in a prepositional phrase.

PATTERN

preposition + noun (no verb)

To identify a prepositional phrase, find a word that appears to be a preposition and ask *what*? Answer with a noun, never a verb. See page G-8.

Through the glimmering twilight beamed the evening star in all its beauty.
Find a preposition. *through* through what? *through the glimmering twilight*
Find a preposition. *in* in what? *in all its beauty*

If a prepositional opener has five words or more, follow it with a comma.

> *Under the table* (no comma) the tiny mouse hid.

> *Under the heavy wooden table,* the tiny mouse hid.

If two or more prepositional phrases open a sentence, follow the last phrase with a comma.

> *Under the heavy wooden table in the kitchen,* the tiny mouse hid.

If a prepositional opener functions as a transition, follow it with a comma.

> *Of course,* the cook was afraid of mice.

If a prepositional opener is followed by a main clause that has the verb before the subject, do not use a comma.

> *Under the heavy wooden table* hid a tiny mouse.

Do not put a comma in front of a prepositional phrase unless the phrase is a transition.

> The mouse hid (no comma) *under a table in the kitchen.*

> The cook was, *of course,* afraid of mice.

Prepositional phrases that function as transitions require commas.

> in fact
> in addition
> by the way
> by contrast
> for example
> for instance
> of course
> on the other hand

Recognizing the basic clause and phrase structure of a sentence will allow students to punctuate their sentences properly. Removing prepositional phrases helps reveal the underlying structure of the sentence.

When a prepositional phrase is misplaced, the meaning is distorted, often humorously. Revise the sentence by moving the prepositional phrase.

> The mouse hid under a table with the long gray tail.

> The mouse, not the table, has the long gray tail.

> The mouse with the long gray tail hid under a table.

 Advanced

When a preposition ends a sentence, it is not wrong. This is a carryover from Latin and not a true rule in English. Andrew Pudewa quips that Winston Churchill gave the definitive answer to this problem when he remarked, "That is a rule up with which I will not put!" If the sentence is more awkward to revise with the preposition placed earlier, it is better to have it at the end.

> I have only a staff to meet you with.

> The alternative is this stilted construction: I have only a staff with which to meet you.

A **verb phrase** is one main verb (action or linking) and one or more helping verbs. The helping verb indicates the tense, mood, and voice. Sometimes the helping verb(s) and the main verb are separated by other words. See page G-9.

> The Little Mermaid *could* (helping verb) not *forget* (action verb) the charming prince.
> The verb phrase *could forget* functions as the verb.

A **participial phrase** begins with a participle (verb + -ing or -ed) and includes its modifiers and complements. A participial phrase functions as an adjective that describes a noun in the sentence.

> *Springing to his feet,* Robin Hood confronted the challenger.
> *Springing to his feet* describes Robin Hood, the subject of the main clause.

> Robin Hood, *thinking of Maid Marian,* whistled merrily.
> *Thinking of Maid Marian* describes Robin Hood, the subject of the main clause.

> *Affronted by their mockery,* Robin challenged the foresters.
> *Affronted by their mockery* describes Robin, the subject of the main clause.

> The path brought them to a broad stream *spanned by a narrow bridge.*
> *Spanned by a narrow bridge* describes stream, the object of the prepositional phrase.

 Use a comma after a participial opener (-ing), even if it is short.
PATTERN -ing word/phrase, main clause

> *Gathering their three gifts,* the soldiers visited the king.
> The thing after the comma is the thing doing the inging.

Place commas around a mid-sentence participial phrase if it is nonessential to the meaning of the sentence.

> David, *playing on the beach,* saw a mermaid. (nonessential, commas)
> The proper noun David defines which child saw a mermaid.

Use a comma when a participial phrase comes at the end of a sentence and describes a noun other than the word it follows.

> Robin whistled, *thinking of Maid Marian.* (describes Robin, comma)

 Do not place commas around a mid-sentence participial phrase if it is essential to the meaning of the sentence. See page G-26.

> The child *playing on the beach* saw a mermaid. (essential, no commas)
> The phrase is essential because it defines which child saw a mermaid.

Do not use a comma when a participial phrase comes at the end of a sentence and describes the word it follows.

> Dorinda saw her ball rolling down the hill. (describes ball, no comma)

Every clause must have an action or a linking verb, not a helping verb.

A #4 -ing opener is a participial opener. See page G-44.

Clause

A clause is a group of related words that contains both a subject and a verb.

A **main clause [MC]** has a subject and a verb. A main clause, sometimes called an independent clause, can stand alone as a sentence because it expresses a complete thought.

> The second solider took the road to the right. [main clause]

A **dependent clause** also has a subject and a verb. However, it cannot stand alone as a sentence because it does not express a complete thought. As a result, a dependent clause, sometimes called a subordinate clause, must be added to a main clause to make sense. Dependent clauses begin with a word that causes them to be an incomplete thought.

> Although the second soldier took the road to the right. (dependent clause)

> One of the keys to punctuating sentences properly is being able to identify dependent clauses accurately. Every dependent clause functions as either an adjective, an adverb, or a noun.

Identify the clause by 1) focusing on the word that begins the dependent clause and 2) checking the placement of the clause in the sentence. Once the clause function has been determined, properly punctuating the sentence is easy.

Main Clause

Contains:
subject + verb

stands alone

Contains:
subject + verb

cannot stand alone

Main Clause [MC]

subject + verb
stands alone

[The frog rescued her ball.]

Dependent Clause

subject + verb
cannot stand alone

Adjective Dependent Clause

[The frog, (who was actually a prince,) rescued her ball.]

who/which clause (*w/w*)
functions as an adjective
begins with *who, which, that*
use commas unless essential

Adverb Dependent Clause

(When her ball fell into the well,) [the frog rescued it.]

[The frog rescued her ball] (when it fell into the well.)

www.asia.b clause (AC)
functions as an adverb
begins with www word
use comma after but not before

Noun Dependent Clause

[Dorinda did not realize] (that the frog was a prince.)

that clause (*that*)
functions as a noun
often begins with *that*
no commas

An **adjective clause** is a dependent clause that functions as an adjective.

> Because the adjective clause is a dependent clause, it must be added to a main clause. Most of the time it directly follows the noun or pronoun that it describes.
>
> An adjective clause begins with a relative pronoun (*who, which, that*) or a relative adverb (*where, when, why*) and contains both a subject and a verb. The subject of the adjective clause is often the word it begins with (such as *who, which, where*). See page G-6.
>
> > Robin, who lived among them, led the outlaws.
> > *Robin led the outlaws* is the main clause.
> > (*Robin* is the subject; *led* is the verb.)
> >
> > *Who lived among* them is the adjective clause.
> > (*Who* is the subject; *lived* is the verb.)

The *who/which* clause is an adjective clause that begins with *who* or *which*. See page G-39.

 Place commas around an adjective clause if it is nonessential to the meaning of the sentence.

> Robin**,** *who was happy and carefree***,** traveled through the forest.
> (nonessential, commas)

 Do not place commas around an adjective clause if it is essential to the meaning of the sentence. See page G-26.

> The men *who followed Robin Hood* could be trusted. (essential, no commas) The clause is essential because it defines which men could be trusted.

An adjective clause that begins with *that* is always essential. Thus, *that* clauses do not take commas.

Advanced

A relative pronoun introduces the adjective clause and connects it to the main clause. It functions as a pronoun because it replaces the noun or pronoun that precedes it.

> *which*
> The woman served brown bread, ~~bread~~ tasted delicious.

An **adverb clause** is a dependent clause that functions as an adverb.

> Because the adverb clause is a dependent clause, it must be added to a main clause. An adverb clause may appear anywhere in a sentence.
>
> An adverb clause begins with a subordinating conjunction (www word) and contains both a subject and a verb. See page G-13.
>
> > Eden admired Quinn while she sang her solo.
> > *Eden admired Quinn* is the main clause.
> > (*Eden* is the subject; *admired* is the verb.)
> >
> > *While she sang her solo* is the adverb clause.
> > (*She* is the subject; *sang* is the verb.)

PATTERN

www word + subject + verb

 Use a comma after an adverb clause that comes before a main clause.
PATTERN AC, MC

> *When it rained***,** Timmy stayed indoors.

 Do not use a comma before an adverb clause.
PATTERN MC AC

> Timmy stayed indoors (no comma) *when it rained.*

A comma is placed before *although*, *while*, or *whereas* when a strong contrast exists. See page G-26.

An adverb clause follows the pattern www word + subject + verb. If a verb is not present, the group of words is likely a prepositional phrase. See page G-18.

A **noun clause** is a dependent clause that functions as a noun.

A noun clause can do any function that a noun can do: subject, object of the preposition, direct object, indirect object, subject complement. See page G-7.

Like the other dependent clauses, the noun clause contains both a subject and a verb. Many noun clauses begin with *that*, but they can also begin with other words, including *how, what, when, where, whether, which, who, why*.

> *What Dorinda said* disappointed her father.
> What Dorinda said is the subject of the main clause.

> Dorinda did not realize *when her actions were unacceptable*.
> When her actions were unacceptable is the direct object of the verb *realize*.

> Dorinda's primary problem was *that she was self-centered*.
> That she was self-centered is the subject complement.

An invisible noun clause occurs when the word *that* is implied, not stated directly.

> Dorinda never seemed to understand [that] she was responsible.
> *She was responsible* is the direct object of the verbal *to understand*. *That* is implied.

> Frederick could tell [that] he would enjoy his stay.
> *He would enjoy his stay* is the direct object of the verb *could tell*. *That* is implied.

 Noun clauses do not take commas.

> People felt (no comma) *that Robin Hood was like them.*

> Robin Hood was pleased (no comma) *that he had escaped.*

Sidebar (right column):

The advanced dress-up noun clause is a noun clause that begins with *that*. See page G-41.

Both noun clauses and adjective clauses can begin with the word *that*.

If *which* can be substituted for *that*, the *that* clause is an adjective clause.

Advanced

The first word of a dependent clause does not always indicate the type of clause. The word *that* can begin both adjective clauses and noun clauses. The words *where, when,* and *why* can begin adjective, adverb, and noun clauses. Accurate identification requires one to consider the way the entire clause is functioning in the sentence.

> The Little Mermaid determined to look *where the prince now lived with his bride.*
> The dependent clause begins with *where* and tells the location of where the Little Mermaid looked. This is an adverb clause, so a comma is not needed.

> The Little Mermaid noticed the sky, *where the rosy dawn glimmered more and more brightly.*
> The dependent clauses begins with *where* and directly follows the noun *sky*. This is a nonessential adjective clause, so a comma is needed.

Punctuation

End Marks . ? !

Period

Use a period at the end of a statement.

He bowed and walked away.

Use a period with some abbreviations.

ea. st. Mrs.

Question Mark

Use a question mark at the end of a question.

Did you ever hear the story of the three poor soldiers?

Exclamation Mark

Use an exclamation mark at the end of a sentence that expresses strong emotion.

No one calls me a coward!

Use an exclamation mark after an interjection that expresses strong emotion.

Yuck! I won't touch another bite.

Use only one end mark.

"You're sure?"
"Hah!" he said.
(correct)

"You're sure?!"
"Hah!," he said.
(incorrect)

Commas ,

Adjectives before a Noun

Use a comma to separate **coordinate adjectives**. Adjectives are coordinate if each adjective independently describes the noun that follows. The order is not important.

> The woman had a pointed, protruding nose.
> It sounds right to say both *protruding, pointed nose* and *pointed and protruding nose*.
> The adjectives are coordinate and the comma is necessary.

Do not use a comma to separate **cumulative adjectives**. Adjectives are cumulative if the first adjective describes the second adjective and the noun that follows. Cumulative adjectives follow this specific order: quantity, opinion, size, age, shape, color, origin, material, purpose.

> The soldiers reached the tall green gate.
> It does not sound right to say *green tall gate* or *tall and green gate*.
> The adjectives are cumulative and should not have a comma.

Only coordinate adjectives need to be separated with a comma.

Adjectives are coordinate if you can reverse their order or add *and* between them.

Adjectives are cumulative if they must be arranged in a specific order.

Noun of Direct Address (NDA)

Place commas around a noun of direct address. See page G-7.

> *My friends,* for fourteen days we have enjoyed no sport.

> For fourteen days, *my friends,* we have enjoyed no sport.

> For fourteen days we have enjoyed no sport, *my friends.*

Items in a Series

PATTERN a, b, and c Use commas to separate three or more items in a series. Place the final comma before the coordinating conjunction. These items must be grammatically the same.

> He *ran* to the window, *opened* it, and *jumped* out.

> The cook removed the *tomatoes, beans,* and *cucumbers.*

PATTERN a and b Do not use a comma before a coordinating conjunction when it connects two items in a series unless they are main clauses.

> The cook removed the *tomatoes* (no comma) and *cucumbers.*

> The cook *yelled* (no comma) and *ran.*

The Oxford Comma is the comma before the coordinating conjunction in three or more items in a series. Although the Oxford comma is optional if there is no danger of misreading, writers do not always recognize potential confusion. It is wise to include it since the addition of the Oxford Comma is rarely wrong.

Compound Verb

PATTERN MC cc 2nd verb Do not use a comma before a coordinating conjunction when it connects two verbs (a compound verb) with the same subject. There is no subject after the cc.

> The cook *yelled* (no comma) and *ran.*

> He *ran* to the window (no comma) and *opened* it.

This is the same as pattern a and b.

Compound Sentence

PATTERN MC, cc MC Use a comma before a coordinating conjunction when it connects two main clauses (a compound sentence). There is a subject and a verb after the cc.

> The *cook yelled,* and the *mouse ran.*

> *He ran* to the window, and *he opened* it.

The comma in the MC, cc MC pattern is optional when the clauses are short and there is no danger of misreading.

Mid-Sentence Prepositional Phrase

Do not put a comma in front of a prepositional phrase unless the phrase is a transition.

> The mouse hid (no comma) *under a table in the kitchen.*

> The cook was, *of course,* afraid of mice.

Prepositional Phrase Opener (#2 Sentence Opener)

If a prepositional opener has five words or more, follow it with a comma.

Under the table (no comma) the tiny mouse hid.

Under the heavy wooden table, the tiny mouse hid.

If two or more prepositional phrases open a sentence, follow the last phrase with a comma.

Under the heavy wooden table in the kitchen, the tiny mouse hid.

If a prepositional opener functions as a transition, follow it with a comma.

Of course, the cook was afraid of mice.

If a prepositional opener is followed by a main clause that has the verb before the subject, do not use a comma.

Under the heavy wooden table hid a tiny mouse.

Prepositional phrases that work as transitions and require commas include

  in fact
  in addition
  by the way
  by contrast
  for example
  for instance
  of course
  on the other hand

Transition and Interrupter

Place commas around a transition and an interrupter.

Of course, Dorinda and Maribella lived in the castle.

As grown-up girls they could, *on the other hand,* leave when they pleased.

They rarely left the palace grounds, *however.*

When transitional words connect two main clauses, put a semicolon before and a comma after. See page G-29.

-ly Adverb Opener (#3 Sentence Opener)

Use a comma if an -ly adverb opener modifies the sentence.

Foolishly, Timmy bit into a hot pepper.
Test: It was foolish that Timmy bit ... makes sense. *Foolishly* modifies the sentence.

Do not use a comma if an -ly adverb opener modifies the verb.

Eagerly Timmy ate a ripe cucumber.
Test: It was eager that Timmy ate ... does not make sense. *Eagerly* modifies the verb *ate*.

Test:

It was ___ that ___.

End-Sentence Participial Phrase

Do not use a comma when the participial phrase (-ing) describes the word directly before it.

Dorinda saw her ball (no comma) *rolling down the hill.*

Robin Hood whistled, *thinking of Maid Marian.*

Participial Phrase Opener (#4 Sentence Opener)

Use a comma after a participial opener (-ing), even if it is short.

Excusing herself from the table, Dorinda hurried away.

Adverb Clause Opener (#5 Sentence Opener)

PATTERN AC, MC Use a comma after an adverb clause opener.

When the cat prowled at night, the mice hid.

Mid-Sentence Adverb Clause

PATTERN AC, MC Use a comma after an adverb clause that comes before a main clause.

Early that morning *when Timmy saw the cat,* he was aghast.

PATTERN MC AC Do not use a comma before an adverb clause.

Early that morning Timmy was aghast (no comma) *when he saw the cat.*

Quotation

Use a comma to separate an attribution from a direct quote.

A throaty voice offered, "I should be honored to find your ball."

"I should be honored," a throaty voice offered, "to find your ball."

"I should be honored to find your ball," a throaty voice offered.

The attribution is the narrative that includes the person speaking and the speaking verb (*he said*).

Comparing Items

Do not use a comma when making a comparison.

Robin was a better shot (no comma) *than the other archers.*

Contrasting Items

Use a comma to separate contrasting parts of a sentence.

The ideas in this story are the rooster's thoughts, *not mine.*

Use a comma to contrast, not compare.

Use a comma even if the contrasting part begins with www words *although, while,* or *whereas.* This rule applies only when there is an extreme contrast and is an exception to **MC AC.**

He seemed interested, *whereas* she did not.

Timmy favored the country, *while* Johnny preferred the city.

Appositive, Adjective Clause, Mid-Sentence Participial Phrase

A nonessential appositive, adjective clause, or mid-sentence participial phrase adds information to a sentence.

Use commas to separate nonessential elements from the rest of the sentence.

Robin Hood, *the archer,* led his men through the forest.

Little John, *who liked a challenge,* readily followed Robin.

The men, *laughing at each other,* hiked through the forest.

An appositive is an invisible *who/which* clause. See page G-39.

A *who/which* clause is an adjective clause.

An essential appositive, adjective clause, or mid-sentence participial phrase defines the noun it follows. If the essential information is removed, the overall meaning of the sentence changes.

Do not use commas with essential elements.

A participial phrase is an -ing phrase.

The archer *Robin Hood* led his men through the forest.

The men *who followed Robin Hood* could be trusted.

The man *walking across the bridge* was a stranger.

To determine if a phrase or clause is essential, remove it from the sentence to see if it changes the meaning of the sentence.

Little John, *who liked a challenge,* readily followed Robin.
Remove the *who/which* clause: Little John readily followed Robin. This does not change the meaning of the sentence. This *who* clause is nonessential. Use commas.

Nonessential items need commas.

The men *who followed Robin Hood* could be trusted.
Remove the *who/which* clause: The men could be trusted. This changes the meaning because the reader does not know which men could be trusted. This *who* clause is essential. Do not use commas.

Essential items eliminate commas.

In some cases, the commas determine the meaning of the sentence.

Even the footmen, *who once obeyed her,* snubbed her.
With commas this sentence indicates all footmen snubbed her and all once obeyed her.

Even the footmen *who once obeyed her* snubbed her.
Without commas this same sentence now indicates that only those footmen who once obeyed her now snubbed her.

Quotation Marks " "

Direct Quotation

Use quotation marks to enclose direct quotations.

> "I want to live above the sea," said the Little Mermaid.

There should not be a space between the quotation mark and the word or punctuation it encloses.

Indirect Quotation

Do not use quotation marks with indirect speech, which usually begins with *that*.

> The Little Mermaid said that she wanted to live above the sea.

Thoughts

When typing, place thoughts in italics. When handwriting, use quotation marks.

> *I do not want a fish's tail*, thought the Little Mermaid.

Punctuating a Quotation

Use a comma to separate an attribution from a direct quote. If a direct quote is an exclamation or question, follow it with an exclamation or question mark.

> Attribution, "Quote." Attribution, "Quote!" Attribution, "Quote?"
>
> "Quote," attribution. "Quote!" attribution. "Quote?" attribution.

The attribution is the narrative that includes the person speaking and the speaking verb (*he said*).

Commas and periods always go inside closing quotation marks.

> "I want to live above the sea," said the Little Mermaid.

> Hans Christian Andersen wrote "The Little Mermaid."

Exclamation marks and question marks go inside closing quotations when they are part of the quoted material; otherwise, they go outside.

> "Can humans live forever?" the Little Mermaid asked.

> Did Grandmother say, "Humans can live forever"?

When a spoken sentence is interrupted, close the first part and begin the second with quotation marks. Do not capitalize the first letter of the continuation.

> "Human beings have a soul," explained Grandmother, "that lives eternally."

In conversation, if someone speaking changes topic, start a new paragraph. Close the first paragraph without a quotation mark to signal the speaker has not finished speaking. Open the new paragraph with a quotation mark to indicate that someone is still speaking.

> The prince responded, "You remind me of a girl I once met.
>
> "Long ago, my ship wrecked, and the waves cast me ashore. A maiden saved my life."

Referencing Words

When typing, place words referred to as words in italics or quotation marks. When handwriting, use quotation marks.

> The king believed *sir* and *madam* should be used when addressing one's elders.

Insert "the word(s)" or "the name" before the word in question to tell if this rule applies.

Single Quotation Marks

Use single quotation marks for quotations within quotations.

> The maid said, "Strip the mattresses since, as the queen put it, 'They might be unclean.'"

This is the only reason to use single quotation marks.

Apostrophes '

Contraction

Use an apostrophe to show where a letter or letters have been removed.

> I'll figure out how to trick them.

> It's too bad, but we'd better go our separate ways.

Possessive Adjective

Use an apostrophe to show possession.

To form singular possessives, add an apostrophe + *s*.

> the second soldier's turn

To form plural possessives, make the noun plural; then add an apostrophe.

> the soldiers' last night at the palace (the last night of all three soldiers)

An exception is irregular plural possessives.

> the children's mittens and the women's scarves

Plural Noun

Do not use an apostrophe to make a word plural.

> The *soldiers* each took a turn.

> The *princesses* received whatever they requested.

Possessive Pronoun

Do not use an apostrophe with possessive pronouns.

> his, hers, its, theirs, ours, yours

Possessive Pronouns	Contractions
its	it's (it is)
their	they're (they are)
theirs	there's (there is)
whose	who's (who is)

Ellipsis Points ...

Fictional Writing

Use ellipsis points to signal hesitation or a reflective pause, especially in dialogue.

> "Ahem ... " Lord Ashton cleared his throat conspicuously.

> "Um ... certainly ... the mattress test," the king sighed.

Nonfictional Writing

Use ellipses only when omitting words from a direct quotation.

Semicolons ;

Main Clauses

PATTERN MC; MC Use a semicolon to join main clauses that are closely related and parallel in construction.

The Little Mermaid pondered golden sunsets; she dreamed of twinkling stars.

Conjunctive Adverb

PATTERN MC; ca, MC. If a conjunctive adverb is used to connect two main clauses that express similar ideas, put a semicolon before the conjunctive adverb and a comma after.

Years of indulgence had spoiled her beyond recognition; *however,* Lady Constance recalled a time in Dorinda's childhood when she had been a lovable child.

Conjunctive adverbs are transition words.

Items in a Series

Use semicolons to separate items in a series when the items contain internal commas.

Highborn women lamented when Troy, that noble city celebrated by Homer, fell through trickery; when Pyrrhus, ancient Greek ruler, seized King Priam by the beard; and when the Romans, ruthless and crazed, torched Carthage to the ground.

Colons :

List

PATTERN MC: list Use a colon after a main clause to introduce a list when a phrase like *for example* is not included.

Robin Hood had two choices: run away or fight.

Colons follow a complete thought and mean *see what follows* or *an example follows.*

Explanation

PATTERN MC: explanation Use a colon after a main clause to introduce an explanation when a phrase like *for example* is not included.

One other thing I ask: please accept this simple souvenir from me.

Quotation

PATTERN MC: quotation Use a colon when a complete thought sets up a quotation.

The innkeeper answered him straightaway: "Sir, your friend left town at dawn."

Contrast this with an attribution. The innkeeper answered, "Sir, your friend left town at dawn."

Titles with Subtitles

PATTERN Title: Subtitle Use a colon to separate a title from a subtitle.

Charles Dickens wrote *Oliver Twist: The Parish Boy's Progress* and *A Christmas Carol: A Ghost Story of Christmas.*

Hyphens -

Numbers

Use a hyphen with compound numbers from twenty-one to ninety-nine and with fractions.

> thirty-seven; one-fourth

Compound Nouns

Use hyphens with some compound nouns.

> lady-in-waiting; mother-in-law; self-restraint

Compound Adjectives

Use a hyphen when two or more words come before a noun they describe and act as a single idea.

> The *nineteenth-century* author enjoyed his fame.

> The *five-year-old* boy cried.

When a compound adjective follows the noun it describes, the adjective may or may not be hyphenated. If in doubt, consult a dictionary.

> The boy was *five years old*.

> Mowgli was *self-confident*.

Em Dashes and Parentheses — ( )

Emphasis

Use em dashes to emphasize something.

> Your word—of all people's—must be trustworthy.

Interruption

Use em dashes to indicate an interruption in speech or a sudden break in thought.

> His younger daughter—now there was another topic that brought red to his face—embarrassed him in front of the guests.

Nonessential Elements

Use em dashes to set off nonessential elements that have commas inside them.

> The poor widow owned a few farm animals—three hefty sows, three cows, and a sheep dubbed Molly—with which she attempted to eke out a living.

Extra Information

Use parentheses to provide extra information.

> "Oh, yes, benevolent frog!" (Notice that in fairy tales, characters don't have great curiosity about such oddities as talking frogs.)

Use em dashes in place of commas when you want to draw attention to something.

Use parentheses in place of commas when you want to offer an aside.

Additional Concepts

Indentation

In copy work, indent by doing two things: 1) start on the next line, and 2) start writing ½ inch from the left margin.

To mark indentation, add the ¶ symbol or an arrow (➜) in front of each sentence that should start a new paragraph.

In fiction (stories), there are four reasons to start a new paragraph.

The paragraph mark (¶) is called a pilcrow.

New Speaker

Start a new paragraph when a new character speaks. Include the attribution with the quotation.

> She cried loudly, "Thieves!"

If a narrative sentence sets up the quotation, it should go in the same paragraph as the quoted sentence.

> The stranger came right to the point. "It is cowardly to stand there with a lethal arrow aimed at my heart."

If a narrative follows a quotation in a separate sentence but points directly back to the quotation, it can also go in the same paragraph.

> "It is cowardly to stand there with a lethal arrow aimed at my heart." The stranger did not mince words.

New Topic

Start a new paragraph when the narrator or a character switches topic or focus.

New Place

Start a new paragraph when the story switches to a new location. If several switches are made in quick succession, such as a character's journey to find something, it may be less choppy to keep in one paragraph.

New Time

Start a new paragraph when the time changes unless there are several time shifts in close succession that make sense together in a single paragraph.

Capitalization

Sentence

Capitalize the first word of a sentence and of a quoted sentence, even when it does not begin the full sentence.

> **T**he princess cried, "**M**y nose has grown too long."

Do not capitalize the first word of an attribution when it follows the quoted sentence.

> "My nose has grown too long," **t**he princess cried.

> "You must be content!" **u**rged grandmother

Quotation Continues

When a spoken sentence is interrupted, do not capitalize the first letter of the continuation.

> "**M**y nose," the princess cried, "**h**as grown too long."

Proper Nouns and Adjectives

Capitalize proper nouns and adjectives derived from proper nouns.

> Sherwood Forest; Robin Hood; English flag

Titles

Capitalize titles that precede a name. Do not capitalize titles that are not used with a name.

> In 1952 *Queen Elizabeth II* became the *queen* of England.

Capitalize titles that substitute for a name in a noun of direct address.

> "Can you clean his wound, *Doctor*?"

Do not capitalize family members unless used as a substitute for a name or with a name.

> He succeeded his *father* as king.

> Did *Father* say that we could play outside?

An exception is *sir* or *madam* as a noun of direct address: "Stand back, sir," demanded Robin.

Calendar Words

Capitalize days of the week and months of the year. Do not capitalize seasons: spring, summer, fall, winter.

> Timmy enjoyed peas on a hot *summer Wednesday* evening in *June*.

Directions

Capitalize compass directions when they refer to a region or proper name. Do not capitalize these words when they indicate direction. Do not capitalize words like *northward* or *northern*.

> On her journey *north* Eden encountered few obstacles.
> Eden is heading in a *northward* direction but not traveling to a region known as the *North*.

Literary Titles and Subtitles

Capitalize the first word and the last word of titles and subtitles. Capitalize all other words except articles, coordinating conjunctions, and prepositions.

> A young girl recited "Mary Had a Little Lamb."

> Read *Mozart: The Wonder Boy* by next week.

Numbers

Words

Spell out numbers that can be expressed in one or two words.

> twenty; fifty-three; three hundred

> Dorinda had racked up *one thousand* text messages on her cell phone in one month.

Spell out ordinal numbers.

> first, second, third

> The next year the *second* sister was permitted to rise to the surface.

Numerals

Use numerals for numbers that use three or more words.

> 123; 204

> That evening 250 rockets rose in the air.

Never begin a sentence with a numeral.

> 1492 is a famous year in history. (incorrect)

> The year 1492 is a famous year in history. (correct)

Use numerals with dates. Do not include *st, nd, rd,* or *th.*

> December 25, not December 25th

> Meet me at the Green Chapel in one year and one day on January 1, 1400.

Use numerals when numbers are mixed with symbols.

> We received $500 in donations last month.

> We can expect at least 40% of those invited to attend.

Homophones and Usage

Homophones

Homophones are words that sound alike but are spelled differently and have different meanings.

there	*There* is an adverb pointing to a place or point: *over there* (there is the spot).
their	*Their* is a possessive pronoun: *their house* (the house belongs to them).
they're	*They're* is a contraction: *they're finished* (they are finished).
your	*Your* is a possessive pronoun: *your weapon* (the weapon belongs to you).
you're	*You're* is a contraction: *you're finished* (you are finished).
to	*To* is a preposition or part of an infinitive: *to the left* (preposition); *to rush* (infinitive).
two	*Two* is a number: *two women* (2 women).
too	*Too* is an adverb meaning also or to an excessive degree: *I'll go too; too far.*
its	*Its* is a possessive pronoun: *its wing* (the wing belongs to the bird).
it's	*It's* is a contraction: *it's too bad* (it is too bad).
then	*Then* is an adverb meaning next or immediately after: *wake and then eat.*
than	*Than* is a word used to show a comparison: *Sam is shorter than Bob.*

Although less common, *there* can function as a noun, pronoun, or adjective.

affect	*Affect* is a verb that means to have an influence or to cause: Dorinda was too self-centered for anyone else to *affect* her deeply.
effect	*Effect* is a noun that refers to the result of some action: Years of indulgence had the obvious *effect* of spoiling Dorinda.

The definitions given for *affect* and *effect* are the most commonly used.

Usage

Usage errors occur when a word is used incorrectly.

between	*Between* is a preposition that refers to two items: She stood *between* the (two) trees.
among	*Among* is a preposition that refers to three or more items: She walked *among* them.
like	*Like* is a preposition that compares a noun to a noun: Waves rose *like* mountains.
as	*As* is a subordinating conjunction that compares a noun to an idea (subject + verb). The waves rose suddenly *as* the storm swelled.
	As is a preposition when it means in the role of: They traveled *as* adults.
farther	*Farther* refers to measurable distance: I jumped *farther* than I did yesterday.
further	*Further* refers to a figurative distance: We want to avoid *further* delays.
	Further functions as a verb when it means to promote: He will *further* the agenda.

Use *farthest* like *farther, furthest* like *further.*

lie	*Lie* is a verb that means to recline or remain: The hen rarely *lies* down.
lay	*Lay* is a verb that means to put something down: Daily, the hen *lays* an egg.

The past tense of *lie* is *lay,* which is the same as the present tense of *to lay.*

infinitive	present	past	past participle
to lie	*lie*	*lay*	*lain*
to lay	*lay*	*laid*	*laid*

Present: The hens *lie* down (recline) after they *lay* eggs (put eggs down).

Past: Yesterday the hens *lay* down (reclined) after they *laid* eggs (put eggs down).

Stylistic Techniques

Fix It! stories teach the stylistic techniques of the Institute for Excellence in Writing. Dress-ups are placed within sentences to strengthen vocabulary and add complex sentence structures. Sentence openers are different ways to begin sentences, encouraging sentence variety. Decorations are stylistic devices that embellish prose.

Dress-Ups

Dress-ups are descriptive words, phrases, and clauses that are placed within a sentence.

Three of the dress-ups encourage stronger vocabulary: -ly adverb, strong verb, quality adjective. The other dress-ups encourage more complex sentence structure: *who/which* clause and *www.asia.b* clause.

-ly Adverb Dress-Up

An -ly adverb is an adverb that ends in -*ly*. Adverbs are words that modify verbs, adjectives, or other adverbs. Most often they tell *how* or *when* something is done. The -ly adverb dress-up is used to enhance the meaning of a word. See page G-15.

See a list of -ly adverbs on page G-43.

Notice how the meaning of this sentence changes when different -ly adverbs are added:

> She masqueraded as a poor girl.
>
> She *cleverly* masqueraded as a poor girl.
>
> She *arrogantly* masqueraded as a poor girl.
>
> She *deceptively* masqueraded as a poor girl.

Not all words that end in -ly are adverbs. Impostor -ly adverbs are adjectives. If the word ending in -ly describes a noun, it is an adjective and not an adverb.

Adjective Test:

the _____ pen

To find -ly adverbs to use in your writing, use a thesaurus or vocabulary words. Alternatively, look at -ly adverb word lists on the *Portable Walls for Structure and Style Students*° or the IEW Writing Tools App.

Common Impostors
These -ly words are adjectives.

chilly	holy	lovely	queenly
friendly	kingly	lowly	ugly
ghastly	knightly	orderly	worldly
ghostly	lonely	prickly	wrinkly

Strong Verb Dress-Up

A strong verb is an action verb that creates a strong image or feeling. It helps a reader picture what someone or something is doing. See page G-9.

Challenge students to distinguish between strong verbs and vague ones.

Verb Test:

I _____ .

It _____ .

The mermaids often *went* to the castle.
The mermaids often *visited* the castle and *toured* its opulent halls.

The horse *was* in the barn.
The horse *buried* itself in the hay.

The mermaids' hands *were nibbled* on by the fish.
The fish *nibbled* the mermaids' hands.

Quality Adjective Dress-Up

A quality adjective is a descriptive word that provides specific details about a noun or pronoun. Like a strong verb, a quality adjective provides a strong image or feeling. See page G-14.

Notice how the image of *brook* changes with the use of different adjectives. In both examples, the first suggested adjective is weak, whereas the other two provide a stronger image or feeling.

Adjective Test:

the _____ pen

He hurdled the *small* brook.
He hurdled the *narrow* brook.
He hurdled the *babbling* brook.

The *big* stranger greeted Robin.
The *confident* stranger greeted Robin.
The *disagreeable* stranger greeted Robin.

To find strong verbs and quality adjectives to use in your writing, use a thesaurus or vocabulary words. Alternatively, look at word lists on the *Portable Walls for Structure and Style Students* or the IEW Writing Tools App.

 Advanced

Deliberate use of dual -ly adverbs, strong verbs, or quality adjectives, especially when the words add a different nuance, enriches prose and challenges students to be precise with words chosen. Classic writers of the past like Charles Dickens and persuasive essayists like Winston Churchill have used duals and triples to convey their meaning most powerfully.

The ship glided away *smoothly* and *lightly* over the tranquil sea.

The wind *filled* and *lifted* the ship's sails.

All who beheld her wondered at her *graceful, swaying* movements.

To punctuate dual adjectives properly, see page G-24.

Who/Which Clause Dress-Up

A *who/which* clause is a dependent clause that provides description or additional information about the noun it follows.

> Robin Hood cut a staff, *which measured six feet in length*.
> Which measured six feet in length describes the staff.

> Frederick hoped to make friends with the princess, *who frequently visited the garden*.
> Who frequently visited the garden describes the princess.

A *who/which* clause is a dependent clause that begins with the word *who* or *which*.

> Use *who* when referring to people, personified animals, and pets.
> Use *which* when referring to things, animals, and places.

Because the *who/which* clause is a dependent clause, it must be added to a sentence that is already complete. If only the word *who* or *which* is added, a fragment is formed.

> The noise alerted Sam. (sentence)
> The noise, *which alerted Sam*. (fragment)
> The noise alerted Sam, *who drove to safety*. (sentence)
> The noise, *which alerted Sam*, alerted him to drive to safety. (sentence)

Place commas around a *who/which* clause if it is nonessential to the meaning of the sentence.

> William**,** *who had little***,** shared with his neighbors. (nonessential, commas)

Do not place commas around a *who/which* clause if it is essential to the meaning of the sentence. See page G-26.

> The students *who finished the test* left early. (essential, no commas)
> The clause is essential because it defines which students left early.

The who/which clause immediately follows the noun it describes.

Forms of who include whom and whose. See page G-6.

If the who/which clause is removed, a sentence must remain.

Although the word that may begin an adjective clause, a that clause is not a who/which clause dress-up.

Advanced

A *who* clause always describes a single noun.

A *which* clause can describe a single noun, or it can describe the entire idea that comes before *which*.

> You have killed the king's deer, *which is a capital offense*.
> It is not the *deer* (noun before *which* clause) that is the offense but killing it—the entire idea expressed in the main clause.

If a *who/which* clause contains a *be* verb, the *who* or *which* and the *be* verb can be removed to form an invisible *who/which* clause. An invisible *who/which* clause is called an appositive or appositive phrase, not a clause because the subject (*who* or *which*) and the be verb have been removed from the written sentence. Follow the same comma rules.

> Dorinda frustrated Lady Constance, ~~who was~~ her companion since childhood.

> All had come to Sherwood Forest, ~~which was~~ a vast, uncharted wood.

www.asia.b Clause Dress-Up

A *www.asia.b* clause is a dependent clause that usually functions as an adverb. It begins with a subordinating conjunction (www word) and contains both a subject and a verb.

> Robin Hood and his band guffawed loudly *until the stranger showed irritation.*
> Remain on the other side *while I make a staff.*

There are many subordinating conjunctions. The most common are taught using the acronym *www.asia.b*: when, while, where, as, since, if, although, because. Other words function as subordinating conjunctions: after, before, until, unless, whenever, whereas, than. See page G-13.

Because the *www.asia.b* clause is a dependent clause, it must be added to a main clause. Although an adverb clause may appear anywhere in a sentence, the *www.asia.b* clause dress-up should not begin a sentence because only sentence openers begin sentences.

PATTERN

**www word +
subject + verb**

Memorize the most common www words using the acronym *www.asia.b:* when, while, where, as, since, if, although, because.

> Use a comma after an adverb clause that comes before a main clause.
> **PATTERN AC, MC**
>
> > That morning *while it rained,* Timmy stayed indoors.
>
> Do not use a comma before an adverb clause.
> **PATTERN MC AC**
>
> > Timmy stayed indoors (no comma) *when it rained.*

An adverb clause follows the pattern www word + subject + verb. If a verb is not present, the group of words is likely a prepositional phrase and not an adverb clause.

> Dorinda prepared the guestroom *after supper.*
> After supper is not a clause because it does not contain a subject and a verb.
> After supper is a prepositional phrase.

> Dorinda prepared the guestroom *after they ate supper.*
> After they ate supper is a clause because it contains both a subject (they) and a verb (ate).

Two tricks help tell the difference between a phrase and a clause.

> Look for a verb. A clause must have a verb. A prepositional phrase will not have a verb.

> Drop the first word of the phrase or clause in question and look at what is left.

> > If it is a sentence, the group of words is an adverb clause; if it is not, the words form a prepositional phrase.
> >
> > > ~~after~~ supper
> > > This does not have a verb. This does not form a sentence. This is a phrase.
> > >
> > > ~~after~~ they ate supper
> > > This has a verb (ate). This forms a sentence. This is a clause.

Advanced

When the www words *as, where, when* begin a clause that follows and describes a noun, the clause is probably an adjective clause. Test by inserting *which is* between the noun and www word. If it sounds correct, the clause is an adjective clause, not an adverb clause. Punctuate accordingly. See pages G-21 and G-26.

> King Arthur decided to climb to the top of the cliff, *where he could drink from the pool of water.*
> King Arthur decided to climb to the top of the cliff, [which is] *where he could drink from the pool of water.*
> This is an adjective clause beginning with the word *where.* Because it is nonessential, it requires commas.

When the www words *although, while,* and *whereas* present an extreme contrast to the main clause in the sentence, insert a comma. This is an exception to the more common rule **MC AC**. See page G-26.

> Timmy favored the country, *while* Johnny preferred the city.

Advanced Dress-Ups

Dual -ly Adverbs, Strong Verbs, Quality Adjectives

Deliberate use of dual -ly adverbs, strong verbs, or quality adjectives, especially when the words add a different nuance, enriches prose and challenges students to be precise with words chosen. Classic writers of the past like Charles Dickens and persuasive essayists like Winston Churchill have used duals and triples to convey their meaning most powerfully.

> The ship glided away *smoothly* and *lightly* over the tranquil sea.
> The wind *filled* the ship's sails and *propelled* the ship through the sea.
> All who beheld her wondered at her *graceful, swaying* movements.

Invisible *Who/Which* Clause

An invisible *who/which* clause is formed when the word *who* or *which* is followed by a *be* verb. Removing *who* or *which* and the *be* verb that follows allows for a more elegant construction. Follow the same comma rules.

> Dorinda frustrated Lady Constance, ~~who was~~ her companion since childhood.

> All had come to Sherwood Forest, ~~which was~~ a vast, uncharted wood.

Not all *who/which* clauses can be made invisible.

Teeter-Totters

The adverb teeter-totter uses a verb as a fulcrum with dual -ly adverbs preceding the verb and a *www.asia.b* clause following it. Both the -ly adverbs and the *www.asia.b* clause modify the same verb. **PATTERN** -ly -ly verb *www.asia.b*

> The tortoise *slowly* yet *steadily* <u>finished</u> the race *as the crowd watched in awe.*

The adjective teeter-totter uses a noun as a fulcrum with dual quality adjectives preceding the noun and a *who/which* clause following it. Both the quality adjectives and the *who/which* clause describe the same noun. **PATTERN** adjective adjective noun *w/w*

> The Little Mermaid placed the prince on the *fine white* <u>sand</u>, *which the sun had warmed.*

dual
-ly adverbs

www.asia.b

verb

dual
adjectives

w/w clause

noun

Noun Clause

A noun clause dress-up is a dependent clause that functions as a noun and begins with the word *that*. It typically follows a verb and answers the question *what*.

If the *that* clause is an adjective clause and not a noun clause, the word *which* can replace *that*.

> The king of the beasts never imagined *that* a puny rodent could help him.
> The king of the beasts never imagined *which* a puny rodent could help him.
> This does not make sense. This is not an adjective clause but a noun clause.

> The king of the beasts was freed from a net *that* a mouse had persistently gnawed.
> The king of the beasts was freed from a net *which* a mouse had persistently gnawed.
> This makes sense. This is an adjective clause. See page G-21.

An invisible noun clause occurs when the word *that* is implied, not stated directly.

> Dorinda never seemed to understand [that] *she was responsible.*

> Frederick could tell [that] *he would relish his palace stay.*

 Noun clauses do not take commas.

> People felt (no comma) *that Robin Hood was like them.*

> Robin Hood was pleased (no comma) *that he had escaped.*

Sentence Openers

Sentence openers are descriptive words, phrases, and clauses that are added to the beginning of a sentence.

There are six openers—six ways to open or begin a sentence. Using various sentence openers forces sentence variety, which will improve writing quality. Learning the sentence opener patterns and their related comma rules will result in sophisticated writing skills.

#1 Subject Opener

A subject opener is simply a sentence that begins with its subject. This is the kind of sentence one most naturally writes. A subject opener begins with the subject of the sentence.

Fish glide among the branches.

There may be an article or adjectives in front of the subject, but that does not change the sentence structure. It is still a #1 subject opener.

The colorful fish glide among the branches.

#2 Prepositional Opener

A prepositional opener is a prepositional phrase placed at the beginning of a sentence. See pages G-8 and G-18.

If a prepositional opener has five words or more, follow it with a comma.

Under the table (no comma) the tiny mouse hid.

Under the heavy wooden table, the tiny mouse hid.

If two or more prepositional phrases open a sentence, follow the last phrase with a comma.

Under the heavy wooden table in the kitchen, the tiny mouse hid.

If a prepositional opener functions as a transition, follow it with a comma.

In fact, the cook was afraid of mice.

If a prepositional opener is followed by a main clause that has the verb before the subject, do not use a comma.

Under the heavy wooden table hid a tiny mouse.

PATTERN

preposition + noun (no verb)

Because of begins prepositional phrases.

Because begins clauses.

Advanced

An invisible prepositional opener is formed when some kind of time is followed by the main clause. The preposition *on* or *during* is implied.

~~On~~ *Wednesday* we will go to the beach.

~~On~~ *The day before yesterday* we visited the park.

~~During~~ *That afternoon* she visited friends.

#3 -ly Adverb Opener

An -ly adverb opener is an -ly adverb placed at the beginning of a sentence. Beginning the sentence with an -ly adverb changes the rhythm of the sentence.

Test:

It was _____ that _____.

Use a comma if an -ly adverb opener modifies the sentence.

Foolishly, Timmy bit into a hot pepper.
Test: It was foolish that Timmy bit … makes sense.
Foolishly modifies the sentence. A comma is required.

Do not use a comma if an -ly adverb opener modifies the verb.

Eagerly Timmy ate a ripe cucumber.
Test: It was eager that Timmy ate a ripe cucumber … does not make sense. *Eagerly* modifies the verb *ate*. A comma is not needed.

Advanced

In some cases, the comma indicates the meaning of the sentence.

Sorrowfully Timmy acceded to the counsel of Johnny.
He acceded, but he did so sorrowfully, with regret.

Sorrowfully, Timmy acceded to the counsel of Johnny.
This opener indicates that Timmy made a mistake in acceding to Johnny's advice.
It is sorrowful that Timmy acceded to his Johnny's counsel.

-ly Adverbs List

angrily	critically	historically	mournfully	sleepily	unhappily
annoyingly	deceptively	hopefully	oddly	slyly	usually
boredly	disappointingly	horribly	proudly	sneakily	viciously
busily	discouragingly	joyfully	rapidly	strangely	vigorously
commonly	excitedly	kindly	repeatedly	suddenly	violently
completely	finally	meanly	sadly	tragically	warmly
constantly	greedily	miraculously	seriously	uncomfortably	willfully
continuously	happily	mostly	shamefully	unexpectedly	wisely

#4 -ing Opener

An -ing opener is a participial phrase placed at the beginning of a sentence.

> Taking up his bow, Robin Hood shot with unparalleled skill.

PATTERN -ing word/phrase, main clause. This is the most sophisticated sentence pattern. It is easily written when the pattern is followed. The sentence must begin with an action word that ends in -ing. This is called a participle. The -ing word/phrase and comma are followed by a main clause. The thing (subject of main clause) after the comma must be the thing doing the inging.

> Gathering their three gifts, the soldiers visited a neighboring king. The sentence begins with an action word that ends in -ing: *Gathering*
> The -ing word/phrase and comma are followed by a main clause: *the soldiers visited a neighboring king.*
> The thing (subejct of main clause) after the comma must be the thing doing the inging: *soldiers* (subject) *are gathering.*

An illegal #4 opener is grammatically incorrect. If the thing after the comma is not the thing doing the inging, the sentence does not make sense. This is known as a dangling modifier.

> Hopping quickly, Dorinda let the frog follow her to the dining hall.
> Who was hopping quickly? *Dorinda.* This is incorrect because the frog was hopping quickly.

An impostor #4 opener begins with an -ing word but does not follow the pattern. There are two types.

> Living at the splendid castle cheered the soldiers.
> This is a #1 subject opener. There is neither a comma nor a subject doing the inging. *Living* is the subject.

> During the dance she twirled him around.
> This is a #2 prepositional opener. *She* (the subject) is not doing the *during.*

Prepositions ending in -ing include *concerning, according to, regarding, during.*

Advanced

An invisible -ing opener is formed when *being* is implied before the first word of the sentence. Removing the word *being* allows for a more elegant construction. Follow the same comma rules.

> ~~Being~~ Quick-witted and agile, Robert compensated for his limitation with an eagerness to please.

> ~~Being~~ Relaxed and untroubled, the stranger genially waited for him.

> ~~Being~~ Encouraged by Samuel's speech, William stepped onto the stage.

A #4 -ing opener is a participial opener.

The thing after the comma must be the thing doing the inging.

#5 Clausal Opener

A clausal opener is an adverb clause placed at the beginning of a sentence. This opener is the same as the *www.asia.b* dress-up. The only difference is placement in the sentence. The opener begins a sentence.

 PATTERN AC, MC Use a comma after an adverb clause opener.

> *If possessions were plundered,* Robin and his men would recapture the goods and return them to the poor.
>
> *As he approached,* Robin Hood noticed a tall stranger on the other side of the stream.
>
> *When Robin attempted to cross the river,* the stranger blocked his way.

PATTERN

www word + subject + verb

Because begins clauses.

Because of begins prepositional phrases.

An adverb clause follows the pattern www word + subject + verb. If a verb is not present, the group of words is likely a prepositional phrase and not an adverb clause.

After supper, Dorinda prepared the guestroom.
After supper is not a clause because it does not contain a subject and a verb.
After supper is a prepositional phrase.

After they ate supper, Dorinda prepared the guestroom.
After they ate supper is a clause because it contains both a subject (they) and a verb (ate).

Two tricks help tell the difference between a phrase and a clause.

Look for a verb. A clause must have a verb. A prepositional phrase will not have a verb.

Drop the first word of the phrase or clause in question and look at what is left. If it is a sentence, the group of words is an adverb clause; if it is not, the words form a prepositional phrase.

~~After~~ supper
This does not have a verb. This does not form a sentence. This is a phrase.

~~After~~ they ate supper
This has a verb (ate). This forms a sentence. This is a clause.

#6 Vss Opener

A very short sentence (vss) is simply a short sentence. It must be short (two to five words), and it must be a sentence (subject + verb and be able to stand alone). It is not a fragment.

Remember that variety in sentence structure is important in good writing. Purposefully adding a very short sentence can help break up the pattern of sentences in a stylish way. It catches the reader's attention. As a result, place it in a spot that needs emphasis.

Robin Hood left.

The blow inflamed him.

King Morton esteemed values.

As an added challenge, include a strong verb so that the very short sentence packs a punch.

Advanced Sentence Openers

#F Fragment Opener

A fragment that does not leave the reader hanging and that fits the flow of the paragraph can be dramatic and effective. This opener is often used in fictional writing.

Timmy saw his dear friend. (sentence)

Greeting him kindly. (unacceptable fragment)

"Hello, Johnny!" (acceptable fragment)

#Q Question Opener

A question is a complete sentence. It must contain a subject and a verb and make sense.

Where could he take a nap?

#T Transitional Opener

The transitional opener may be an interjection or a transitional word or phrase.

 Place commas after a transitional expression.

Meanwhile, Robin's men rested near the river.

Of course, Dorinda and Maribella lived in the castle.

When an interjection expresses a strong emotion, use an exclamation mark. When an interjection does not express a strong emotion, use a comma.

Help! My golden ball has vanished.

Oh, I see it now.

List of Common Transitions

however	first
therefore	next
then	also
thus	moreover
later	hence
now	furthermore
otherwise	henceforth
indeed	likewise

Decorations

Used sparingly, as an artist might add a splash of bright color to a nature painting, these stylistic techniques daringly or delicately decorate one's prose.

Alliteration Decoration

Alliteration is using three or more words close together that begin with the same consonant sound. Our ear likes the repetition of sound. The alliterative words may be separated by conjunctions, articles, short pronouns, or prepositions.

> Samuel was *seeking some* shady relief from the *sweltering sun*.
> *Shady* is not part of the alliteration because it does not have the same initial sound as the other *s* words. It is not the letter that matters but the sound. Thus, *celery* and *sound* are alliterative, but *shady* and *sound* are not.

Question Decoration

The question may be a rhetorical question, which means the answer is understood and does not need to be given, or it may be a question that the writer answers soon after asking. If a character in the story asks a question of another character, that is simply conversation. The question decoration is directed towards the reader, causing the reader to stop and think.

> Someone suddenly appeared on the path. *Who was it?* It was Johnny!

Conversation/Quotation Decoration

Conversation appears in narrative writing when characters talk.

> "You're finally here, Johnny!" exclaimed Timmy.

A quotation appears when the writer uses the exact words that someone else has used. A quotation includes a well-known expression, words stated by a famous person, or words found in another source. When a quotation is used as a decoration, it does not require a citation, but the source should be included as a lead-in. Punctuate correctly. See page G-27.

> As Mark Twain noted, "History may not repeat itself, but it sure does rhyme."

3sss Decoration

3sss stands for three short staccato sentences. The 3sss is simply three #6 very short sentences in a row. Using short sentences together, especially among longer sentences, can be a powerful stylistic technique because the short sentences will draw attention to themselves.

A 3sss will have the most impact when the number of words in each of the sentences is the same or decreasing. Increasing patterns have less impact.

> 4:3:2 Killer bees invaded America. Viciously they attacked. Humans suffered.

> 3:3:3 Savage bees attacked. Violently they killed. Nobody was spared.

> 2:2:2 Bees invaded. They marauded. Humans perished.

Simile/Metaphor Decoration

Both a simile and a metaphor are figures of speech which compare two items that are very different from each other. The well-known simile *her cheeks are like roses* compares cheeks to roses, two very different things. A simile makes the comparison by using the words *like* or *as*. A metaphor does not use *like* or *as*. It simply refers to one thing as if it is another.

The key to recognizing these figures of speech is that they compare unlike things. For example, to say that a cat is like a tiger is a comparison but not a simile.

> The ship dove like a swan between them. (simile)

> The waves rose mountains high. (metaphor)

Dramatic Open-Close Decoration

> The vss open-close decoration frames a single paragraph. The vss open-close decoration contains two very short sentences two to five words long. One is placed at the beginning of the paragraph, and the other is placed at the end.

> > Hungry flames roared. (vss open) The farm lay in ashes. (vss close)

> > Peter sighed. (vss open) Peter had an idea. (vss close)

> > The mystery was solved! (vss open) The truth was told. (vss close)

The anecdotal open-close decoration frames a composition or essay that includes an introduction and conclusion. An anecdote is a very short story meant to amuse or teach. To use this decoration, begin the introduction with a story to draw in the reader. Revisit the story somewhere in the conclusion.

Anecdotal open (beginning of introduction):

> With a bushel of cranberries slung over her shoulder, eight-year-old Jennie Camillo trod through the cranberry bog toward the bushel man who would collect her load. When the infamous photographer Lewis Hine asked her to stop so he could take a picture, she stopped for a brief moment to humor the man. Concernedly Jennie glanced toward her toiling father, who was regarding her stop with annoyance.

Anecdotal close (in the conclusion):

> Working during the harvest season, Jennie missed the first six weeks of school. Due to her family's financial struggles, the Camillos were forced to take the whole family to Theodore Budd's bog near Philadelphia before returning home to New Jersey after the harvest.

Triple Extensions

Classic writers of the past have used duals and triples to convey their meaning most powerfully. The trick is to remember "thrice, never twice."

Repeating Words (same word)

Fearing for his sheep, *fearing* that the villagers would not arrive in time, and ultimately *fearing* for his own life, Peter screamed, "Help!" as he bolted down the hill.

Never in the field of conflict was *so* much owed by *so* many to *so* few (Churchill).

Villainy is *the matter*; baseness is *the matter*; deception, fraud, conspiracy are *the matter* (Dickens).

With a *common* origin, a *common* literature, a *common* religion and *common* drinks, what is longer needful to the cementing of the two nations together in a permanent bond of brotherhood (Mark Twain)?

Repeating Clauses

They lived in a land *where* the winter was harsh, *where* food became scarce, and *where* provisions had to be stored.

Repeating Prepositional Phrases

We have not journeyed all this way *across* the centuries, *across* the oceans, *across* the mountains, *across* the prairies, because we are made of sugar candy (Churchill).

Repeating -ings

Gnawing, jerking, and *yanking,* the mouse freed the lion from the thick rope.

The Little Mermaid could be seen *holding* the prince while *kissing* his brow and *stroking* his hair.

Repeating -ly Adverbs

Robin Hood *cheerfully, boldly,* and *fearlessly* led his men.

The mouse *vigorously* gnawed at the tough fibers and *tenaciously* jerked at the rope while he *continuously* assured the lion of escape.

Repeating Adjectives

The *patient, persistent,* and *personable* tortoise determined that at least he would have a chance.

Repeating Nouns

Peter's deceptive cries for help finally determined the *attitude, behavior,* and *actions* of the village people.

Repeating Verbs

With all his might, the mouse *gnawed, jerked,* and *yanked* at the thick rope.

What's next

Little Mermaid LEVEL 6

IEW.com/FIX-L6

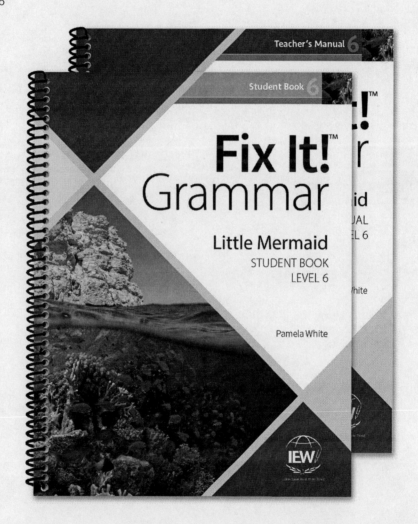